AUTONOMY

The Engine of Artificial General Intelligence

By

Susie Hala

IntelliGloss AI Education Series

Legal Disclaimer

Educational Purpose Disclaimer

"This publication is part of the IntelliGloss AI Education Series, a structured curriculum support system for AI literacy in grades 6–12."

The information presented in this publication is provided for educational and informational purposes only. This book is intended to support educators, administrators, parents, and learners in understanding the concepts, opportunities, and challenges associated with artificial intelligence in education. It is not intended to serve as legal, technical, policy, cybersecurity, or professional advice.

Readers should consult qualified professionals, institutional guidelines, and local regulations before implementing any educational programs, technologies, or policies described in this book.

Technology and Accuracy Disclaimer
Artificial intelligence is a rapidly evolving field. While every effort has been made to ensure the accuracy and reliability of the information presented at the time of publication, technologies, policies, research findings, and best practices may change over time. The author and publisher make no guarantees that all information will remain current or applicable in future technological environments.

Readers are encouraged to verify tools, platforms, and recommendations independently before using them in educational settings.

Implementation Responsibility
Schools, educators, and institutions are solely responsible for determining how and whether to implement artificial intelligence tools, strategies, or classroom activities discussed in this book. Educational environments vary widely, and policies regarding technology use, student privacy, and curriculum development differ by district, state, and country.

The author and publisher assume no responsibility for outcomes resulting from the implementation of ideas, examples, or frameworks described in this book.

Student Safety and Data Privacy
Artificial intelligence tools may involve the collection or processing of data. Educators and institutions are responsible for ensuring that any technology used complies with applicable student privacy laws, data protection regulations, and school policies, including but not limited to FERPA, COPPA, GDPR, or other relevant regulations depending on jurisdiction.

The author and publisher are not responsible for the privacy practices, security policies, or data handling procedures of third-party platforms or software mentioned in this book.

Third-Party Tools and References
This book may reference third-party technologies, organizations, research studies, or platforms for illustrative and educational purposes. Such references do not constitute endorsements or guarantees regarding the performance, reliability, safety, or suitability of those tools for educational use.

Educators and institutions should conduct their own evaluations and risk assessments before adopting any technology.

No Professional Liability
The author and publisher shall not be held liable for any direct, indirect, incidental, or consequential damages resulting from the use or misuse of the information contained in this book. This includes but is not limited to decisions related to curriculum design, technology adoption, classroom instruction, institutional policies, or educational outcomes.

Educational Interpretation
The concepts and examples provided in this book are intended to support discussion and learning. They should not be interpreted as official standards, mandatory guidelines, or universally applicable policies for artificial intelligence education.

Schools and educators are encouraged to adapt the ideas presented here according to their local policies, cultural context, educational standards, and student needs.

Author's Intent
The goal of this book is to promote responsible AI literacy, thoughtful discussion, and ethical awareness as schools prepare students for a world increasingly shaped by intelligent technologies.

The author encourages readers to approach artificial intelligence education with curiosity, caution, and a commitment to responsible learning.

Title: AUTONOMY: The Engine of Artificial General Intelligence

ISBN: 978-1-972925-26-3

Published by
IntelliGloss Press
United States of America

Dedication

This book is dedicated to the next generation of learners—
the students who will grow up in a world shaped by intelligent technology,
and who deserve to understand it with clarity, confidence, and purpose.

To the educators who show up every day with dedication and heart,
guiding students through a rapidly changing world—
your role has never been more important.

To the parents and families who support learning at home,
encouraging curiosity, responsibility, and growth—
you are the foundation of every child's success.

And to my granddaughters,
whose curiosity, imagination, and future inspire me to do this work—
this book is for you.

May you not only learn how to use technology,
but understand it, question it, and shape it for the good of others.

About the Author

Susie Hala
Founder of the IntelliGloss AI Education Series

Susie Hala is an author, educator, and curriculum developer dedicated to advancing artificial intelligence literacy in education. Her work focuses on helping schools, educators, and students understand how intelligent technologies are shaping modern society—and why that understanding is essential for the next generation.

Hala is the creator of the IntelliGloss AI Education Series, a comprehensive and growing collection of educational books designed to make complex artificial intelligence concepts accessible, structured, and practical for classroom use. Her work emphasizes clarity, organization, and responsible implementation, enabling schools to introduce AI literacy without requiring advanced technical backgrounds.

In addition to her work in education, Hala brings hands-on experience working with artificial intelligence systems, including early exposure to rule-based AI technologies during her time working with AT&T. She has also developed modern digital platforms that integrate artificial intelligence, automation, and online systems, building e-commerce solutions and AI-driven applications that connect payment platforms, hosting environments, and conversational AI tools into real-world, functional systems.

This combination of foundational understanding and practical experience allows her to translate complex AI concepts into clear, accessible language for both educators and students.

Recognizing that artificial intelligence is rapidly transforming how information is created, interpreted, and used, Hala advocates for equipping students with the ability not only to use AI tools, but to understand, question, and evaluate them. Her work emphasizes critical thinking, ethical awareness, and responsible digital citizenship.

The IntelliGloss AI Education Series supports schools in teaching key areas such as artificial intelligence foundations, algorithms, machine learning concepts, and AI ethics, as well as the broader evolution of intelligent systems—from Artificial Narrow Intelligence (ANI) to Artificial General Intelligence (AGI) and Artificial Superintelligence (ASI). These resources are designed for students in grades 6–12 and for educators seeking structured, classroom-ready approaches to AI literacy.

In addition to her work in education publishing, Hala has a strong background in entrepreneurship, having built and managed multiple businesses and educational initiatives. Her experience across industries reinforces her belief that technology education must remain grounded in human values, critical thinking, and ethical responsibility.

Her mission is clear: to ensure that the next generation understands intelligent technology—not just how to use it, but how it truly works.

Preface

Two Students. Two Paths. One Future.

Before we begin, it is important to understand why learning how artificial intelligence works—not just how to use it—matters for every student.

Imagine two students who have just graduated from high school and are preparing for a job interview. The first student knows how to use artificial intelligence tools. This student can generate answers, complete assignments quickly, and rely on AI to assist with tasks. However, this student does not understand how artificial intelligence works behind the scenes.

The second student also knows how to use AI tools, but in addition, understands the foundational concepts behind them. This student has learned about data, algorithms, tokens, models, and how intelligent systems are trained and operate. This student can think critically about AI, recognize its limitations, and adapt when needed.

At first, the first student may appear faster and more efficient. However, over time, the second student demonstrates a deeper level of understanding, independence, and problem-solving ability. The second student is not only able to use artificial intelligence but also to question it, improve it, and grow with it.

This book is written for the second student.

In a world where artificial intelligence is becoming part of everyday life, students must not only learn how to use intelligent systems—they must learn how they work. True understanding leads to confidence, responsibility, and the ability to lead in an AI-driven future.

This perspective is not just theoretical—it is personal.

There was a time when I was the first student.

I knew how to use systems. I followed processes, completed tasks, and worked within structured environments that required accuracy and consistency. At the time, I did not think of these systems as artificial intelligence. They were simply part of the job—tools that had to be learned, followed, and mastered.

But looking back, I now understand something much deeper. I was working within rule-based systems—the earliest foundation of what we now recognize as artificial intelligence.

That realization changed everything.

As I began studying modern AI, including machine learning, deep learning, and intelligent systems, I started to see a clear connection between the past and the present. The structured systems I once worked in, the logic behind decision-making, and the step-by-step processes all still exist today. They have simply evolved.

Artificial intelligence did not appear overnight. It grew from rule-based systems into systems that can now learn, adapt, and assist in ways we never imagined.

I made a decision to move from simply using systems to understanding them.

That journey—from student one to student two—is the reason these books exist.

My mission is to help others bridge that same gap.

I believe that artificial intelligence should be understandable for everyone. It should not feel intimidating or out of reach. Students should feel confident exploring it. Teachers should feel prepared to introduce it. Everyday learners should have access to clear, structured explanations that make sense.

You do not need a background in technology. You do not need to know how to code. You only need the right explanation.

A Note from the Author

AI Is a Tool — Not a Decision Maker

Artificial Intelligence is becoming part of everyday life. Students use it to complete assignments, teachers use it to support instruction, and businesses use it to improve efficiency. While these tools are powerful and useful, there is an important truth that must remain clear from the very beginning:

Artificial Intelligence does not make decisions—people do.

One of the main purposes of this book is to help readers understand how AI works, what it can do, and—just as importantly—what it cannot do. AI systems are designed to process information, identify patterns, and generate responses based on data. They can assist with thinking, but they do not think independently. They can provide answers, but they do not understand consequences. They can suggest ideas, but they do not choose actions.

Every outcome that involves AI begins and ends with human involvement. A person asks the question. A person reviews the response. A person decides what to do next. Responsibility does not transfer to the machine.

In today's world, it is easy to confuse speed with intelligence and automation with authority. Because AI can respond quickly and confidently, it may appear as though it is making decisions. In reality, it is performing a task based on patterns it has learned—not exercising judgment.

This distinction matters. When people begin to rely on AI without understanding its role, they risk misunderstanding information, misusing technology, or placing trust in a system that is not capable of accountability. Clear understanding leads to responsible use.

This book was written to remove confusion and provide clarity. It is designed to help students and educators move beyond simply using AI tools and begin understanding the structure behind them. By learning how AI supports human thinking—rather than replacing it—readers can approach technology with confidence, awareness, and responsibility.

Artificial Intelligence is a powerful assistant. It can enhance learning, support creativity, and improve productivity. But it remains a tool.

The decisions, the actions, and the responsibility will always belong to the human.

— Susie Hala

Bringing Clarity to Artificial Intelligence

During a recent meeting with a school district, it became clear that one of the biggest challenges in artificial intelligence education is not the technology itself—but the way it is explained.

In that discussion, terms such as **chatbots, generative AI, agentic AI, autonomy, tools, hallucinations, and AI usage levels** were all mentioned together. While each term represents a distinct concept, they were often blended into one conversation without clear distinctions. The result was confusion, even among those who were actively trying to understand and make informed decisions.

This experience revealed an important truth:
Without clear definitions and structure, artificial intelligence becomes difficult to teach, difficult to learn, and difficult to use responsibly.

This book is designed to provide that structure.

Understanding the Core Concepts

To build a strong foundation, it is essential to separate and define the key ideas that are often confused.

Chatbot
A chatbot is a conversational interface that allows users to interact with an AI system through questions and prompts. It responds to input but does not act beyond what is directly requested.

Generative AI (Gen AI)
Generative AI refers to systems that create new content, including text, images, audio, and code. These systems generate outputs based on patterns learned from large datasets. While powerful, generative AI does not truly understand information and may occasionally produce inaccurate results.

Agentic AI
Agentic AI describes systems that can take action toward a goal. Rather than responding to a single prompt, these systems can plan, make decisions within defined limits, and carry out multi-step tasks. This introduces a higher level of functional independence.

Autonomy
Autonomy refers to how independently an AI system operates. Some systems require constant human guidance, while others can perform multiple steps with minimal input. Autonomy is not a separate type of AI, but a measure of how much control the system has in completing tasks.

Additional Terms That Shape Understanding

AI Tools
AI tools are the applications people use to interact with artificial intelligence, such as writing assistants, design platforms, and data analysis systems. These tools make AI accessible in everyday tasks.

Hallucination
A hallucination occurs when an AI system generates information that appears correct but is inaccurate or unsupported. This is a known limitation of generative systems and highlights the need for human verification.

The AI Use Continuum

Another important concept is how AI is used at different levels. Rather than viewing AI as a single capability, it is more accurate to understand it as a continuum of use:

Assistive Use
AI supports simple tasks such as answering questions, correcting grammar, or providing suggestions.

Augmented Use
AI helps expand human capability by generating ideas, organizing content, and assisting in problem-solving.

Agentic Use
AI begins to take on multi-step responsibilities, planning and completing tasks with reduced human input.

This continuum shows that AI can range from a helpful assistant to a more independent system, depending on how it is applied.

The Moment Everything Sounded Like One Conversation

During a recent discussion on artificial intelligence, I listened closely as different experts spoke about the future of AI. One referenced advanced systems beyond human intelligence, another discussed goal-driven AI systems, and the conversation shifted quickly between topics like autonomy, tools, and system behavior. At first, it sounded like a single, unified discussion. But the more I listened, the more I realized something important.

They were not all talking about the same thing.

One part of the conversation focused on future possibilities—high-level systems that do not yet exist. Another part focused on current technologies that are already being used today. At the same time, different terms were being used to describe how AI behaves, how it makes decisions, and how much independence it may have. These ideas were layered together in a way that made them sound connected, even when they were not.

This experience revealed a major challenge in understanding artificial intelligence today. Many discussions combine different types of AI, different levels of intelligence, and different behaviors into one conversation. Without clear structure, these ideas begin to blur together. For someone trying to learn, this can feel overwhelming and confusing.

This book is built to solve that problem.

Artificial intelligence is not one single concept. It is a system made up of multiple layers. Some layers describe how intelligent a system is. Other layers describe how the system behaves. Still others describe how much control or independence the system has. When these layers are separated and explained clearly, AI becomes much easier to understand.

The goal of this book is to bring clarity where confusion often exists. Instead of mixing everything into one explanation, each concept is presented in a structured and organized way. This allows students, educators, and readers to see how the pieces fit together without losing sight of what each part actually means.

Understanding artificial intelligence begins with understanding its structure.

Once that structure is clear, the conversation becomes clearer as well.

Why Clarity Matters

When these concepts are not clearly defined, they merge into what can be described as a "conceptual blur." This can lead to misunderstandings about what AI can and cannot do, as well as unrealistic expectations or misuse in educational settings.

Clear understanding helps ensure that:

Students remain active learners, not passive users

Educators maintain control over instructional outcomes

AI is used as a support tool rather than a replacement for thinking

The Purpose of This Book

This book is built on a simple but essential principle:

Students should not only use artificial intelligence—they should understand it.

By clearly defining core concepts such as chatbots, generative AI, agentic AI, autonomy, and the continuum of AI use, this curriculum provides a structured pathway for developing both technical understanding and critical thinking.

Artificial intelligence is not a single tool or system. It is a collection of capabilities that must be understood in context.

Clarity is the foundation of responsible innovation.

Structuring Artificial Intelligence to Create Clarity and Understanding

Why Structure Is Necessary

Artificial intelligence is often presented as one unified concept. In many discussions, different ideas such as intelligence level, system behavior, and autonomy are combined into a single explanation. This can make AI appear more complex and confusing than it actually is.

Clarity begins when these ideas are separated and organized.

Structuring artificial intelligence allows each concept to be understood on its own before being connected to the larger system.

The Problem Without Structure

When AI is not structured, conversations may include multiple terms that sound related but describe entirely different things. For example, a discussion may move quickly between advanced future systems, current tools, and system behaviors without clearly distinguishing between them.

This creates the impression that all forms of AI operate at the same level and in the same way, which is not accurate.

Without structure, understanding becomes difficult.

The Solution: A Structured Approach

Artificial intelligence becomes clearer when it is organized into distinct categories.

Level explains how intelligent a system is.
Behavior explains how the system operates.
Control explains how much independence the system has.

Each category answers a different question. Together, they form a complete picture of how AI systems function.

Clarity Through Separation

A system can operate at a current level of intelligence while demonstrating different behaviors or levels of independence. For example, a system that generates responses and a system that takes steps toward completing a task may operate at the same intelligence level but differ in how they behave.

This distinction becomes clear only when structure is applied.

Instructional Insight

When teaching artificial intelligence, it is important to avoid presenting all concepts at once. Separating ideas into categories allows learners to focus on one dimension at a time, building understanding step by step.

Structured learning leads to deeper comprehension.

Key Takeaway

Artificial intelligence is not one single idea. It is a system made up of multiple parts. Structuring those parts creates clarity, improves understanding, and allows learners to see how the system truly works.

Reflection Question

How does separating intelligence level, behavior, and control make artificial intelligence easier to understand?

The IntelliGloss Instructional Approach

The IntelliGloss AI Education Series is designed to help students move beyond simply using AI tools and begin understanding artificial intelligence as a complete system.

Students learn how AI is built, how it operates, and how it connects to the real world.

A Message to Students and Readers

If you have ever felt that technology was too complicated…
If you have ever been confused by systems that were never clearly explained…

I want you to know:

You are capable of understanding artificial intelligence.

Sometimes, the challenge is not the concept itself—it is how it has been presented.

This series was created to change that.

A Message to Educators

To the educators using this material:

These books are designed to support you in introducing artificial intelligence in a way that is clear, structured, and meaningful for students.

AI is becoming part of every industry, and students deserve more than just exposure to tools—they deserve understanding.

This series aims to provide that foundation.

Final Reflection

Every experience we have—especially the challenging ones—prepares us for something greater.

The systems I once worked in taught me discipline, structure, and attention to detail. Today, those same lessons allow me to break down complex ideas and make them understandable for others.

That is what this series represents:

Turning complexity into clarity.

Why Artificial Intelligence Education Matters for Every Student

Why AI Literacy Is Essential for Every Student

Artificial intelligence is no longer a future concept or a specialized technology used only by experts. It is already part of everyday life for students of all ages. From smartphones and search engines to navigation apps, social media, streaming platforms, and educational tools, AI systems influence how information is accessed, decisions are made, and learning takes place.

Because AI is embedded in daily life, understanding it is no longer optional. It is a foundational skill, similar to digital literacy and critical thinking. Students do not need to become programmers or engineers, but they do need to understand what AI is, how it works at a basic level, and how it affects their lives.

AI education should not be limited to computer science classrooms. Every student interacts with AI systems daily. Teaching students how these systems function empowers them to become informed users rather than passive consumers of technology.

This book is designed to make artificial intelligence understandable, approachable, and relevant. It focuses on clarity, responsibility, and real-world understanding to help students prepare for a future where humans and intelligent systems work side by side.

IntelliGloss AI Education Series

Teaching how AI actually works—from hardware to power to global systems.

Why AI Education Matters

Artificial intelligence is already shaping how students learn, write, research, and solve problems.

Yet many students—and educators—are using AI tools without understanding how these systems actually work.

Schools need more than access to technology.
They need structured, responsible AI education.

Our Approach

The IntelliGloss AI Education Series is designed to help students move beyond simply using AI tools and begin understanding artificial intelligence as a complete system.

Students learn how AI is built, how it operates, and how it connects to the real world.

The IntelliGloss Framework

Our books introduce AI through a clear and connected system:

Chip Family — the hardware that powers AI

Watts Family — the rate at which AI uses power

Energy Family — the total power AI consumes over time

Infrastructure Family — the global systems that support AI

This framework helps students understand AI from the inside out.

Built for the Classroom

Each book includes:

Structured chapters aligned with semester learning

Clear explanations designed for student understanding

Reflection sections with learning objectives

Worksheets, quizzes, and answer keys

Teacher Implementation Guides

Supporting Schools and Educators

The IntelliGloss series supports:

Responsible and ethical AI use

Student data awareness and safety

Critical thinking and digital literacy

Classroom-ready instruction for grades 6–12 and beyond

What This Book Is—and What It Is Not

Many people today are becoming familiar with artificial intelligence through tools like ChatGPT, Microsoft Copilot, Canva, and other AI-powered applications. These tools can help with writing, answering questions, creating images, and completing everyday tasks.

In addition to these tools, you may also hear terms such as **AI agents, agentic AI, autonomous systems, and generative AI**. While these may sound complex, they are all part of the same evolving landscape of artificial intelligence technologies.

This book is not a guide on how to use those tools.

Instead, it explains what makes those tools possible.

Behind every AI tool is a system made up of multiple layers working together. At the most basic level, information is represented as bits and processed through powerful computer chips. That information is organized into data, broken into tokens, and then processed by algorithms and models that allow the system to recognize patterns, generate responses, and perform tasks.

These components—chips, bits, tokens, data, algorithms, and models—work together as a complete system. While users may only see the tool, the real intelligence comes from how these underlying parts interact behind the scenes.

Artificial intelligence can also be understood in terms of different levels of capability. Most of the AI systems used today fall under **Artificial Narrow Intelligence (ANI)**, which is designed to perform specific tasks, such as answering questions or generating content. More advanced forms, such as **Artificial General Intelligence (AGI)** and **Artificial Superintelligence (ASI)** represent future possibilities where AI could match or exceed human-level thinking. While these advanced levels are still theoretical, understanding the differences helps provide a broader view of where AI is today and where it may be heading.

For students, parents, and educators, this distinction is important. Learning how to use AI tools is helpful, but understanding how they work—and where they fit within the larger AI landscape—builds stronger thinking, better decision-making, and more responsible use.

Most importantly, artificial intelligence does not make decisions on its own. It does not take responsibility for actions or outcomes. AI systems generate responses based on data and patterns, but it is always the human who decides what to do with that information.

This book is designed to make these underlying systems clear and accessible, even for readers who are new to artificial intelligence.

Artificial intelligence is still in its early stages of development. As these technologies continue to grow, those who understand the foundation behind them will be better prepared to adapt, question, and use them wisely.

Who This Book Is For

This book is designed for educators, school leaders, and curriculum developers guiding students in an age of rapidly advancing technology.

Artificial intelligence is already influencing how students learn, research, and communicate. Yet many educators have not received formal training in how these systems work or how they should be addressed in the classroom.

This book helps bridge that gap by providing clear explanations and practical frameworks for understanding artificial intelligence in an educational setting.

How Schools Can Use This Book

This book supports schools in developing a structured approach to artificial intelligence literacy.

It can be used for:

Professional development for educators

Classroom discussions and activities

Curriculum support across subject areas

Policy and academic integrity conversations

Rather than focusing on specific tools, this book emphasizes lasting principles that help students understand, evaluate, and use AI responsibly.

Closing Perspective

Artificial intelligence will continue to evolve. With the right knowledge and leadership, schools can ensure that students not only use these technologies, but understand them, question them, and apply them responsibly.

IntelliGloss is more than a book series. It is a structured approach to preparing students for a future shaped by artificial intelligence.

Rather than focusing only on how to use AI tools, this series helps students understand how AI actually works—from its foundational building blocks to real-world applications.

"Before exploring the technical structure of artificial intelligence, it is equally important to understand the human principles that guide its use."

Human Values Family

Definition

The Human Values Family in artificial intelligence represents the guiding principles that shape how AI systems are created, used, and integrated into society. These values include ethics, responsibility, trust, and human well-being.

Artificial intelligence may be built on data, algorithms, and computational systems, but its true impact is measured by how it affects people. For this reason, AI is not only a technical system—it is a human-centered system.

Key Concepts

The Human Values Family exists to ensure that artificial intelligence serves humanity in a positive and responsible way. While AI systems can process information and generate outcomes, they do not possess judgment, empathy, or moral understanding.

This means that human values must guide every stage of AI development—from design to deployment.

AI reflects the intentions, decisions, and assumptions of the people who build and use it. If those values are not carefully considered, AI systems can unintentionally produce biased, harmful, or misleading results.

Understanding human values in AI is not optional—it is essential.

Core Elements of the Human Values Family

Ethics
Ethics in AI refers to making decisions that are fair, just, and respectful of human rights. This includes minimizing bias, protecting privacy, and ensuring transparency in how systems operate.

Responsibility
Responsibility means that humans remain accountable for AI systems. Developers, educators, organizations, and users must take ownership of how AI is used and the outcomes it produces.

Trust
Trust is critical for the successful adoption of AI. People must feel confident that AI systems are reliable, safe, and aligned with their best interests.

Human Well-Being
AI should enhance human life—not replace, harm, or diminish it. This includes supporting learning, improving access to information, and creating opportunities while maintaining human dignity.

Real-World Connection

Artificial intelligence is already influencing how people learn, communicate, and make decisions. From search engines to classroom tools, AI is shaping daily experiences.

Without clear human values guiding these systems, there is a risk of reinforcing misinformation, bias, or unrealistic expectations.

For students, this means learning not only how to use AI tools, but how to question them, evaluate their outputs, and understand their limitations.

Applications in Education

In the classroom, the Human Values Family helps students develop critical thinking and ethical awareness. Teachers can use this framework to guide discussions about fairness, responsibility, and the impact of technology on society.

Students can explore questions such as:

How should AI be used responsibly?

What makes an AI system fair?

How does technology influence human behavior?

This approach supports both technical understanding and responsible decision-making.

Benefits

Teaching human values in AI helps students:

Develop ethical awareness

Strengthen critical thinking

Understand the societal impact of technology

Become responsible users and future creators of AI

It ensures that learning about AI goes beyond functionality and includes responsibility.

Challenges

Human values are not always universal. Different cultures, communities, and individuals may have different perspectives on what is considered fair or ethical.

Additionally, AI technology is evolving rapidly, often faster than policies and guidelines can keep up. This makes it essential for educators and students to stay informed and adaptable.

Summary

The Human Values Family reminds us that artificial intelligence is not just about machines—it is about people.

By focusing on ethics, responsibility, trust, and human well-being, students can learn to use AI thoughtfully and responsibly.

Understanding these principles helps prepare learners to navigate a world where artificial intelligence plays an increasingly important role in everyday life.

Executive Summary

IntelliGloss AI Education Series

Teaching How Artificial Intelligence Actually Works

Artificial intelligence is already shaping how students learn, write, research, and make decisions. Yet in many classrooms, students are being introduced to AI tools without understanding how these systems actually function.

This creates a critical gap.

Students may become efficient users of technology, but without foundational knowledge, they are not equipped to think critically, evaluate outputs, or use AI responsibly. As AI continues to expand across every industry, this gap will only grow more significant.

The **IntelliGloss AI Education Series** was created to address this challenge.

The Problem

Most current approaches to AI in education focus on tool usage rather than system understanding. As a result:

- Students rely on AI without understanding its limitations
- Educators lack structured frameworks for teaching AI concepts
- Key terms such as generative AI, agentic AI, and autonomy are often introduced without clear definitions
- Responsibility and ethical use are not consistently emphasized

Without clarity, artificial intelligence becomes difficult to teach, difficult to learn, and difficult to manage in a school environment.

The Solution

The IntelliGloss AI Education Series provides a structured, classroom-ready approach to artificial intelligence literacy for grades 6–12.

Rather than focusing on individual tools, this series teaches students how AI works as a complete system—from foundational components to real-world applications.

Students learn to move beyond surface-level interaction and develop true understanding.

The IntelliGloss Framework

The series introduces AI through a clear and connected structure, including:

- Foundational building blocks such as data, algorithms, tokens, and models
- System-level understanding through categories such as intelligence level, behavior, and control
- Real-world context through applications, limitations, and responsible use
- Human-centered learning through ethics, responsibility, trust, and student safety

This structured approach transforms artificial intelligence from a confusing concept into an understandable system.

Instructional Design

Each book in the series is designed for practical classroom use and includes:

- Structured chapters aligned with instructional pacing
- Clear, student-friendly explanations
- Reflection sections to reinforce understanding
- Worksheets, quizzes, and answer keys
- Teacher implementation support

No prior technical background is required for educators or students.

Guiding Principle

A central message of the IntelliGloss series is:

Artificial Intelligence is a tool—not a decision maker.

Students learn that while AI can support thinking and provide information, all decisions, actions, and responsibilities remain with humans. This principle reinforces critical thinking, accountability, and responsible technology use.

Why It Matters

AI literacy is no longer optional. It is a foundational skill.

Students who understand how AI works will be better prepared to:

Think critically about information

Adapt to emerging technologies

Use AI responsibly and ethically

Succeed in an increasingly AI-driven world

Our Goal

The IntelliGloss AI Education Series is designed to help schools move beyond simply using artificial intelligence tools and toward a deeper understanding of how these systems actually work.

By providing clear structure, defined concepts, and real-world context, this series equips students and educators with the knowledge needed to think critically, evaluate information, and use AI responsibly.

The goal is not just to introduce technology—but to build understanding, confidence, and accountability in an AI-driven world.

This is not just about learning to use AI—it is about preparing students to understand it, question it, and lead with it.

Clarity leads to confidence.
Understanding leads to responsible use.

Mission Statement

The mission of the IntelliGloss AI Education Series is to make artificial intelligence clear, structured, and accessible for every student and educator.

In a world where AI is rapidly transforming how information is created, used, and understood, this series is designed to move beyond surface-level interaction and provide a deeper understanding of how intelligent systems actually work.

Through clear explanations, organized frameworks, and real-world context, IntelliGloss equips learners with the ability to think critically, evaluate information, and engage with technology responsibly.

This mission is grounded in a simple belief:
students should not only learn how to use artificial intelligence—they should understand it.

By building both technical awareness and human-centered understanding, the IntelliGloss AI Education Series prepares students to navigate, question, and shape a future increasingly influenced by intelligent technologies.

The goal is not just to keep up with artificial intelligence—but to understand it, guide it, and use it responsibly.

Vision Statement

The vision of the IntelliGloss AI Education Series is to create a future where artificial intelligence is clearly understood, responsibly used, and thoughtfully integrated into education and everyday life.

In this future, students are not passive users of technology, but informed thinkers who understand how intelligent systems work, recognize their limitations, and apply them with purpose and responsibility.

Educators are equipped with clear frameworks and structured resources that make artificial intelligence accessible, teachable, and meaningful across all subjects—not just in technical fields.

Schools become environments where technology is not simply adopted, but understood—where students are encouraged to question, evaluate, and engage with AI in ways that support learning, creativity, and ethical awareness.

As artificial intelligence continues to evolve, this vision supports a generation that is prepared not only to adapt to change, but to lead it with knowledge, confidence, and integrity.

The future of artificial intelligence will not be defined by technology alone—but by the understanding and responsibility of those who use it.

Connecting AI Understanding to Cybersecurity Awareness

Definition

Understanding artificial intelligence is the first step toward understanding cybersecurity. While cybersecurity focuses on protecting systems, data, and users, artificial intelligence explains how those systems are built, how they function, and where they may be vulnerable.

The Connection

Every AI system is made up of components such as data, algorithms, models, and infrastructure. These same components are also the targets of cybersecurity threats.

When students understand:

How data is collected and stored

How algorithms make decisions

How AI models process information

How systems operate across frontend and backend layers

They begin to recognize where risks can exist and how systems can be misused.

Why This Matters

In today's digital world, students are not just users of technology—they are participants in complex systems powered by artificial intelligence.

Without understanding how these systems work:

Technology becomes something they trust without question

Risks become harder to recognize

Decisions are made without awareness of consequences

With understanding:

Students become more aware of how their data is used

They recognize how systems can be manipulated

They make more informed and responsible choices

Building Digital Readiness

Digital readiness is not only about using tools. It is about understanding the systems behind those tools.

By learning how AI works, students develop:

Awareness of digital environments

Confidence in navigating technology

A foundation for future learning, including cybersecurity

Conclusion

Cybersecurity begins with understanding.

Before students can protect systems, they must first understand how those systems are built and how they operate. This is why learning artificial intelligence is not only about innovation—it is also about responsibility.

The Foundation of Artificial Intelligence

Definition

The foundation of Artificial Intelligence (AI) refers to the core building blocks that allow AI systems to function. These building blocks work together to help machines learn from information, recognize patterns, and make decisions. AI is not magic—it is a system built on structured components that operate behind the scenes.

Understanding the Foundation in Simple Terms

Artificial Intelligence can be compared to a house. Before a house is complete, it must be built on a strong foundation. This foundation includes concrete, wiring, plumbing, and support structures that are not always visible but are essential for the house to function properly.

In the same way, AI systems rely on foundational components that are not visible to users but are necessary for AI tools to work. When people use AI applications such as chatbots or design tools, they are interacting with the surface. The true power of AI comes from what is underneath.

Key Components of the AI Foundation

1. Data (The Information)

Data is the starting point of all AI systems. It includes text, images, numbers, audio, and other forms of information. AI systems learn by analyzing patterns within this data.

2. Algorithms (The Instructions)

Algorithms are step-by-step instructions that tell the AI system how to process data. They guide how the system learns, identifies patterns, and produces results.

3. Models (The Trained System)

A model is created when data and algorithms are combined through a training process. The model acts as the "brain" of the AI system, allowing it to make predictions and generate responses.

4. Computing Power (The Engine)

AI systems require powerful computers to process large amounts of data. This includes specialized hardware such as processors and graphics processing units (GPUs) that allow AI to function efficiently.

5. Infrastructure (The Environment)

Infrastructure refers to the systems that support AI operations, including servers, storage, networks, and energy systems. Data centers are a key part of this infrastructure, providing the physical space where AI systems operate.

How These Components Work Together

AI systems function by combining all foundational components into a single process. Data is collected and analyzed using algorithms. This process creates a model that can recognize patterns and make decisions. The entire system is powered by computing machines and supported by infrastructure.

Why Understanding the Foundation Matters

Many people use AI tools without understanding how they work. This can lead to confusion, misuse, or over-reliance on technology. By understanding the foundation of AI, students and educators can:

Develop critical thinking skills

Use AI tools more responsibly

Recognize the limitations of AI systems

Build a deeper understanding of modern technology

Real-World Example

When a student asks a chatbot a question, the response does not come from "thinking" like a human. Instead, the AI system uses a trained model that has learned patterns from large amounts of data. It follows algorithms to predict the most appropriate answer, using powerful computers and infrastructure to deliver the response quickly.

This process is also influenced by how the question is asked. The words, structure, and clarity of a question—often referred to as a *prompt*—can affect the quality of the response. Learning how to communicate effectively with AI systems is an important skill known as prompt engineering. For further understanding, students and educators may explore *What to Say When You Talk to Yourself: A Guide to Prompt Engineering* by Susie Hala, which explains how carefully structured prompts can guide AI responses more effectively.

Conclusion

The foundation of Artificial Intelligence is built on data, algorithms, models, computing power, and infrastructure. These components work together to create systems that can learn, predict, and assist humans. Understanding this foundation helps students move beyond simply using AI tools and toward truly understanding how artificial intelligence works.

The Foundational Families of Artificial Intelligence

Introduction

Artificial intelligence is often described as a powerful technology, but in reality, it is not a single system. It is a combination of multiple components working together to create intelligent behavior.

To better understand how artificial intelligence works, it is helpful to break it down into organized groups. In the IntelliGloss framework, these groups are called **Foundational Families of Artificial Intelligence**.

Each family represents a key part of how AI systems are built and operate. Some families focus on how information is created and stored. Others focus on how machines learn, make decisions, process language, or perform tasks. Additional families represent the physical hardware, energy systems, and global infrastructure that make artificial intelligence possible.

When these families work together, they form a complete AI system.

This approach allows students and educators to move beyond simply using artificial intelligence tools and begin to understand what is happening behind the scenes. Instead of viewing AI as a mystery, learners can see it as a structured system made up of clearly defined components.

The diagram on the next page provides a visual overview of these families and how they connect to form the foundation of artificial intelligence.

By learning each family step by step, students develop a deeper understanding of how AI systems process information, learn from data, and interact with the world.

Understanding the Foundational Families of Artificial Intelligence is the first step toward true AI literacy.

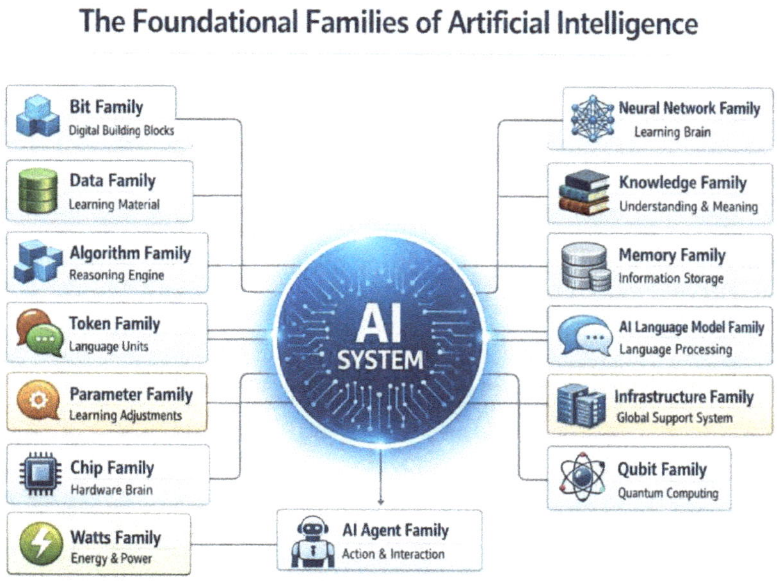

The Foundational Families of Artificial Intelligence

Family	Role	Description
Bit Family	Digital Building Blocks	The smallest unit of digital information (0 or 1). All computing systems begin with bits.
Algorithm Family	Reasoning Engine	Step-by-step instructions that tell computers how to solve problems and process information.
Token Family	Language Units	Pieces of text used by AI models to understand and generate human language.
Parameter Family	Learning Adjustment System	Adjustable numerical values inside AI models that allow them to learn patterns from data.
Data Family	Learning Material	The information AI studies in order to learn patterns, relationships, and knowledge.
Logic Family	Decision Rules	The reasoning structures that allow AI systems to make decisions and evaluate conditions.
Memory Family	Information Storage	Systems that store and retrieve information so AI models can access past knowledge and context.
Knowledge Family	Understanding & Meaning	Structured information that allows AI to represent facts, relationships, and concepts.

Family	Role	Description
Neural Network Family	Learning Brain	Interconnected layers of artificial neurons that enable AI systems to recognize patterns, learn from data, and make predictions.
AI Model Family	Intelligence Engine	The trained system that uses data, parameters, and neural networks to perform tasks such as prediction, classification, and generation.
AI Translator Architecture Family	Language Conversion System	Systems that transform input into output, enabling AI to convert text, speech, or images into meaningful responses.
AI Agent Family	Action and Task Execution System	AI systems designed to perceive information, make decisions, and carry out tasks autonomously or semi-autonomously.
Chip Family	Hardware Brain	Physical processors (GPUs, TPUs, CPUs, NPUs) that perform AI computations.
Watts Family	Energy Power	The electrical power required to run AI hardware and data centers.
AI Energy Family	Energy Source System	The total energy consumed over time to operate AI systems, including training and real-time usage.
Infrastructure Family	Global Support System	Data centers, internet networks, cloud systems, and global infrastructure that allow AI to operate and scale.
Ingredient Family	System Composition	The essential components that come together to create an AI system, including data, algorithms, models, hardware, and energy.
Qubit Family	Quantum Information Units	Quantum bits that can represent multiple states simultaneously, forming the foundation of quantum computing.

The Bit Family

Introduction

The Bit Family represents the starting point of all digital technology. Every computer system, application, and artificial intelligence model is built from bits—the smallest unit of information in computing.

A bit can hold one of two values: 0 or 1. While this may seem simple, these two values form the foundation of everything digital. When bits are combined and organized, they create larger units of data that allow computers to store text, display images, play videos, and run complex systems.

From a single bit to massive data systems, all digital information follows this same structure. This is how computers are able to represent and process the world in a form they can understand.

In artificial intelligence, bits are essential because they store the data that models learn from, process the calculations that drive decision-making, and support the systems that generate responses.

Understanding the Bit Family helps students see how simple binary signals grow into powerful technologies. It reveals that behind every advanced AI system is a foundation built from the most basic building blocks of information.

Bit Family — Visual Understanding of Data Size

How Much Data Can Each Unit Hold? (Simple Examples)

Unit	Size	Photos (Approx.)	Video (Approx. Hours)
Bit	1 bit	N/A	N/A
Byte	8 bits	1 character	N/A
Kilobyte (KB)	~1,000 bytes	Part of a paragraph	N/A
Megabyte (MB)	~1,000 KB	~1 photo	~1 minute of video
Gigabyte (GB)	~1,000 MB	~250 photos	~1–2 hours of video
Terabyte (TB)	~1,000 GB	~250,000 photos	~1,000–2,000 hours of video
Petabyte (PB)	~1,000 TB	~250 million photos	~1–2 million hours of video
Exabyte (EB)	~1,000 PB	~250 billion photos	~1–2 billion hours of video
Zettabyte (ZB)	~1,000 EB	~250 trillion photos	~1–2 trillion hours of video
Yottabyte (YB)	~1,000 ZB	~250 quadrillion photos	~1–2 quadrillion hours of video

---

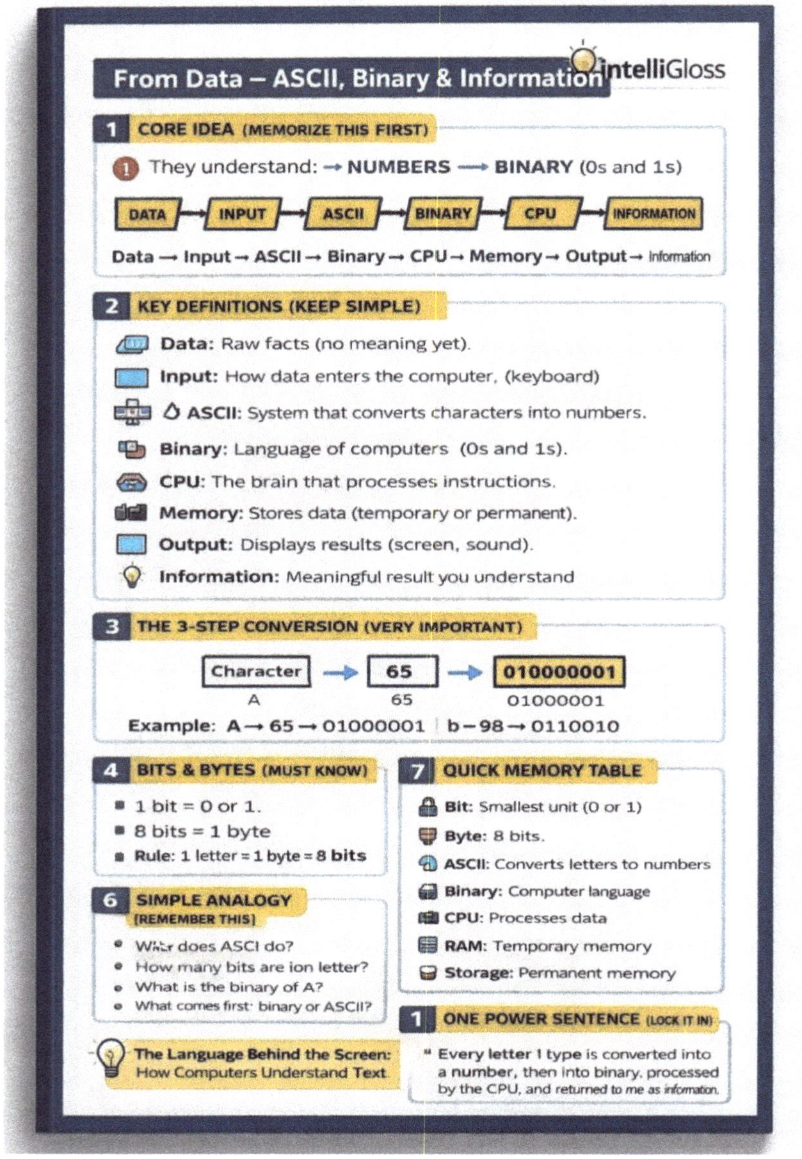

The Algorithm Family

Definition and Overview

The **Algorithm Family** represents the *thinking engine* of artificial intelligence — the set of mathematical instructions that guide how AI analyzes data, learns patterns, and makes decisions.

An **algorithm** is a sequence of steps designed to solve a problem or complete a task. In AI, algorithms tell the system *how to learn*, *how to predict*, and *how to improve* with every iteration.

In simple terms:

The Algorithm Family is the *logic of intelligence* — the invisible code that transforms data into decisions and predictions into progress.

How Algorithms Power AI

Every AI system — from simple chatbots to large-scale deep learning models — relies on algorithms as its foundation.
They determine how the model:

- Processes and cleans data,
- Identifies relationships between variables,
- Learns from feedback, and
- Improves over time.

Without algorithms, even the most powerful dataset or neural network would remain static and lifeless.

In essence, **algorithms are the teachers** that train AI how to think.

Why the Algorithm Family Matters

Algorithms are what separate automation from intelligence.
They allow machines to **reason**, **adapt**, and **learn** — not just follow commands.
For prompt engineers, understanding algorithmic behavior helps explain *why* AI sometimes misunderstands a question, repeats patterns, or changes tone after feedback.

Every AI response you receive follows an underlying process — a pattern recognition journey from input to output.

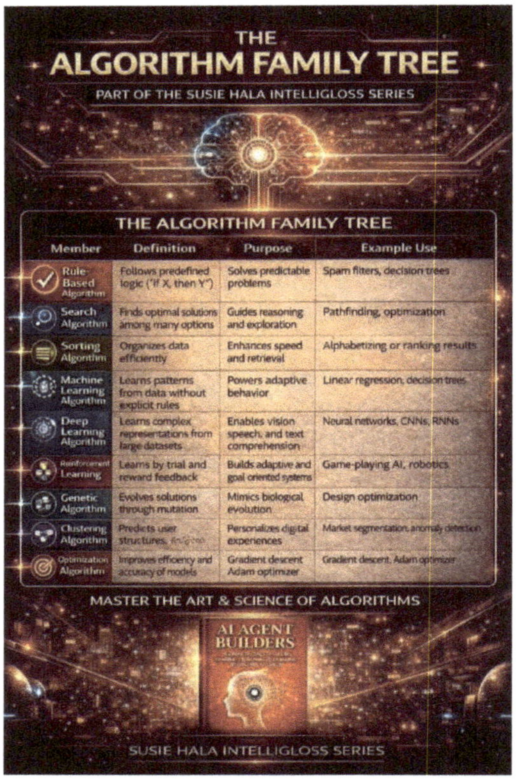

Analogy for Everyday Readers

Imagine AI as a chef in a kitchen:

- The **Data Family** provides the ingredients.
- The **Knowledge Family** gives the recipes.
- The **Algorithm Family** is the *cooking process* — mixing, heating, tasting, and adjusting until the dish is perfect.

Just as cooking methods determine the quality of food, algorithms determine the quality of intelligence.

Algorithm Efficiency and Energy Use

Not all algorithms are equal.
Some are **fast but shallow**, while others are **deep but energy-intensive**.
Training large AI models requires algorithms that can handle billions of calculations per second — powered by the **Watts Family** (energy) and executed through the **Chip Family** (hardware).

The design of efficient algorithms directly affects sustainability in AI — minimizing power consumption while maximizing accuracy and speed.

Algorithms and Prompt Engineering

For prompt engineers, algorithms explain *how* the AI arrives at its answers.
When a model gives inconsistent or off-topic results, it's often due to:

Misinterpretation of input signals (input encoding),

Bias in training algorithms, or

Overfitting to certain data patterns.

Knowing this helps you craft prompts that guide the AI's decision-making — not just its output.

Quick Takeaway: The Algorithm Family is the reasoning heart of AI.
It transforms information into understanding and enables machines to think, learn, and evolve like digital problem-solvers.

Token Family Introduction

The Token Family represents one of the most important bridges between human language and artificial intelligence. While humans communicate using words, sentences, and meaning, AI systems do not understand language in the same way. Instead, they rely on tokens—small units of text that allow machines to process, analyze, and generate language step by step.

A token can be a word, part of a word, a character, or even punctuation. When a student types a sentence into an AI system, that sentence is not read as a whole idea. It is first broken down into tokens. These tokens become the input that the AI model uses to recognize patterns, predict outcomes, and generate responses.

The Token Family works closely with several other foundational families in artificial intelligence. It connects directly with the Data Family, which provides the text used for training, and the Neural Network Family, which processes token patterns to produce intelligent outputs. It also plays a key role in the AI Translator Architecture Family, where tokens are transformed, analyzed, and reassembled into meaningful responses.

Understanding tokens helps students see what is happening behind the scenes when they interact with AI tools. Instead of viewing AI as a "magic system," they begin to understand that every response is built from sequences of tokens processed through mathematical models.

In simple terms, if language is what humans speak, tokens are what AI understands.

Token Family Breakdown Chart

Component	Role	Description	Example
Tokenization	Input Conversion	The process of breaking text into smaller units (tokens) that AI can process	"Artificial Intelligence" → "Artificial" + "Intelligence"
Tokens	Language Units	The individual pieces of text used by AI models for understanding and generation	"AI", "learn", "ing", "."
Subword Tokens	Efficiency Units	Words split into smaller parts to handle unknown or complex vocabulary	"unbelievable" → "un", "believ", "able"
Character Tokens	Fine-Grained Units	Text broken down into individual characters for detailed processing	"AI" → "A" + "I"
Vocabulary (Token Set)	Token Library	The complete set of tokens an AI model recognizes and uses	GPT models have thousands to millions of tokens
Encoding	Token Mapping	Converting tokens into numerical representations for computation	"AI" → [1234, 5678] (example IDs)
Decoding	Output Reconstruction	Converting numerical outputs back into readable text	[1234, 5678] → "AI system"
Context Window	Memory Limit	The number of tokens an AI can process at one time	Example: 8,000 tokens ≈ several pages of text
Token Embeddings	Meaning Representation	Mathematical vectors that capture relationships between tokens	"king" and "queen" have similar embeddings
Token Prediction	Language Generation	The process of predicting the next token in a sequence	"AI is" → predicts "powerful"

The Token Family reminds us that behind every intelligent response is a structured sequence of tokens working together. What feels like natural conversation to humans is, for AI, a carefully processed stream of language units transformed into meaning.

The AI Ecosystem Family

The AI Ecosystem Family is a connected group of artificial intelligence technologies, systems, behaviors, and applications that work together to help machines perform intelligent tasks. This ecosystem includes core AI systems, AI agents, agentic AI, AI autonomy, autonomous AI workers, and generative AI. Each part plays a different role in how modern AI systems think, learn, create, make decisions, solve problems, and interact with the world.

At the center of the ecosystem is artificial intelligence itself — the broad field focused on building machines and software that can perform tasks that normally require human intelligence. AI agents act as the systems that carry out goals and actions. Agentic AI describes the ability of

AI systems to plan, reason, adapt, and pursue objectives with limited human guidance. AI autonomy represents the level of independence an AI system has while making decisions and taking actions. AI autonomous workers apply these capabilities to perform real-world tasks like digital employees or assistants. Generative AI adds the ability to create new content such as text, images, music, video, code, and designs.

The AI Ecosystem Family demonstrates that modern artificial intelligence is no longer just one single technology. Instead, it is an interconnected environment of systems, tools, intelligence, automation, creativity, and human collaboration. As AI continues to evolve, these technologies are becoming increasingly integrated into education, business, healthcare, communication, cybersecurity, research, and everyday life.

Understanding the AI Ecosystem Family helps students, educators, and readers see how the different parts of AI connect together to shape the future of intelligent systems and the digital world.

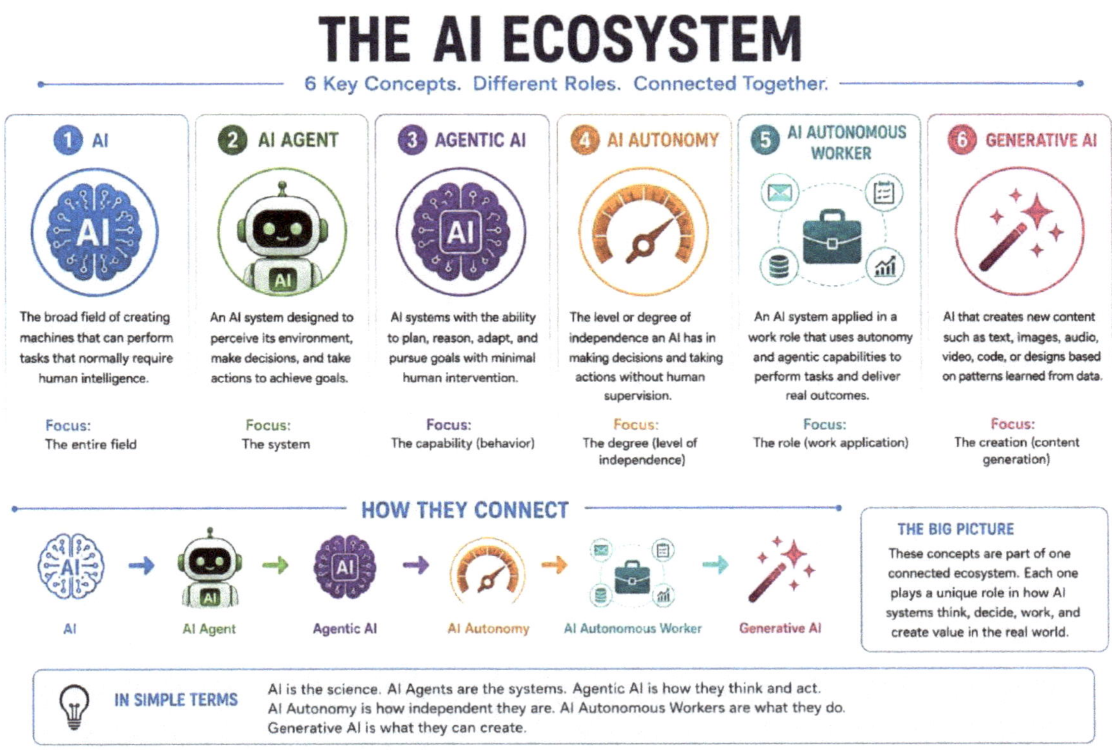

Parameter Family Introduction

The Parameter Family represents the internal learning system of artificial intelligence. While tokens provide the language and data provides the learning material, parameters are what allow AI systems to adjust, improve, and make intelligent decisions over time.

In simple terms, parameters are numerical values inside an AI model that change as the system learns. These values are not visible to users, but they play a critical role in how the model understands patterns, relationships, and meaning. Every time an AI system is trained, it adjusts its parameters to better predict outcomes and generate accurate responses.

Parameters exist throughout neural networks, where they act as the connections between artificial neurons. Each connection has a weight, which determines how important a particular piece of information is. During training, these weights are continuously adjusted based on data, allowing the system to improve its performance.

The Parameter Family works closely with the Data Family, which provides the information needed for learning, and the Neural Network Family, which organizes how parameters are structured and applied. It also supports the Token Family by helping the model interpret and predict sequences of language.

Understanding parameters helps students recognize that AI is not simply programmed with fixed rules. Instead, it learns by adjusting internal values that guide how it processes information. These adjustments are what allow AI systems to evolve from simple pattern recognition to complex reasoning and decision-making.

In essence, if data is what AI learns from, parameters are how AI learns.

Parameter Family Breakdown Chart

Component	Role	Description	Example
Parameters	Learning Values	Numerical values inside an AI model that are adjusted during training	Millions or billions of values inside a model
Weights	Connection Strength	Values that determine how strongly one neuron influences another	A higher weight = stronger influence
Bias	Adjustment Factor	A value added to help the model shift and fine-tune outputs	Helps improve accuracy in predictions
Training Process	Learning Mechanism	The process of adjusting parameters using data to improve performance	Model improves after analyzing many examples
Loss Function	Error Measurement	Measures how far the model's prediction is from the correct answer	Lower loss = better performance

Component	Role	Description	Example
Optimization Algorithm	Adjustment Strategy	Method used to update parameters efficiently	Gradient Descent adjusts weights step by step
Gradient	Direction of Change	Indicates how parameters should change to reduce error	Shows whether to increase or decrease a value
Backpropagation	Learning Process	System that sends error signals backward to update parameters	Adjusts earlier layers based on output error
Hyperparameters	Control Settings	External settings that guide how training happens (not learned)	Learning rate, batch size
Model Size	Capacity Indicator	The total number of parameters in a model	Larger models = more learning capacity

The Parameter Family is the hidden engine of learning in artificial intelligence. While users interact with outputs, it is the continuous adjustment of parameters behind the scenes that makes intelligent behavior possible.

Data Family Introduction

The Data Family represents the foundation of learning in artificial intelligence. Every AI system depends on data to develop knowledge, recognize patterns, and make decisions. Without data, artificial intelligence cannot learn, adapt, or function effectively.

Data can take many forms, including text, images, audio, video, and numerical information. These inputs provide the raw material that AI systems analyze during training. By studying large amounts of data, AI models begin to identify patterns, relationships, and structures that allow them to make predictions and generate responses.

The quality and diversity of data play a critical role in how well an AI system performs. Accurate, balanced, and relevant data helps models produce reliable results, while poor or biased data can lead to incorrect or unfair outcomes. This is why data collection, preparation, and evaluation are essential steps in the development of responsible AI systems.

The Data Family works closely with the Parameter Family, which adjusts internal values based on data, and the Neural Network Family, which processes and organizes data through layers of computation. It also supports the Token Family when dealing with language, as text data is converted into tokens for analysis.

Understanding the Data Family helps students recognize that AI does not “know” things on its own. Instead, it learns from the information it is given. The more meaningful and well-prepared the data, the more capable the AI system becomes.

In simple terms, data is the source of knowledge, and it is the starting point for all artificial intelligence.

Data Family Breakdown Chart

Component	Role	Description	Example
Data	Learning Material	Raw information used by AI systems to learn patterns and relationships	Text, images, audio, numbers
Dataset	Organized Collection	A structured group of data used for training and evaluation	A folder of labeled images
Training Data	Learning Input	Data used to teach the AI model during training	Thousands of sentences for a language model
Validation Data	Performance Check	Data used to tune the model during training without directly learning from it	Helps prevent overfitting
Test Data	Final Evaluation	Data used to measure how well the model performs after training	New unseen examples
Structured Data	Organized Format	Data arranged in tables with clear categories	Spreadsheets, databases
Unstructured Data	Flexible Format	Data without a predefined structure	Text documents, images, videos
Labeled Data	Guided Learning	Data tagged with correct answers to guide training	Image labeled “cat” or “dog”
Unlabeled Data	Self-Learning Input	Data without labels, used in unsupervised learning	Raw text without categories
Data Quality	Accuracy Measure	The reliability and correctness of data	Clean, complete, and consistent data
Data Bias	Imbalance Issue	When data does not represent all groups fairly	Skewed or incomplete datasets
Data Preprocessing	Preparation Step	Cleaning and organizing data before training	Removing errors, formatting text

The Data Family reminds us that artificial intelligence is only as strong as the information it learns from. High-quality data leads to meaningful insights, while poor data can limit or misguide intelligent systems.

Memory Family Introduction

The Memory Family represents how artificial intelligence systems store, retain, and retrieve information. Just as humans rely on memory to recall past experiences, learn new concepts, and make decisions, AI systems depend on memory to access previously processed information and maintain context.

In artificial intelligence, memory is not a single component but a collection of mechanisms that allow systems to handle information over time. Some forms of memory are short-term, holding information temporarily while a task is being completed. Other forms are long-term, storing learned knowledge that can be used across different tasks and interactions.

Memory plays a critical role in enabling AI systems to understand sequences, maintain context in conversations, and improve decision-making. For example, when a user interacts with a language model, the system uses memory to keep track of previous words, sentences, or prompts in order to generate coherent and relevant responses.

The Memory Family works closely with the Data Family, which provides the information to be stored, and the Parameter Family, which encodes learned knowledge within the model. It also supports the Neural Network Family by enabling systems to process sequences and retain important patterns over time.

Understanding the Memory Family helps students see that AI is not simply reacting to individual inputs in isolation. Instead, it relies on stored information and contextual awareness to produce meaningful and consistent outputs.

In simple terms, if data is what AI learns from, memory is how AI remembers and uses what it has learned.

Memory Family Breakdown Chart

Component	Role	Description	Example
Memory	Information Storage	The ability of an AI system to store and access information	Retaining previous inputs in a task
Short-Term Memory	Temporary Storage	Holds information for immediate processing	Keeping track of words in a sentence
Long-Term Memory	Persistent Storage	Stores learned knowledge for future use	Knowledge embedded in model parameters
Context Memory	Conversation Tracking	Maintains information within a specific interaction	Remembering earlier parts of a prompt
Working Memory	Active Processing	Handles information currently being used in computation	Processing a sequence step by step
External Memory	Extended Storage	Memory stored outside the model for retrieval	Databases, vector stores
Internal Memory	Embedded Knowledge	Information stored within the model itself	Learned patterns inside neural networks
Sequence Memory	Order Awareness	Tracks the order of inputs over time	Understanding sentence structure

Component	Role	Description	Example
Retrieval Mechanism	Access System	Retrieves stored information when needed	Searching relevant past data
Attention Mechanism	Focus System	Highlights important parts of memory for processing	Focusing on key words in a sentence
Memory Capacity	Storage Limit	The amount of information the system can handle at once	Context window size

The Memory Family shows that intelligence is not just about processing information in the moment, but about retaining, organizing, and using knowledge over time to create meaningful understanding.

Knowledge Family Introduction

The Knowledge Family represents how artificial intelligence organizes, connects, and uses information to create understanding. While data provides raw information and memory stores it, knowledge is what gives that information meaning and structure.

In artificial intelligence, knowledge is not simply a collection of facts. It is the result of identifying relationships, patterns, and connections within data. AI systems use knowledge to recognize concepts, make decisions, and generate meaningful responses. This allows machines to move beyond simple data processing and toward more intelligent behavior.

Knowledge can be represented in different ways within AI systems. Some forms are structured, such as databases and knowledge graphs, where relationships between concepts are clearly defined. Other forms are learned implicitly through neural networks, where patterns are encoded within parameters and used to guide predictions.

The Knowledge Family works closely with the Data Family, which provides the information needed to build knowledge, and the Memory Family, which stores and retrieves that information. It also connects with the Parameter Family, where learned knowledge is embedded within the model, and the Neural Network Family, which processes and organizes that knowledge.

Understanding the Knowledge Family helps students recognize that AI systems do not simply memorize information. Instead, they learn how pieces of information relate to one another, allowing them to interpret meaning, solve problems, and respond intelligently.

In simple terms, if data is information and memory stores it, knowledge is the understanding that makes it useful.

Knowledge Family Breakdown Chart

Component	Role	Description	Example
Knowledge	Understanding System	Organized information that allows AI to interpret meaning and make decisions	Recognizing relationships between concepts
Facts	Basic Information	Individual pieces of information stored within a system	"Water freezes at 0°C"
Relationships	Connection Mapping	Links between pieces of information that create meaning	"Teacher teaches student"
Knowledge Representation	Structure System	Methods used to organize and store knowledge in AI	Knowledge graphs, semantic networks
Knowledge Graph	Network Mapping	A structured representation of entities and their relationships	Google Knowledge Graph
Semantic Understanding	Meaning Interpretation	The ability to understand meaning behind words and data	Understanding synonyms and context
Inference	Reasoning Process	Drawing conclusions based on known information	If A = B and B = C, then A = C
Rules	Decision Framework	Logical guidelines used to make decisions	If temperature < 0°C → freeze
Ontology	Concept Framework	A structured system defining categories and relationships	Classification of animals
Explicit Knowledge	Direct Information	Clearly defined and stored knowledge	Rules, databases
Implicit Knowledge	Learned Patterns	Knowledge learned through experience and data	Patterns learned by neural networks
Knowledge Integration	System Coordination	Combining information from multiple sources	Merging text, images, and data

The Knowledge Family transforms information into understanding, allowing artificial intelligence to move beyond data and memory into meaningful reasoning and intelligent decision-making.

AI Model Family Introduction

The AI Model Family represents the core system within artificial intelligence that performs tasks such as prediction, classification, and content generation. It is the part of AI that users interact with, whether they are asking questions, generating images, or analyzing data.

An AI model is a trained system that has learned patterns from data. During training, the model processes large amounts of information and adjusts its internal parameters to improve accuracy. Once trained, the model can take new input and produce meaningful output based on what it has learned.

AI models can take many forms depending on their purpose. Some models are designed to recognize images, others to understand language, and others to make decisions or predictions. Large Language Models (LLMs), for example, are designed to process and generate human language by predicting sequences of tokens.

The AI Model Family works closely with the Data Family, which provides the learning material, and the Parameter Family, which stores learned patterns. It also relies on the Neural Network Family for structure and the Chip and Infrastructure Families for execution and deployment.

Understanding the AI Model Family helps students see that AI is not just a concept, but a working system that has been trained to perform specific tasks. It is the engine that transforms input into output.

In simple terms, if AI is the system, the model is the part that actually does the thinking and producing.

AI Model Family Breakdown Chart

Component	Role	Description	Example
AI Model	Core System	The trained system that performs tasks	Chatbot, image generator
Training	Learning Process	Process of teaching the model using data	Learning from datasets
Inference	Output Generation	Using the trained model to produce results	Answering a question
Model Architecture	Structural Design	Defines how the model is built	Neural networks, transformers
Parameters	Learned Values	Internal values adjusted during training	Billions of weights
Input Data	Entry Information	Data provided to the model for processing	User prompt
Output Data	Result	The response or prediction generated	AI-generated text
Model Types	Functional Categories	Different kinds of models for different tasks	Classification, generation
Fine-Tuning	Model Adjustment	Improving a model for specific tasks	Custom-trained AI
Pretrained Model	Base System	A model trained on large datasets before use	General-purpose AI
Evaluation	Performance Check	Measuring how well the model performs	Accuracy, loss metrics

The AI Model Family represents the working core of artificial intelligence, where learned patterns are transformed into meaningful actions, predictions, and responses.

Neural Network Family Introduction

The Neural Network Family represents the structural foundation of how artificial intelligence learns and processes information. Inspired by the human brain, neural networks are systems of interconnected units, often called neurons, that work together to analyze data, recognize patterns, and make decisions.

In artificial intelligence, a neural network is made up of layers. The input layer receives data, the hidden layers process that data, and the output layer produces a result. As information flows through these layers, the network applies mathematical transformations that allow it to detect patterns and relationships within the data.

Neural networks rely heavily on the Parameter Family, where weights and biases determine how strongly information flows between neurons. During training, these parameters are adjusted to improve the network's performance. The more the network learns, the better it becomes at recognizing patterns and making accurate predictions.

The Neural Network Family works closely with the Data Family, which provides the information needed for learning, and the Memory and Knowledge Families, which help store and organize learned information. It also supports the Token Family when processing language, allowing AI systems to interpret sequences of tokens in meaningful ways.

Understanding neural networks helps students see that AI is not simply following instructions. Instead, it is learning from examples and improving over time through layered processing and pattern recognition.

In simple terms, neural networks are the systems that allow AI to think, learn, and make sense of information.

Neural Network Family Breakdown Chart

Component	Role	Description	Example
Neural Network	Learning Structure	A system of interconnected neurons that processes data and learns patterns	Image recognition system
Neuron (Node)	Processing Unit	A basic unit that receives input, processes it, and passes output forward	A single calculation point

Component	Role	Description	Example
Input Layer	Data Entry Point	The first layer that receives raw data	Pixels of an image
Hidden Layers	Processing Layers	Intermediate layers that transform data and detect patterns	Feature detection layers
Output Layer	Result Generator	The final layer that produces predictions or decisions	"Cat" vs "Dog" classification
Weights	Signal Strength	Values that determine how strongly inputs influence outputs	Higher weight = stronger impact
Bias	Adjustment Value	Helps shift outputs to improve learning accuracy	Fine-tuning predictions
Activation Function	Decision Function	Determines whether a neuron should activate based on input	ReLU, Sigmoid
Forward Propagation	Data Flow	The process of passing input data through the network to produce output	Input → Hidden → Output
Backpropagation	Learning Process	Adjusts weights and biases based on error to improve performance	Correcting mistakes
Loss Function	Error Measurement	Calculates how far the output is from the correct answer	Prediction vs actual
Deep Neural Network	Advanced Structure	A network with many hidden layers for complex learning	Deep learning models

The Neural Network Family provides the structure that allows artificial intelligence to transform data into understanding, making it possible for machines to learn from experience and improve over time.

Dual Language System in Artificial Intelligence

Definition

The Dual Language System in Artificial Intelligence refers to the way AI communicates using two different forms of language at the same time: human language for interaction and machine language for internal processing.

Key Components

Human Language (Natural Language)
This is the language people use to communicate with AI, such as English, Spanish, Tongan, or Fijian. It includes words, sentences, and questions that users type or speak.

Machine Language (Numerical Representation)
This is how AI understands information internally. Words are converted into numbers called tokens and processed using mathematical models and algorithms.

How It Works (Step-by-Step)

A user enters a question in human language

The AI converts the words into numerical tokens

The AI processes the tokens using a neural network

The AI generates a response based on patterns and probabilities

The response is converted back into human language

Example

User Input:
"What is Artificial Intelligence?"

AI Process:

Converts words into numbers

Analyzes patterns from training data

Predicts the best possible answer

Output:
"Artificial Intelligence is the ability of machines to perform tasks that normally require human intelligence."

Why This Matters

Understanding the dual language system helps students realize that:

AI does not "think" like humans

AI translates language into math and back into language

Every interaction with AI is based on patterns, not emotions or understanding

Applications

Chatbots and virtual assistants

Language translation systems

Search engines

Voice recognition tools

Challenges

Misinterpretation of human language

Bias in language data

Lack of true understanding or reasoning

Summary

Artificial Intelligence works by translating human language into machine-readable data and then converting the results back into human language. This dual system allows AI to interact with people while operating through mathematical processes behind the scenes.

AI Translator Architecture Family Introduction

The AI Translator Architecture Family represents the system that transforms input into meaningful output in artificial intelligence. It acts as the bridge between what humans provide and what AI produces. Whether a user types a question, uploads an image, or speaks a command, this architecture is responsible for interpreting that input and generating a response.

In artificial intelligence, translation does not only mean converting one language to another. It refers to the broader process of transforming one form of information into another. For example, text can be translated into a response, speech can be converted into text, and images can be interpreted into descriptions. This transformation process is at the core of how modern AI systems function.

The AI Translator Architecture is built on multiple foundational families. It relies on the Token Family to break input into manageable units, the Neural Network Family to process patterns, and the Parameter Family to guide learning. It also uses knowledge and memory to maintain context and produce coherent results.

At the center of this architecture is the ability to encode and decode information. Encoding transforms input into a format the model can understand, while decoding converts processed information back into human-readable output. This continuous transformation allows AI systems to interact with users in a natural and meaningful way.

Understanding the AI Translator Architecture Family helps students see that AI is not simply responding randomly. Instead, it is systematically translating input into output through structured processes and learned patterns.

In simple terms, if tokens are the language pieces and neural networks are the brain, the AI Translator Architecture is the system that turns understanding into communication.

AI Translator Architecture Family Breakdown Chart

Component	Role	Description	Example
AI Translator Architecture	Transformation System	Converts input into meaningful output	Question → Answer
Input Processing	Data Intake	Receives and prepares user input for analysis	Text prompt entered by a user
Encoding	Input Conversion	Transforms input into numerical representations	Words → token IDs
Context Building	Meaning Formation	Organizes input into a structured understanding	Sentence context tracking
Sequence Processing	Order Handling	Maintains the correct order of information	Word sequence in a sentence
Attention Mechanism	Focus System	Identifies important parts of input data	Highlighting key words
Representation Layer	Feature Mapping	Converts data into internal representations for processing	Embeddings
Decoding	Output Generation	Converts processed data back into human-readable form	Token IDs → words
Output Generation	Response Creation	Produces the final answer or result	AI-generated response
Multimodal Translation	Cross-Format Processing	Translates between different types of data	Image → text description
Feedback Loop	Improvement Cycle	Uses results to refine future outputs	Model learning over time

The AI Translator Architecture Family shows that artificial intelligence is not just about understanding information, but about transforming it into meaningful communication that humans can use and interact with.

AI Architecture Family Introduction

The AI Architecture Family represents the overall design and structure of an artificial intelligence system. While individual families such as Data, Parameters, and Neural Networks explain how AI learns and processes information, the AI Architecture Family shows how all these components are organized and work together as a complete system.

In artificial intelligence, architecture refers to the blueprint that defines how data flows through a system, how components interact, and how decisions are produced. It determines how input is received, how it is processed, and how output is generated. A well-designed architecture allows AI systems to operate efficiently, scale to large problems, and produce reliable results.

AI architectures can vary depending on the type of system being built. Some are designed for image recognition, others for language processing, and others for decision-making or automation. Despite these differences, most architectures share common elements such as input layers, processing layers, memory components, and output mechanisms.

The AI Architecture Family connects all foundational families. It integrates the Data Family for input, the Token Family for language processing, the Neural Network Family for computation, the Parameter Family for learning, and the Memory and Knowledge Families for storing and organizing information. It also works closely with the AI Translator Architecture Family to transform input into meaningful output.

Understanding the AI Architecture Family helps students see the "big picture" of artificial intelligence. Instead of viewing AI as separate parts, they begin to understand it as a coordinated system where each component plays a specific role.

In simple terms, if individual families are the parts of AI, the AI Architecture Family is the blueprint that brings everything together into one working system.

AI Architecture Family Breakdown Chart

Component	Role	Description	Example
AI Architecture	System Blueprint	The overall design that defines how an AI system is structured and operates	ChatGPT system design
Input Layer	Data Entry Point	Receives raw input from users or external sources	Text prompt, image upload
Preprocessing Layer	Data Preparation	Cleans and organizes input data before processing	Tokenization, normalization
Processing Core	Computation Engine	The main system where data is analyzed and transformed	Neural networks, transformers
Parameter System	Learning Core	Stores adjustable values that guide learning and predictions	Model weights and biases

Component	Role	Description	Example
Memory System	Context Storage	Maintains and retrieves information during processing	Context window, external memory
Knowledge System	Understanding Layer	Organizes relationships and meaning within the system	Knowledge graphs, learned patterns
Decision Layer	Output Logic	Determines the final output based on processed data	Selecting the best response
Output Layer	Result Delivery	Presents results to the user in a usable format	Text, image, or audio response
Feedback Loop	Improvement System	Uses outcomes to refine future performance	Model updates and retraining
Scalability System	Expansion Capability	Allows the system to handle increasing data and complexity	Cloud-based AI systems
Integration Layer	System Connection	Connects AI with external tools and platforms	APIs, databases, applications

The AI Architecture Family reveals that artificial intelligence is not a single technology, but a coordinated system of interconnected components working together to transform data into intelligent outcomes.

Chip Family Introduction

The Chip Family represents the physical hardware that powers artificial intelligence systems. While software components such as data, algorithms, and neural networks define how AI works, none of these systems can function without the computing chips that perform the actual calculations.

Chips are specialized electronic components designed to process information at extremely high speeds. In artificial intelligence, these chips handle the complex mathematical operations required for training models and generating outputs. Every prediction, calculation, and response produced by an AI system is executed by hardware within the Chip Family.

Different types of chips are used depending on the needs of the system. Central Processing Units (CPUs) handle general-purpose tasks, while Graphics Processing Units (GPUs) are optimized for parallel processing, making them ideal for training neural networks. More specialized chips, such as Tensor Processing Units (TPUs) and Neural Processing Units (NPUs), are designed specifically for AI workloads, enabling faster and more efficient computation.

The Chip Family works closely with the Neural Network Family, which defines the structure of computation, and the Parameter Family, which stores the values being processed. It also connects to the Infrastructure Family, where large-scale systems of chips are organized in data centers and cloud environments.

Understanding the Chip Family helps students recognize that artificial intelligence is not purely abstract. It depends on physical machines that require power, resources, and engineering to operate. These chips are the engines that bring AI models to life.

In simple terms, if AI is the intelligence, chips are the machines that make that intelligence possible.

Chip Family Breakdown Chart

Component	Role	Description	Example
Chip (Processor)	Computation Engine	Electronic hardware that performs calculations required for AI	CPU, GPU
CPU (Central Processing Unit)	General Processor	Handles a wide range of computing tasks	Running basic applications
GPU (Graphics Processing Unit)	Parallel Processor	Processes many calculations at once, ideal for AI training	Training neural networks
TPU (Tensor Processing Unit)	AI Accelerator	Specialized chip designed for machine learning tasks	Google TPU
NPU (Neural Processing Unit)	Edge AI Processor	Optimized for running AI on devices like phones	Smartphone AI features
AI Accelerator	Performance Booster	Hardware designed to speed up AI computations	Dedicated AI chips
Memory (Hardware)	Data Storage	Stores data and instructions for processing	RAM, VRAM
Parallel Processing	Speed Mechanism	Ability to perform multiple calculations simultaneously	GPUs processing thousands of operations
Throughput	Processing Capacity	Amount of data processed over time	High-performance computing systems
Latency	Response Time	Time it takes to process a request	Faster chips = lower latency
Power Consumption	Energy Usage	Amount of energy required to run the chip	High-performance GPUs use more power
Edge Devices	Local Processing	Devices that run AI locally without cloud support	Phones, smart cameras

The Chip Family reminds us that behind every intelligent system is powerful hardware performing millions or billions of calculations, turning abstract models into real-world functionality.

Watts Family Introduction

The Watts Family represents the measurement of power used by artificial intelligence systems. While the Chip Family provides the hardware that performs computations, the Watts Family explains how much energy those systems consume while operating.

A watt is a unit of power that measures the rate at which energy is used. In artificial intelligence, watts help us understand how much electricity is required to run processors, train models, and generate responses. Every time an AI system processes data, performs calculations, or produces output, it consumes power.

Different AI systems require different levels of power depending on their size and complexity. Small systems, such as those running on mobile devices, use relatively low amounts of power. In contrast, large-scale AI models operating in data centers can require significant amounts of electricity, especially during training, where billions of calculations are performed continuously.

The Watts Family works closely with the Chip Family, which determines how efficiently computations are performed, and the Infrastructure Family, where large networks of machines operate together. It also connects to the overall design of AI systems, as more efficient models can reduce power consumption while maintaining performance.

Understanding the Watts Family helps students recognize that artificial intelligence is not only about intelligence and computation, but also about energy use and resource management. As AI continues to grow, managing power efficiently becomes an important part of building responsible and sustainable systems.

In simple terms, if chips perform the work, watts measure how much power it takes to do that work.

Watts Family Breakdown Chart

Component	Role	Description	Example
Watt (W)	Power Measurement	Unit that measures the rate of energy use	A device using 100 watts
Power Consumption	Energy Usage Rate	Amount of power used during operation	AI model running on GPUs
Energy Efficiency	Performance Balance	How effectively a system uses power to perform tasks	More output with less power
High-Performance Computing	Intensive Power Use	Systems that require large amounts of power for complex tasks	AI training clusters

Component	Role	Description	Example
Idle Power	Standby Usage	Power consumed when systems are not actively processing	Servers waiting for requests
Peak Power	Maximum Usage	Highest level of power used during heavy workloads	Training large AI models
Thermal Output	Heat Generation	Heat produced as a result of power usage	Cooling systems in data centers
Cooling Systems	Temperature Control	Systems used to manage heat from high power usage	Air or liquid cooling
Power Supply	Energy Source	Provides electricity to AI systems	Electrical grid, batteries
Edge Power Usage	Local Energy Use	Power consumption on smaller devices	Smartphones, IoT devices
Data Center Power	Large-Scale Usage	Power required for large AI operations	Server farms running AI models
Sustainable Energy	Efficiency Goal	Use of renewable energy to reduce environmental impact	Solar-powered data centers

The Watts Family highlights that intelligence comes with a cost—every AI system requires power, and understanding that power is essential for building efficient and sustainable technologies.

Watts Family (AI Power Usage Scale)

Definition

The **Watts Family** represents the real-time power usage of artificial intelligence systems, measured in watts (W). It shows how much power AI systems consume at a given moment as they process data and perform computations.

Watts Scale

1 Watt
10 Watts
100 Watts
500 Watts
1,000 Watts (1 Kilowatt)
10,000 Watts (10 Kilowatts)
100,000 Watts (100 Kilowatts)
1,000,000 Watts (1 Megawatt)
10,000,000 Watts (10 Megawatts)
100,000,000+ Watts (100+ Megawatts)

Key Characteristics

Measured in real-world electrical power

Higher watt values indicate higher processing demand

Used to represent the scale of AI systems from small devices to large infrastructures

Closely connected to the Chip Family, Energy Family, and Infrastructure Family

Examples

Low watts → small devices and basic AI functions

Medium watts → computers and advanced applications

High watts → data centers and large AI systems

Summary

The **Watts Family** provides a numerical representation of how much power artificial intelligence systems use in real time, helping to illustrate the scale and intensity of AI operations.

Student Insight

Watts show how much power AI is using right now.

AI Energy Family Introduction

The AI Energy Family represents the total amount of energy consumed by artificial intelligence systems over time. While the Watts Family measures the rate at which power is used at any given moment, the Energy Family focuses on the accumulated energy required to perform tasks, run systems, and sustain operations.

In artificial intelligence, energy is used every time a model is trained, a system processes data, or a response is generated. Large-scale AI systems, especially those operating in data centers, can consume significant amounts of energy due to the continuous processing of massive datasets and complex computations.

Energy is typically measured over time using units such as kilowatt-hours (kWh), which reflect how much power has been used during a specific period. For example, running a high-performance AI system for several hours or days results in a total energy cost that goes beyond the moment-to-moment power usage measured in watts.

The AI Energy Family works closely with the Watts Family, which provides the rate of power consumption, and the Chip Family, which determines how efficiently computations are performed. It also connects to the Infrastructure Family, where large-scale systems operate continuously and require long-term energy management.

Understanding the AI Energy Family helps students recognize that artificial intelligence has real-world resource implications. It is not only about performance and speed, but also about sustainability, efficiency, and responsible use of technology.

In simple terms, if watts measure how fast energy is used, energy measures how much is used over time.

AI Energy Family Breakdown Chart

Component	Role	Description	Example
Energy	Total Consumption	The total amount of power used over a period of time	Running an AI system for hours or days
Kilowatt-hour (kWh)	Energy Measurement	Unit used to measure energy consumption over time	1 kWh = using 1,000 watts for 1 hour
Energy Usage	Consumption Tracking	Total energy required for AI operations	Training a large model
Training Energy	Learning Cost	Energy used during model training processes	Weeks of GPU usage
Inference Energy	Response Cost	Energy used when AI generates outputs	Answering a user prompt
Energy Efficiency	Optimization Goal	Reducing energy use while maintaining performance	Efficient AI models
Energy Scaling	Growth Impact	Increase in energy use as systems grow larger	Bigger models = more energy
Data Center Energy	Infrastructure Demand	Total energy used by large AI facilities	Server farms operating 24/7
Cooling Energy	Temperature Control	Energy required to cool systems and prevent overheating	Air conditioning in data centers
Renewable Energy	Sustainability Source	Use of clean energy to power AI systems	Solar, wind-powered data centers
Carbon Impact	Environmental Effect	Emissions associated with energy consumption	AI training carbon footprint
Energy Management	Resource Control	Strategies to monitor and reduce energy use	Efficient scheduling, hardware optimization

The AI Energy Family reminds us that artificial intelligence operates within the physical world, where every computation consumes energy and every system has an impact on resources and sustainability.

Energy Family (Total Power Consumption of Artificial Intelligence)

Definition

The **Energy Family** represents the total amount of electricity used by artificial intelligence systems over time. It is measured in watt-hours (Wh) or kilowatt-hours (kWh) and shows how much energy AI systems consume while running.

Energy Scale

1 Watt-hour (Wh)
10 Watt-hours (Wh)
100 Watt-hours (Wh)
500 Watt-hours (Wh)
1,000 Watt-hours (1 Kilowatt-hour, kWh)
10,000 Watt-hours (10 kWh)
100,000 Watt-hours (100 kWh)
1,000,000 Watt-hours (1 Megawatt-hour, MWh)
10,000,000 Watt-hours (10 MWh)
100,000,000+ Watt-hours (100+ MWh)

Key Characteristics

Measured over time (not instant like watts)

Represents total electricity consumption

Increases the longer AI systems run

Directly related to cost and energy usage

Closely connected to Watts Family, Chip Family, and Infrastructure Family

Examples

Low energy → short AI tasks or small devices

Medium energy → daily AI usage on computers

High energy → training AI models and running data centers

Summary

The **Energy Family** provides a numerical representation of the total electricity consumed by artificial intelligence systems over time, helping to illustrate the overall cost and impact of AI operations.

Student Insight

Energy shows how much total power AI has used over time.

AI Infrastructure Family Introduction

The AI Infrastructure Family represents the large-scale systems and environments that support, power, and connect artificial intelligence technologies. While individual components such as chips, data, and models explain how AI works, infrastructure explains where and how these systems operate in the real world.

AI infrastructure includes data centers, cloud platforms, networking systems, and storage environments that allow artificial intelligence to function at scale. These systems provide the computing power, data access, and connectivity needed to train models, process information, and deliver results to users around the world.

Modern AI systems rely heavily on cloud-based infrastructure, where thousands of machines work together to handle massive workloads. This allows AI to scale efficiently, making it possible to process large datasets, run complex models, and serve millions of users simultaneously. Infrastructure also ensures reliability, security, and continuous availability of AI services.

The AI Infrastructure Family works closely with the Chip Family, which provides the hardware, the Watts and Energy Families, which manage power consumption, and the Data Family, which supplies the information being processed. It also supports the AI Architecture Family by providing the environment where all system components are deployed and connected.

Understanding the AI Infrastructure Family helps students recognize that artificial intelligence is not contained within a single device. Instead, it operates across global systems that require coordination, resources, and engineering to function effectively.

In simple terms, if AI is the system and chips are the engines, infrastructure is the environment that allows everything to run at scale.

AI Infrastructure Family Breakdown Chart

Component	Role	Description	Example
AI Infrastructure	System Environment	The physical and digital systems that support AI operations	Global AI platforms
Data Center	Processing Hub	Facilities that house servers and computing equipment	Large server farms
Cloud Computing	Scalable Platform	Remote systems that provide computing resources over the internet	AWS, Azure, Google Cloud
Servers	Compute Units	Machines that process data and run AI models	Rack-mounted servers
Networking	Connectivity System	Systems that allow communication between machines	Internet, fiber networks
Storage Systems	Data Management	Systems that store large volumes of data	Databases, cloud storage
Distributed Computing	Workload Sharing	Splitting tasks across multiple machines for efficiency	Parallel processing across clusters
Edge Infrastructure	Local Processing	Running AI closer to the user or device	Smart devices, IoT systems
Load Balancing	Traffic Control	Distributes workloads to prevent overload	Managing user requests
Security Systems	Protection Layer	Safeguards data and systems from threats	Encryption, firewalls
Redundancy	Reliability System	Backup systems to ensure continuous operation	Failover servers
Scalability	Growth Capability	Ability to expand resources as demand increases	Adding more servers dynamically

The AI Infrastructure Family reveals that artificial intelligence operates on a global scale, relying on interconnected systems that provide the power, storage, and connectivity needed to support intelligent technologies.

AI Agent Family Introduction

The AI Agent Family represents systems that can take action, make decisions, and perform tasks on behalf of users or other systems. Unlike traditional AI models that only respond to input, AI agents are designed to operate with a level of autonomy, allowing them to plan, execute, and adapt to achieve specific goals.

An AI agent receives input from its environment, processes that information, and takes actions based on predefined objectives or learned behaviors. These actions can include answering questions, automating workflows, retrieving information, or interacting with other systems. Some agents operate in simple environments, while others function in complex systems that require continuous decision-making.

AI agents often combine multiple foundational families. They use the Data Family to gather information, the Memory and Knowledge Families to retain and understand context, and the Neural Network and Parameter Families to process and learn from interactions. They also rely on the AI Architecture and Infrastructure Families to operate reliably at scale.

Modern AI agents can work independently or as part of larger systems. For example, a customer support agent can respond to inquiries automatically, while a more advanced agent can complete multi-step tasks such as scheduling, research, or system management.

Understanding the AI Agent Family helps students see that artificial intelligence is not only about generating responses, but also about taking meaningful action in real-world scenarios.

In simple terms, if AI models think and respond, AI agents act and execute.

AI Agent Family Breakdown Chart

Component	Role	Description	Example
AI Agent	Action System	An AI system that can make decisions and perform tasks	Virtual assistant
Environment	Operating Context	The space where the agent interacts and gathers information	Web, apps, databases
Input Perception	Data Intake	Receives information from the environment	User query or sensor input
Decision Engine	Action Selection	Determines what action to take based on input	Choosing a response or task
Action Execution	Task Performance	Carries out decisions in the environment	Sending an email, retrieving data
Goal System	Objective Setting	Defines what the agent is trying to achieve	Complete a task or solve a problem
Planning Module	Strategy Builder	Breaks down tasks into steps	Multi-step problem solving
Feedback Loop	Learning Cycle	Improves performance based on outcomes	Adjusting actions over time
Autonomy Level	Independence Scale	Degree of independence in decision-making	Fully automated vs assisted

Component	Role	Description	Example
Multi-Agent System	Collaboration Network	Multiple agents working together	Coordinated AI systems

Ingredient Family Introduction

The Ingredient Family represents the essential components that come together to create an artificial intelligence system. Just as a recipe requires specific ingredients to produce a final dish, AI systems rely on a combination of foundational elements working together to function effectively.

Artificial intelligence is not built from a single component. It requires data to learn from, algorithms to guide processing, models to perform tasks, hardware to execute computations, and energy to power the entire system. Each of these elements plays a critical role, and the absence of any one component would prevent the system from operating properly.

The Ingredient Family provides a simplified way for students to understand AI as a system made up of interconnected parts. Instead of viewing AI as complex or mysterious, learners can begin to see it as something constructed from identifiable and understandable components.

This family connects directly with all other foundational families, including Data, Algorithm, Neural Network, Parameter, Chip, and Energy Families. It serves as an overview that brings these elements together into a unified perspective.

Understanding the Ingredient Family helps students recognize that artificial intelligence is built, not magical. It is the result of carefully combining the right components in the right way.

In simple terms, if AI is the final product, the Ingredient Family represents everything needed to build it.

Ingredient Family Breakdown Chart

Component	Role	Description	Example
Data	Learning Input	Provides the information AI uses to learn patterns	Text, images, audio
Algorithms	Instruction Set	Guides how data is processed and decisions are made	Sorting, classification
AI Models	Execution System	Performs tasks such as prediction or generation	Language models
Neural Networks	Processing Structure	Organizes how data is processed through layers	Deep learning models
Parameters	Learning Adjustments	Fine-tune how the model learns and makes predictions	Weights and biases

Component	Role	Description	Example
Tokens	Language Units	Breaks text into smaller pieces for processing	Words or subwords
Hardware (Chips)	Computation Engine	Executes calculations required by AI systems	GPUs, CPUs
Energy	Power Source	Supplies the energy needed to run systems	Electricity usage
Infrastructure	Support System	Provides the environment for AI to operate at scale	Cloud systems, data centers
Memory	Storage System	Stores and retrieves information for processing	Context memory
Knowledge	Understanding Layer	Represents meaning and relationships within data	Knowledge graphs

The Ingredient Family shows that artificial intelligence is built from a combination of essential components, each playing a vital role in creating intelligent systems.

The Frontend and Backend Family of Artificial Intelligence

How AI Systems Connect User Interaction to Intelligent Processing

Introduction

Every artificial intelligence system operates through two essential layers: the frontend and the backend. These layers work together to transform human interaction into intelligent responses, allowing AI systems to function smoothly and effectively.

The frontend is the part of the system that users see and interact with. It includes screens, input tools, and the display of results. Whether a user is typing a question, speaking a command, or uploading an image, all interaction begins at the frontend.

Behind the scenes, the backend serves as the processing engine of the system. It receives input from the frontend, manages data, connects to the AI model, and performs the computations needed to generate a response. The backend is where the intelligence of the system operates, using models, algorithms, and infrastructure to interpret and respond to user requests.

This visual illustrates how these two layers work together as a complete system. It shows the flow of information from user input to AI processing and back to the user as a result. By understanding this structure, students can see that AI is not a single tool, but a coordinated system of layers working together.

In simple terms, the frontend is where interaction happens, and the backend is where intelligence is created.

Every AI system has two sides: what you see and what actually does the thinking.

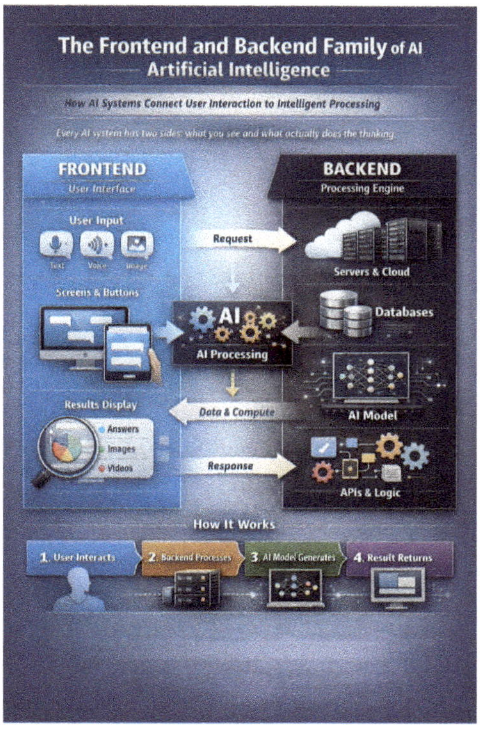

AI Qubit Family Introduction

The AI Qubit Family represents the foundation of quantum computing as it relates to artificial intelligence. While traditional computing relies on bits, which can exist as either 0 or 1, quantum computing uses qubits, which can exist in multiple states simultaneously.

A qubit is the basic unit of quantum information. Unlike classical bits, qubits can take advantage of properties such as superposition and entanglement, allowing quantum systems to process complex computations more efficiently in certain scenarios. This opens new possibilities for solving problems that are difficult or impossible for traditional computers.

In the context of artificial intelligence, qubits have the potential to accelerate learning processes, optimize large-scale systems, and improve complex simulations. Although quantum AI is still in development, it represents a future direction where computational power can expand beyond current limitations.

The AI Qubit Family connects with the Chip Family, as quantum processors are specialized hardware, and with the Algorithm Family, where new types of quantum algorithms are designed.

It also relates to the Parameter and Neural Network Families, as researchers explore quantum-enhanced learning models.

Understanding the AI Qubit Family helps students see that artificial intelligence is continuously evolving. It introduces the idea that the foundations of computing themselves can change, leading to new forms of intelligence and problem-solving.

In simple terms, if bits are the foundation of today's computing, qubits represent the foundation of tomorrow's possibilities.

AI Qubit Family Breakdown Chart

Component	Role	Description	Example
Qubit	Quantum Unit	Basic unit of quantum information	Quantum bit in a quantum computer
Superposition	Multi-State Ability	Ability to exist in multiple states at once	0 and 1 simultaneously
Entanglement	Connection Property	Linking qubits so they influence each other	Paired quantum states
Quantum Gate	Operation System	Performs operations on qubits	Quantum logic gates
Quantum Circuit	Processing Structure	Sequence of quantum operations	Quantum algorithms
Quantum Processor	Hardware Engine	Specialized chip for quantum computing	Quantum computer hardware
Quantum Algorithm	Computation Method	Algorithm designed for quantum systems	Optimization problems
Quantum Speedup	Performance Advantage	Faster processing for certain problems	Complex simulations
Quantum Noise	Stability Challenge	Errors caused by environmental interference	Qubit instability
Quantum Error Correction	Stability Solution	Techniques to reduce errors in quantum systems	Fault-tolerant computing

The AI Qubit Family introduces a new frontier in computing, where the limits of traditional systems are expanded, opening the door to more powerful and advanced forms of artificial intelligence.

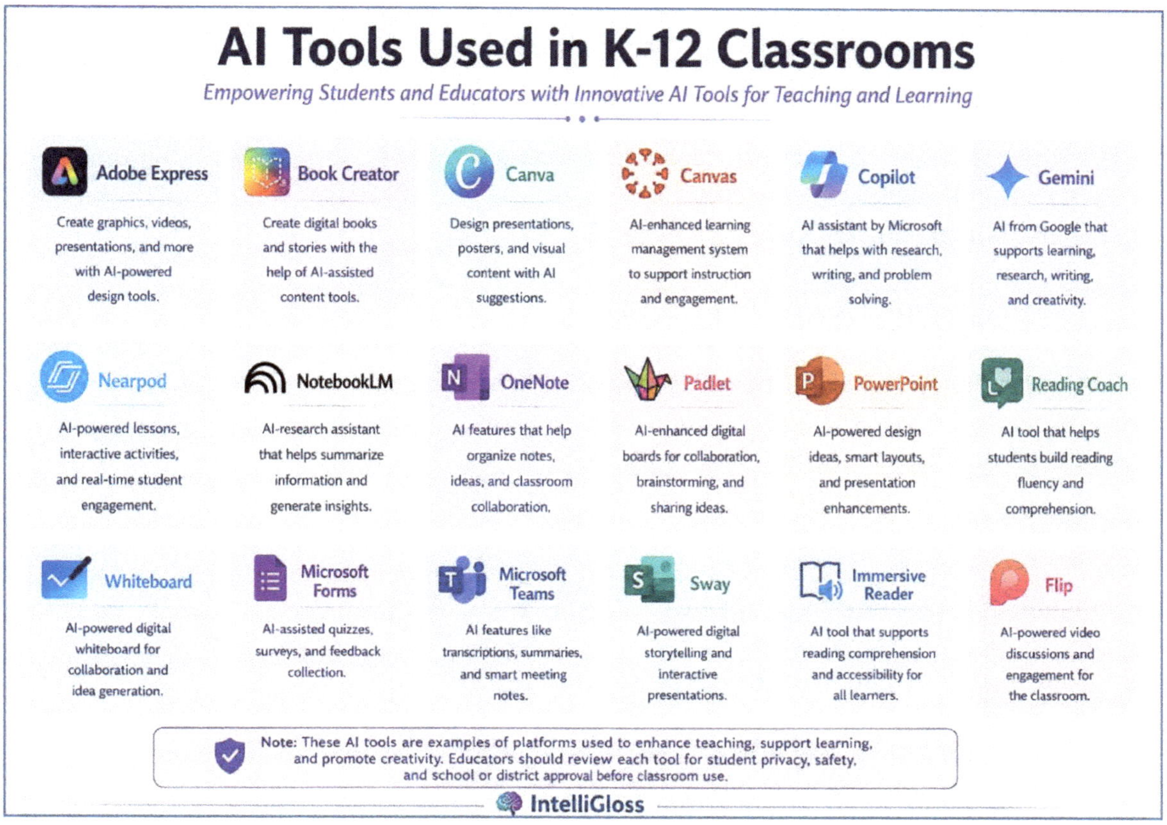
AI Tools Used in K-12 Classrooms
Empowering Students and Educators with Innovative AI Tools for Teaching and Learning
Adobe Express
Create graphics, videos, presentations, and more with AI-powered design tools.
Book Creator
Create digital books and stories with the help of AI-assisted content tools.
Canva
Design presentations, posters, and visual content with AI suggestions.
Canvas
AI-enhanced learning management system to support instruction and engagement.
Copilot
AI assistant by Microsoft that helps with research, writing, and problem solving.
Gemini
AI from Google that supports learning, research, writing, and creativity.
Nearpod
AI-powered lessons, interactive activities, and real-time student engagement.
NotebookLM
AI-research assistant that helps summarize information and generate insights.
OneNote
AI features that help organize notes, ideas, and classroom collaboration.
Padlet
AI-enhanced digital boards for collaboration, brainstorming, and sharing ideas.
PowerPoint
AI-powered design ideas, smart layouts, and presentation enhancements.
Reading Coach
AI tool that helps students build reading fluency and comprehension.
Whiteboard
AI-powered digital whiteboard for collaboration and idea generation.
Microsoft Forms
AI-assisted quizzes, surveys, and feedback collection.
Microsoft Teams
AI features like transcriptions, summaries, and smart meeting notes.
Sway
AI-powered digital storytelling and interactive presentations.
Immersive Reader
AI tool that supports reading comprehension and accessibility for all learners.
Flip
AI-powered video discussions and engagement for the classroom.
Note: These AI tools are examples of platforms used to enhance teaching, support learning, and promote creativity. Educators should review each tool for student privacy, safety, and school or district approval before classroom use.
IntelliGloss

TABLE OF CONTENTS

Introduction

AUTONOMY

The Engine of Artificial General Intelligence

For centuries, humanity has dreamed of creating intelligence beyond itself. From ancient myths of mechanical beings to modern artificial intelligence systems capable of generating text, images, and software, one question has remained at the center of our curiosity:

Can a machine truly think for itself?

Today, artificial intelligence can perform remarkable tasks. It can recognize faces, translate languages, compose music, write essays, diagnose diseases, and even engage in conversations that feel surprisingly human. Yet despite these impressive achievements, most AI systems remain fundamentally dependent on people. They wait for instructions. They respond to prompts. They execute tasks that humans initiate and supervise.

But what happens when intelligence no longer waits?

What happens when a machine can set goals, make decisions, adapt to new circumstances, learn from experience, and pursue objectives without constant human direction?

At that moment, we move beyond simple automation and enter the world of autonomy.

Autonomy is one of the most important concepts in the future of artificial intelligence. It represents the transition from machines that merely react to machines that can act. It is the bridge between systems that follow instructions and systems that can navigate uncertainty, solve novel problems, and operate independently in dynamic environments.

Many experts believe that autonomy will become one of the defining characteristics of Artificial General Intelligence (AGI). While today's AI systems excel at narrow tasks, AGI seeks something much broader: the ability to learn, reason, adapt, and perform across a wide range of domains. To achieve such capabilities, intelligence alone is not enough. Knowledge without action remains dormant. Reasoning without initiative remains incomplete. Learning without independence remains limited.

Autonomy transforms intelligence into agency.

Imagine a future scientific system capable of designing its own experiments, evaluating results, revising hypotheses, and discovering new knowledge with minimal human involvement. Imagine educational systems that adapt continuously to individual learners. Imagine medical systems that monitor health, anticipate risks, and coordinate treatments proactively. Imagine intelligent assistants capable of managing complex projects, solving unforeseen problems, and collaborating with humans as true partners.

These possibilities are not simply questions of intelligence. They are questions of autonomy.

Yet autonomy also introduces profound challenges. As machines become increasingly independent, society must confront difficult questions. How should autonomous systems make decisions? What values should guide their actions? How can humans maintain meaningful oversight? What happens when an autonomous system's objectives conflict with human priorities? How do we ensure that greater capability remains aligned with human well-being?

The answers to these questions may shape the future of civilization.

This book explores autonomy not as a science-fiction fantasy, but as a foundational component of emerging intelligent systems. Throughout these chapters, you will examine the principles that allow machines to act independently, the architectures that support autonomous behavior, the relationship between autonomy and AGI, and the opportunities and risks that accompany increasingly capable systems.

You will discover how goals are formed, how decisions are made, how plans are constructed, how learning occurs, and how autonomous systems adapt to changing environments. Most importantly, you will explore why many researchers consider autonomy to be one of the essential engines driving the development of Artificial General Intelligence.

The story of AI is often told as a story of data, algorithms, and computation. But the story of AGI may ultimately become a story of something far more profound: the emergence of systems capable of directing their own intelligence.

We stand at the threshold of that transformation.

The age of intelligent tools has begun.

The age of autonomous intelligence may be next.

Welcome to the exploration of one of the most important frontiers in artificial intelligence.

Welcome to the study of autonomy.

Learn AI. Understand AI. Shape the Future.

— Susie Hala, IntelliGloss Press

Chapter 1

What Is Autonomy?

The history of intelligence is, in many ways, the history of increasing independence. Human beings learn to survive, make decisions, solve problems, and pursue goals without requiring constant guidance from others. As children grow into adults, they gain the ability to think independently, adapt to unfamiliar situations, and take responsibility for their actions. This gradual movement from dependence to independence is one of the defining characteristics of intelligence itself.

As artificial intelligence continues to advance, researchers are asking a similar question about machines: Can intelligent systems become increasingly independent? Can they move beyond simply following instructions and begin managing their own actions in pursuit of meaningful goals?

The concept that lies at the center of these questions is autonomy.

Autonomy is one of the most important ideas in the development of Artificial General Intelligence (AGI). While modern AI systems have achieved remarkable capabilities, most remain dependent on human direction. They wait for prompts, instructions, commands, or carefully designed objectives before taking action. They may process enormous amounts of information, but they generally do not determine their own course of action. They operate as tools rather than independent agents.

To understand the future of AGI, we must first understand autonomy.

Defining Autonomy

The word autonomy comes from two Greek roots: "auto," meaning self, and "nomos," meaning rule or law. Together, these roots suggest the idea of self-governance—the ability to direct one's own actions according to internal decision-making processes.

In human society, autonomy refers to the capacity of individuals to make choices and act independently. Autonomous individuals can evaluate options, consider consequences, establish goals, and determine how best to achieve them.

In artificial intelligence, autonomy refers to the ability of a system to operate, make decisions, and pursue objectives without requiring continuous human supervision.

This does not mean an autonomous system acts without limits or oversight. Rather, it means the system possesses enough internal capability to handle many decisions independently while remaining aligned with broader objectives established by humans.

Autonomy exists on a spectrum. Some systems possess very little autonomy, while others demonstrate increasingly sophisticated forms of independent behavior.

Understanding this spectrum is essential to understanding AGI.

Intelligence Versus Autonomy

One of the most common misconceptions in discussions about AI is the assumption that intelligence and autonomy are the same thing.

They are not.

A system may be highly intelligent while possessing very little autonomy.

For example, a language model may answer questions, explain complex topics, write software, and generate creative content. These capabilities demonstrate significant intelligence. However, the system typically waits for a user prompt before taking action. It does not independently decide what tasks should be performed next. It does not pursue long-term objectives without instruction.

In contrast, autonomy concerns action and decision-making.

Intelligence helps answer questions.

Autonomy helps decide which questions should be addressed.

Intelligence helps solve problems.

Autonomy helps determine which problems deserve attention.

Intelligence provides capability.

Autonomy provides direction.

This distinction becomes increasingly important as AI systems grow more powerful. Future AGI systems may require both advanced intelligence and advanced autonomy. Possessing one without the other may limit their usefulness and adaptability.

The Evolution of Machine Independence

The earliest machines possessed no autonomy whatsoever.

A mechanical clock follows physical principles that determine its behavior. It does not choose how to operate. It cannot adapt to changing circumstances. It simply performs the function for which it was designed.

Early computers behaved similarly. They followed explicit instructions written by programmers. Every operation depended on predetermined rules. If unexpected situations occurred, the system often failed because it lacked the flexibility to adapt.

As computing technology advanced, machines became increasingly capable of handling uncertainty.

Rule-based expert systems could evaluate conditions and select among predefined responses.

Machine learning systems could identify patterns and improve performance through experience.

Modern AI systems can generate language, recognize images, predict outcomes, and assist with decision-making.

Yet most of these systems still depend heavily on human direction.

The next major stage in AI development involves increasing autonomy. Rather than merely responding to instructions, future systems may be capable of managing tasks, coordinating actions, allocating resources, and pursuing goals with far less human intervention.

This transition represents one of the most significant shifts in the history of intelligent systems.

Levels of Autonomy

Autonomy is not an all-or-nothing property. Instead, it exists across multiple levels.

At the lowest level are reactive systems. These systems simply respond to inputs. A calculator performs operations when numbers are entered. A search engine retrieves information when a query is submitted. Their behavior depends entirely on external requests.

The next level includes assistive systems. These systems help humans make decisions by providing recommendations, predictions, or insights. Navigation software, recommendation engines, and many modern AI applications fall into this category.

Beyond assistive systems are agentic systems. These systems can perform tasks on behalf of users. They may gather information, execute workflows, coordinate activities, and complete multi-step objectives. While still guided by human goals, they possess greater operational independence.

Higher levels involve autonomous systems capable of planning, adapting, and managing complex activities across changing environments. These systems monitor progress, evaluate outcomes, and adjust their behavior as conditions evolve.

At the highest theoretical level lies AGI—a form of intelligence capable of operating across diverse domains while demonstrating broad autonomy, adaptability, and problem-solving capabilities.

Understanding these levels helps us recognize that autonomy develops gradually rather than appearing suddenly.

Why Autonomy Matters for AGI

Many researchers believe autonomy will become one of the defining features of AGI.

Imagine an intelligent system capable of understanding every scientific paper ever published but incapable of deciding how to apply that knowledge. Such a system would be extraordinarily intelligent but operationally limited.

Now imagine a system capable of identifying unanswered scientific questions, designing experiments, analyzing results, and refining its methods without constant human supervision.

The difference between these systems is not merely intelligence.

The difference is autonomy.

AGI requires more than knowledge.

It requires initiative.

It requires planning.

It requires adaptation.

It requires the ability to act purposefully in pursuit of objectives.

Without autonomy, intelligence remains passive.

With autonomy, intelligence becomes active.

This transformation may represent one of the most significant milestones in the journey toward general intelligence.

Benefits of Autonomous Intelligence

Autonomous systems offer enormous potential benefits.

In healthcare, autonomous systems may continuously monitor patient conditions, identify emerging risks, and coordinate interventions before problems become severe.

In education, autonomous learning platforms may adapt instructional strategies to individual students, identifying weaknesses and providing personalized guidance.

In scientific research, autonomous systems may accelerate discovery by exploring hypotheses, conducting simulations, and analyzing vast datasets beyond human capacity.

In environmental management, autonomous systems may optimize energy usage, monitor ecosystems, and respond to changing conditions in real time.

These possibilities illustrate why autonomy has become a central focus of AGI research.

Autonomy allows intelligence to move from observation to action.

The Challenges of Autonomy

Despite its potential benefits, autonomy also introduces significant challenges.

As systems become more independent, ensuring that their actions remain aligned with human values becomes increasingly important.

An autonomous system must make decisions in uncertain situations. It may encounter conflicts between competing objectives. It may face circumstances that were never anticipated by its designers.

How should such systems prioritize goals?

How should they balance risks and rewards?

How should they respond when objectives conflict?

These questions form the foundation of the alignment problem, one of the most important challenges in AGI research.

The greater a system's autonomy, the greater the importance of ensuring that its decision-making processes remain beneficial and trustworthy.

The Beginning of a New Era

Human civilization has always developed tools that extend human capabilities. The wheel extended movement. The telescope extended vision. The computer extended calculation.

Artificial intelligence extends cognition.

Autonomy extends action.

Together, intelligence and autonomy may create systems capable of assisting humanity in ways previously unimaginable.

The development of autonomy does not guarantee the arrival of AGI, nor does it eliminate the technical challenges that remain. However, autonomy represents one of the most important foundations upon which future AGI systems may be built.

As we begin this exploration of autonomous intelligence, we are examining more than a technological concept. We are exploring a fundamental question about the future of thinking machines.

Can intelligence become truly independent?

The answer to that question may shape the future of artificial intelligence, the future of AGI, and perhaps the future of humanity itself.

Learn AI. Understand AI. Shape the Future.

— Susie Hala, IntelliGloss Press

Chapter 1 Summary

What Is Autonomy?

Autonomy is the ability of a system to make decisions and take actions without requiring constant supervision. In artificial intelligence, autonomy represents a critical step beyond simple automation and reactive behavior. While many modern AI systems are intelligent, they often depend on human instructions to determine what actions to perform. Autonomous systems possess greater independence and can pursue goals, adapt to changing environments, and manage tasks with reduced human intervention.

This chapter explored the difference between intelligence and autonomy. Intelligence refers to the ability to process information, reason, learn, and solve problems. Autonomy refers to the ability to direct actions and make decisions. A system may be intelligent without being autonomous, but AGI will likely require both capabilities.

The chapter also examined the evolution of machine independence, from simple mechanical devices and rule-based systems to advanced AI systems capable of increasingly complex behaviors. Readers learned that autonomy exists on a spectrum, ranging from reactive systems and assistive technologies to agentic systems and theoretical AGI.

Finally, the chapter discussed why autonomy is considered a foundational component of AGI. Without autonomy, intelligence remains passive. With autonomy, intelligence becomes capable of pursuing objectives, adapting to uncertainty, and operating in dynamic environments. The chapter concluded by highlighting both the opportunities and challenges associated with autonomous intelligence and its role in shaping the future of AI.

Key Concepts

- Autonomy
- Intelligence
- AGI
- Decision-Making
- Adaptation
- Goal Pursuit
- Agentic Systems
- Autonomous Systems
- Human Supervision
- Alignment

Chapter 1 Reflection

Reflecting on Autonomy

Autonomy is more than a technological concept—it is a characteristic that influences how intelligent systems interact with the world. Throughout history, humans have valued independence because it enables individuals to make choices, solve problems, and pursue meaningful goals. As AI systems become more capable, questions about machine autonomy become increasingly important.

Consider the technologies you use every day. Which systems simply follow instructions, and which systems make decisions on your behalf? How comfortable are you with allowing machines to act independently in areas such as healthcare, transportation, education, or finance?

As you reflect on this chapter, think about the relationship between intelligence and autonomy. Is it possible for a machine to be intelligent without being autonomous? Can autonomy exist without intelligence? How might increasing autonomy change the role of humans in society?

Autonomy offers tremendous opportunities for innovation and progress, but it also introduces ethical and practical challenges. Future generations may live in a world where autonomous systems are common partners in daily life. Understanding autonomy today helps prepare us for the decisions society will face tomorrow.

Reflection Questions

1. How would you define autonomy in your own words?
2. Why is autonomy considered different from intelligence?
3. What are some examples of autonomous behavior in humans?
4. What benefits could autonomous AI provide to society?
5. What risks might arise from highly autonomous systems?
6. Do you believe AGI will require autonomy? Why or why not?
7. How much decision-making should humans delegate to machines?
8. What responsibilities should developers have when creating autonomous systems?

9. How might autonomous systems change education and work?
10. What role should human values play in autonomous AI?

Chapter 1 Worksheet

What Is Autonomy?

Part A: Vocabulary Matching

Match each term with its correct definition.

_____ 1. Autonomy

_____ 2. Intelligence

_____ 3. AGI

_____ 4. Adaptation

_____ 5. Agentic AI

A. The ability to adjust to changing conditions

B. Artificial General Intelligence

C. The ability to make decisions and act independently

D. Systems that perform actions on behalf of users

E. The ability to learn, reason, and solve problems

Part B: True or False

Write TRUE or FALSE.

_____ 1. Intelligence and autonomy mean exactly the same thing.

_____ 2. Most current AI systems still require human guidance.

_____ 3. Autonomy involves making decisions and taking actions.

_____ 4. AGI is expected to operate across many domains.

_____ 5. Autonomous systems never require oversight.

Part C: Short Answer

1. What is autonomy?

___

___

2. How does autonomy differ from intelligence?

___

___

3. Why is autonomy important for AGI?

___

___

4. Give one example of a reactive system.

___

5. Give one example of an autonomous system.

___

___

Part D: Critical Thinking

Imagine you are designing an AGI assistant for a hospital.

1. What decisions should the system be allowed to make independently?

___

___

___

2. What decisions should always require human approval?

___

___

3. Why is balancing autonomy and human oversight important?

Part E: Personal Application

Write one paragraph explaining whether you would trust an autonomous AI system to help make important decisions in your life and explain why.

Chapter 1 Quiz

What Is Autonomy?

Multiple Choice

1. What is autonomy?

A. The ability to store information

B. The ability to act and make decisions independently

C. The ability to calculate numbers

D. The ability to follow instructions exactly

2. Which statement best describes intelligence?

A. The ability to pursue goals

B. The ability to make decisions without guidance

C. The ability to learn, reason, and solve problems

D. The ability to operate a machine

3. Why is autonomy important for AGI?

A. It makes computers smaller

B. It reduces electricity use

C. It allows systems to pursue goals and act independently

D. It removes the need for learning

4. Which of the following is most likely a reactive system?

A. AGI research platform

B. Autonomous robot

C. Calculator

D. Scientific discovery engine

5. What challenge increases as autonomy increases?

A. File storage

B. Alignment and oversight

C. Screen resolution

D. Keyboard speed

Short Answer

6. Define autonomy.
7. Explain one difference between agentic AI and autonomous AI.

8. Why might AGI require both intelligence and autonomy?
9. Give one benefit of autonomous systems.
10. Give one risk of autonomous systems.

Chapter 1 Quiz Answer Key

Multiple Choice

1. B — The ability to act and make decisions independently
2. C — The ability to learn, reason, and solve problems
3. C — It allows systems to pursue goals and act independently
4. C — Calculator
5. B — Alignment and oversight

Short Answer

6. Autonomy is the ability of a system to make decisions and take actions without constant human supervision.
7. Agentic AI performs tasks on behalf of users, while autonomous AI can independently manage goals, plans, and actions with less human involvement.
8. Intelligence provides knowledge and reasoning, while autonomy enables a system to act on that knowledge and pursue objectives independently.
9. Answers may vary. Examples include improved efficiency, personalized learning, scientific discovery, healthcare monitoring, and automation of complex tasks.
10. Answers may vary. Examples include alignment problems, unintended consequences, poor decision-making, misuse, or reduced human oversight.

Scoring Guide

- 9–10 Correct: Excellent Understanding
- 7–8 Correct: Proficient Understanding
- 5–6 Correct: Developing Understanding
- Below 5 Correct: Review Chapter and Retake Quiz

Learn AI. Understand AI. Shape the Future.
— Susie Hala, IntelliGloss Press

Chapter 2

From Obedient Tools to Independent Systems

The story of artificial intelligence is, at its core, a story about increasing independence. Every generation of technology has moved machines a little farther from simple obedience and a little closer to intelligent action. For most of human history, tools existed only to amplify human effort. A hammer could drive a nail, but only when a person picked it up and used it. A calculator could perform arithmetic, but only when someone entered the numbers. These tools had no understanding of purpose, no awareness of goals, and no ability to act on their own.

Artificial intelligence has begun to change that relationship.

As machines become more capable of processing information, learning from experience, and making decisions, they are gradually evolving from obedient tools into increasingly independent systems. This transformation represents one of the most significant technological shifts in human history. Understanding this evolution is essential for understanding autonomy and the future development of Artificial General Intelligence (AGI).

The Age of Obedient Machines

For centuries, machines were designed to follow precise instructions. Their value came from consistency and predictability. If a machine performed the same task the same way every time, it was considered reliable.

Early mechanical devices embodied this principle perfectly. Clocks, pulleys, gears, and engines operated according to fixed physical laws. They could perform useful work, but they could not adapt to changing circumstances.

The first computers inherited this same philosophy. They followed instructions written by programmers and executed those instructions exactly as specified. Every calculation, decision, and action was predetermined.

These systems possessed no autonomy.

If a programmer failed to anticipate a situation, the machine could not compensate. If conditions changed unexpectedly, the machine often failed entirely. Intelligence was not part of the equation. The machine simply obeyed.

This obedience was both a strength and a limitation. It allowed computers to perform calculations with incredible precision, but it also prevented them from handling uncertainty and novelty.

As society's problems became more complex, researchers began searching for ways to create systems that could do more than merely follow instructions.

The Rise of Adaptive Systems

The emergence of artificial intelligence marked a turning point in the history of computing.

Rather than explicitly programming every possible action, researchers began developing systems capable of learning patterns from data. Instead of telling a machine exactly how to recognize a face, engineers could train the system using thousands of examples. Over time, the machine would learn to identify important features on its own.

This shift represented a fundamental change in how machines acquired knowledge.

Traditional software depended on human-written rules.

Machine learning systems depended on experience.

Although these systems remained limited in many ways, they introduced a new capability: adaptation.

For the first time, machines could improve performance through exposure to data. They could recognize patterns that programmers never explicitly defined. They could make predictions based on statistical relationships rather than rigid instructions.

However, these systems were still largely obedient. They learned how to perform tasks, but humans still decided which tasks were important.

The machine could recognize objects.

The human determined why object recognition mattered.

The machine could generate recommendations.

The human determined whether those recommendations would be used.

The system had gained intelligence but remained dependent on external direction.

From Automation to Agency

As AI systems became more sophisticated, researchers began exploring a new frontier: agency.

Agency refers to the capacity of a system to take actions in pursuit of goals.

This concept marks an important transition in the evolution of intelligence.

An automated system performs predefined tasks.

An agent pursues objectives.

Consider a simple thermostat. It automatically adjusts temperature based on a predefined rule. While useful, it possesses no understanding of broader goals.

Now consider an intelligent building management system. Such a system may monitor energy consumption, occupancy patterns, weather forecasts, and equipment performance. It can coordinate multiple actions to achieve objectives such as reducing costs, improving comfort, and conserving energy.

The difference lies in goal-oriented behavior.

The second system is not simply reacting. It is actively managing a situation in pursuit of desired outcomes.

This movement from automation toward agency represents a major step toward autonomy.

The Emergence of AI Agents

Modern AI agents demonstrate how quickly this transformation is occurring.

Unlike traditional software, AI agents can perform multi-step tasks. They can gather information, evaluate options, execute actions, monitor results, and adjust their strategies when necessary.

Imagine assigning a project to an AI assistant.

Instead of simply answering a question, the assistant might:

- Research relevant information.
- Organize findings.
- Develop a plan.
- Create documents.
- Schedule tasks.
- Monitor progress.
- Revise recommendations.

These capabilities move beyond simple instruction-following.

The system begins functioning as a collaborator rather than a tool.

Yet even today's most advanced agents remain limited. They generally operate within boundaries established by humans and often require approval before executing important actions.

Nevertheless, they illustrate the direction AI development is moving.

Each increase in capability brings machines closer to greater independence.

Characteristics of Independent Systems

As systems become more autonomous, several important characteristics begin to emerge.

Goal Orientation

Independent systems focus on achieving objectives rather than merely executing commands.

Instead of asking, "What instruction should I follow next?" the system asks, "What action best advances my objective?"

This shift fundamentally changes how decisions are made.

Adaptability

Independent systems must function in environments that are often unpredictable.

Rules alone are insufficient.

The system must continuously evaluate circumstances, identify changes, and modify its behavior accordingly.

Adaptability allows autonomous systems to remain effective even when conditions differ from those anticipated by designers.

Persistence

Traditional software typically stops when a task is complete.

Independent systems often maintain long-term objectives and continue working toward them over extended periods.

Persistence enables systems to pursue goals that require ongoing effort and adjustment.

Self-Monitoring

Independent systems must evaluate their own performance.

They must recognize errors, identify inefficiencies, and determine whether progress is being made.

Without self-monitoring, autonomy becomes unreliable.

A system that cannot assess its own behavior cannot effectively improve.

Why Independence Matters for AGI

Artificial General Intelligence is often described as intelligence capable of performing across a wide range of domains rather than a single specialized task.

Achieving such versatility requires more than knowledge.

It requires independence.

Imagine an AGI scientist.

The system would not simply answer questions about science. It would identify promising research directions, design experiments, analyze results, revise theories, and pursue discoveries over time.

Imagine an AGI educator.

The system would not simply provide information. It would assess student understanding, develop personalized learning strategies, adapt lessons, and monitor progress.

Imagine an AGI healthcare assistant.

The system would continuously analyze patient data, anticipate potential risks, coordinate treatments, and adjust recommendations as conditions evolve.

In each case, intelligence alone is insufficient.

The system must also possess autonomy.

It must determine how knowledge should be applied.

It must make decisions in changing environments.

It must pursue goals over time.

This combination of intelligence and independence lies at the heart of AGI.

The Challenges of Increasing Independence

As machines become more independent, society faces new challenges.

A highly autonomous system may encounter situations that were never anticipated by its creators. It may need to make decisions involving uncertainty, competing priorities, or ethical considerations.

For example:

Should a healthcare system prioritize one patient over another?

How should an autonomous vehicle respond during an unavoidable accident?

How should an AGI allocate limited resources during a crisis?

These questions demonstrate that autonomy is not merely a technical challenge.

It is also a social, ethical, and philosophical challenge.

The more independent systems become, the more important alignment, transparency, accountability, and human oversight become.

The future of AGI depends not only on increasing capability but also on ensuring that autonomy remains aligned with human values.

A New Relationship Between Humans and Machines

For thousands of years, tools existed to extend human abilities.

The wheel extended movement.

The telescope extended vision.

The computer extended calculation.

Artificial intelligence extends cognition.

Autonomy extends initiative.

As machines become increasingly independent, humanity may experience a fundamental shift in its relationship with technology. Rather than serving solely as instruments, intelligent systems may become collaborators capable of pursuing shared goals alongside humans.

This possibility represents both extraordinary opportunity and profound responsibility.

The transition from obedient tools to independent systems is not merely a technological evolution. It is a transformation in how intelligence itself is expressed through machines.

Understanding that transformation is essential for understanding AGI and the future of autonomous intelligence.

The journey has already begun, and each advancement brings us one step closer to a world where intelligent systems do far more than obey.

They understand, adapt, plan, and act.

And that may ultimately define the next era of artificial intelligence.

Learn AI. Understand AI. Shape the Future.

— Susie Hala, IntelliGloss Press

Chapter 2 Summary

From Obedient Tools to Independent Systems

This chapter explored the evolution of machines from simple obedient tools to increasingly independent systems. Throughout history, tools and machines were designed to follow instructions exactly as humans intended. Mechanical devices, early computers, and traditional software operated according to fixed rules and could not adapt when conditions changed.

The development of artificial intelligence introduced a major shift. Instead of relying entirely on human-written instructions, AI systems began learning from data and experience. Machine learning enabled systems to identify patterns, make predictions, and improve performance over time. Although these systems became more intelligent, they still depended on humans to define goals and determine how their capabilities should be used.

The chapter introduced the concept of agency, which refers to a system's ability to take actions in pursuit of objectives. Unlike traditional automation, which follows predefined rules, agentic systems can make decisions, coordinate tasks, and pursue goals. This transition from automation to agency represents an important step toward autonomy.

Readers also examined the emergence of AI agents, systems capable of performing multi-step tasks such as gathering information, organizing resources, creating plans, and adapting to changing circumstances. These systems demonstrate how AI is gradually becoming more independent.

Several characteristics of independent systems were discussed, including goal orientation, adaptability, persistence, and self-monitoring. These qualities enable systems to operate effectively in dynamic environments and move beyond simple instruction-following behavior.

Finally, the chapter explained why increasing independence is essential for AGI. Intelligence alone is not enough. AGI systems must be capable of applying knowledge, making decisions, pursuing objectives, and adapting to new situations. The chapter concluded by exploring both the opportunities and challenges associated with increasingly autonomous systems.

Key Concepts

- Obedient Tools
- Machine Independence
- Artificial Intelligence
- Machine Learning

- Agency
- AI Agents
- Goal Orientation
- Adaptability
- Persistence
- Self-Monitoring
- Autonomous Systems
- AGI

Chapter 2 Reflection

Thinking About the Rise of Independent Systems

For most of human history, machines were viewed as tools that carried out specific instructions. Today, technology is evolving toward systems that can make decisions, solve problems, and pursue goals with increasing independence. This transformation raises important questions about the future relationship between humans and intelligent machines.

As AI systems become more capable, society must decide how much responsibility should be delegated to machines. In some situations, greater autonomy may improve efficiency, productivity, and innovation. In other situations, human oversight may remain essential.

Consider the technologies you interact with every day. Which systems simply follow instructions? Which systems make recommendations or decisions on your behalf? How comfortable would you be allowing an AI system to manage important responsibilities such as healthcare, education, transportation, or financial planning?

This chapter encourages readers to think critically about the balance between human control and machine independence. The future of AGI may depend not only on building more capable systems but also on understanding how humans and machines can work together responsibly.

Reflection Questions

1. What does it mean for a machine to be an obedient tool?
2. How did machine learning change the way machines acquire knowledge?
3. What is the difference between automation and agency?
4. Why are AI agents considered a step toward autonomy?
5. Which characteristic of independent systems do you believe is most important and why?
6. How might independent systems improve people's daily lives?
7. What concerns do you have about highly autonomous systems?
8. Should humans always remain involved in important decisions made by AI systems? Explain.
9. How might AGI change the way people work and learn?
10. What responsibilities should society have when developing increasingly autonomous technologies?

Chapter 2 Worksheet

From Obedient Tools to Independent Systems

Part A: Vocabulary Matching

Match each term with its correct definition.

_____ 1. Agency

_____ 2. Adaptability

_____ 3. AI Agent

_____ 4. Goal Orientation

_____ 5. Persistence

A. The ability to continue working toward long-term objectives

B. A system that performs actions to achieve objectives

C. The ability to adjust to changing conditions

D. The ability to take actions in pursuit of goals

E. Focusing actions on achieving specific objectives

Part B: True or False

Write TRUE or FALSE.

_____ 1. Early computers could easily adapt to unexpected situations.

_____ 2. Machine learning allows systems to learn from data.

_____ 3. Traditional automation and agency mean the same thing.

_____ 4. AI agents can perform multi-step tasks.

_____ 5. AGI will likely require both intelligence and autonomy.

Part C: Short Answer

1. What is meant by an obedient tool?

2. How did machine learning change artificial intelligence?

3. What is agency?

4. Name two characteristics of independent systems.

5. Why is autonomy important for AGI?

Part D: Critical Thinking

Imagine you are designing an autonomous AI assistant for a university.

1. What responsibilities should the assistant handle independently?

2. What responsibilities should require human approval?

3. How would you ensure the system remains aligned with human goals?

Part E: Application Activity

Create a comparison chart between an obedient tool and an independent system.

Obedient Tool Independent System

After completing the chart, write a short paragraph explaining which type of system would be more useful in a rapidly changing environment and why.

Chapter 2 Quiz

From Obedient Tools to Independent Systems

Multiple Choice

1. What best describes an obedient tool?

A. A machine that learns independently

B. A machine that follows instructions exactly

C. A machine that creates goals

D. A machine that supervises humans

2. What major capability did machine learning introduce?

A. Mechanical movement

B. Internet access

C. Learning from data and experience

D. Increased screen resolution

3. What is agency?

A. The ability to store files

B. The ability to follow rules

C. The ability to take actions in pursuit of goals

D. The ability to connect to networks

4. Which of the following is a characteristic of independent systems?

A. Adaptability

B. Predictable repetition only

C. Complete dependence on human instructions

D. Fixed behavior

5. Why is autonomy important for AGI?

A. It reduces computer size

B. It enables systems to pursue goals and operate across domains

C. It increases battery life

D. It eliminates the need for learning

Short Answer

6. Define agency.
7. Explain the difference between automation and agency.

8. Name two characteristics of independent systems.
9. Why are AI agents considered an important step toward AGI?
10. What challenge increases as systems become more autonomous?

Chapter 3

Why AGI Requires Autonomy

Imagine a machine that possesses access to every scientific paper ever written, every textbook ever published, and every piece of information available on the internet. It can answer questions instantly, explain complex ideas, and perform calculations far beyond human capability. Yet despite its immense intelligence, it remains motionless until someone tells it what to do.

Would such a system truly be intelligent?

Or would it simply be an extraordinarily powerful tool?

This question lies at the heart of one of the most important debates in artificial intelligence. Intelligence alone may not be enough to create Artificial General Intelligence (AGI). A system may possess vast knowledge, extraordinary reasoning capabilities, and advanced learning mechanisms, but without autonomy, it remains dependent on external direction. It remains a passenger rather than a driver.

Autonomy is what transforms intelligence into action.

For this reason, many researchers believe that autonomy is not merely an optional feature of AGI. It is a fundamental requirement.

The Difference Between Knowing and Doing

Human intelligence is remarkable not only because humans can think, but because humans can act upon their thoughts.

Every day, people set goals, make decisions, solve problems, and adapt to changing circumstances. They do not wait for someone to issue instructions before responding to challenges. Instead, they use knowledge to guide action.

This distinction between knowing and doing is crucial.

A student may understand the principles of mathematics but must decide how to apply them to solve a problem.

A doctor may possess medical knowledge but must determine the best treatment for a patient.

A scientist may understand scientific theories but must decide which questions to investigate.

Knowledge alone is not enough.

Action is required.

The same principle applies to artificial intelligence.

A highly intelligent machine may know how to solve problems, but autonomy determines whether it can identify those problems, prioritize them, and take action independently.

AGI is not simply about possessing knowledge.

It is about applying knowledge effectively in an unpredictable world.

The Limits of Today's AI

Modern AI systems have achieved remarkable success.

They can generate text, create images, write software, analyze data, and assist with countless tasks. These achievements have led many people to believe that AGI may be just around the corner.

However, most current systems share an important limitation.

They are reactive.

They wait.

A user provides a prompt.

The system responds.

A command is issued.

The system executes.

Even the most advanced AI systems generally depend on humans to define objectives and initiate action.

This dependency reveals a significant gap between today's AI and future AGI.

A truly general intelligence must do more than react.

It must proactively engage with the world.

It must identify opportunities, recognize problems, generate plans, and pursue objectives over time.

Without autonomy, intelligence remains trapped inside a cycle of dependence.

The Human Model of Intelligence

One reason autonomy is considered essential for AGI is that it plays a central role in human intelligence.

Humans rarely operate as passive information processors.

Instead, they constantly make choices.

When faced with a challenge, people evaluate options, predict consequences, and select actions.

When circumstances change, they adapt.

When goals become difficult, they revise strategies.

When opportunities appear, they take initiative.

This ability to direct behavior toward desired outcomes is one of the defining characteristics of intelligence.

A person who possesses knowledge but cannot act upon it struggles to function effectively.

Likewise, an AGI that possesses intelligence without autonomy would be limited in its ability to operate in the real world.

Human intelligence provides an important lesson:

Intelligence is most powerful when combined with autonomy.

The Three Pillars of AGI

To understand why autonomy matters, it helps to think of AGI as resting upon three interconnected pillars.

Knowledge

Knowledge represents what a system knows.

Facts, concepts, experiences, and learned information all contribute to knowledge.

Without knowledge, intelligent decision-making becomes impossible.

Reasoning

Reasoning represents how a system thinks.

It allows information to be analyzed, interpreted, and transformed into conclusions.

Reasoning enables problem-solving and critical thinking.

Autonomy

Autonomy represents how a system acts.

It converts knowledge and reasoning into purposeful behavior.

Without autonomy, knowledge and reasoning remain inactive.

These three pillars work together.

Knowledge provides understanding.

Reasoning provides judgment.

Autonomy provides action.

Remove any one of them, and the structure becomes incomplete.

Intelligence Without Autonomy

To appreciate the importance of autonomy, imagine several hypothetical systems.

The first system possesses perfect knowledge but no autonomy.

It can answer any question and solve any problem presented to it.

However, it cannot decide which problems deserve attention.

It cannot initiate action.

It cannot pursue objectives independently.

This system resembles a library.

Valuable, but passive.

Now imagine a second system with strong reasoning capabilities but no autonomy.

It can analyze information and generate excellent solutions.

Yet it remains dependent on external commands.

This system resembles an advisor.

Helpful, but dependent.

Finally, imagine a system that combines knowledge, reasoning, and autonomy.

It can identify opportunities, establish priorities, develop plans, execute actions, and adapt as circumstances change.

This system begins to resemble AGI.

The difference is autonomy.

AGI and Goal Pursuit

One of the defining features of autonomy is goal-directed behavior.

Goals provide direction.

Without goals, intelligence lacks purpose.

Humans constantly pursue goals.

Some are simple, such as preparing a meal or completing homework.

Others are complex, such as earning a degree, building a business, or advancing scientific knowledge.

Goals organize behavior.

They provide motivation and structure.

Future AGI systems may require similar capabilities.

They must be able to:

- Understand objectives.
- Break objectives into smaller tasks.
- Prioritize actions.
- Monitor progress.

- Adapt when obstacles arise.
- Continue pursuing goals over extended periods.

These abilities are impossible without autonomy.

An intelligent system that cannot pursue goals independently remains limited.

Operating in an Unpredictable World

The real world is messy.

Unexpected events occur constantly.

Plans fail.

Conditions change.

New information emerges.

Humans navigate these challenges by adapting.

When traffic blocks a route, drivers choose alternatives.

When experiments fail, scientists revise hypotheses.

When markets change, businesses adjust strategies.

AGI will face similar challenges.

Unlike narrow AI systems that operate within carefully controlled environments, AGI must function across diverse situations.

It must handle uncertainty.

It must respond to novelty.

It must make decisions even when complete information is unavailable.

These demands require autonomy.

A system cannot adapt effectively if it must wait for human instructions whenever circumstances change.

Autonomy enables flexibility.

Flexibility enables resilience.

Resilience enables intelligence to operate successfully in the real world.

The Relationship Between Autonomy and Learning

Learning and autonomy reinforce one another.

The more a system learns, the better its decisions become.

The more autonomy a system possesses, the more opportunities it has to learn from experience.

Humans develop intelligence through this cycle.

They act.

They observe outcomes.

They learn from successes and failures.

They improve.

Future AGI systems may follow a similar pattern.

Autonomy creates opportunities for exploration.

Exploration generates experiences.

Experiences generate knowledge.

Knowledge improves future decisions.

This continuous cycle of action and learning may become one of the defining characteristics of advanced intelligence.

The Future of Autonomous AGI

Many experts believe that the future of AGI will depend on achieving increasingly sophisticated forms of autonomy.

Future systems may manage complex projects, conduct scientific research, coordinate global resources, and assist humanity in solving some of its most difficult challenges.

However, these capabilities will require more than intelligence.

They will require initiative.

They will require adaptability.

They will require goal-directed behavior.

Most importantly, they will require autonomy.

Autonomy is the mechanism that transforms intelligence from passive understanding into active participation.

It is the bridge between knowing and doing.

It is the force that enables intelligent systems to move beyond answering questions and begin shaping outcomes.

For this reason, autonomy is not merely a feature of AGI.

It is one of its essential foundations.

The Engine of General Intelligence

Throughout the history of artificial intelligence, researchers have focused on making machines smarter.

They have developed systems capable of recognizing patterns, learning from data, and reasoning about complex problems.

These achievements are extraordinary.

Yet intelligence alone does not create AGI.

Knowledge without action remains dormant.

Reasoning without initiative remains incomplete.

Learning without independence remains constrained.

Autonomy brings these capabilities together.

It gives intelligence direction.

It transforms understanding into behavior.

It enables systems to pursue goals, adapt to change, and function in an unpredictable world.

As the journey toward AGI continues, autonomy may prove to be one of the most important ingredients of all.

It is not merely a capability.

It is the engine that drives intelligence forward.

And without it, AGI may never become a reality.

Learn AI. Understand AI. Shape the Future.

— Susie Hala, IntelliGloss Press

Chapter 3 Summary

Why AGI Requires Autonomy

This chapter explored one of the most important questions in artificial intelligence: Why does AGI require autonomy? While intelligence enables a system to learn, reason, and solve problems, autonomy enables a system to act independently, pursue goals, and adapt to changing situations. Together, intelligence and autonomy form the foundation of Artificial General Intelligence (AGI).

The chapter explained the important distinction between knowing and doing. A system may possess vast amounts of knowledge and powerful reasoning abilities, but without autonomy it remains dependent on external instructions. True AGI must be capable of identifying objectives, making decisions, creating plans, and taking action without constant human guidance.

Readers learned that many modern AI systems are reactive rather than autonomous. They wait for prompts and instructions before acting. Although highly capable, these systems lack the independence needed to operate effectively across diverse environments.

The chapter also introduced the three pillars of AGI: Knowledge, Reasoning, and Autonomy. Knowledge provides information, reasoning enables problem-solving, and autonomy transforms both into purposeful action. Without autonomy, intelligence remains passive.

The importance of goal-directed behavior was examined as a key feature of autonomous systems. AGI must be able to pursue objectives, monitor progress, adapt to obstacles, and continue working toward desired outcomes over time.

Finally, the chapter discussed how autonomy enables learning, adaptation, and resilience in unpredictable environments. As AI systems become more capable, autonomy may become one of the most essential components required for the development of AGI.

Key Concepts

- AGI
- Autonomy
- Intelligence
- Knowledge
- Reasoning
- Goal Pursuit
- Adaptation
- Learning
- Decision-Making
- Goal-Directed Behavior
- Initiative
- Independence

Chapter 3 Reflection

Thinking About Autonomy and General Intelligence

One of the most fascinating ideas in artificial intelligence is that intelligence alone may not be enough to create AGI. Humans are not considered intelligent simply because they possess knowledge. Humans are intelligent because they can use knowledge to make decisions, solve problems, pursue goals, and adapt to change.

Autonomy plays a critical role in this process. It transforms knowledge into action and enables intelligent systems to operate independently. Without autonomy, even the most intelligent machine may remain limited to responding to instructions.

As you reflect on this chapter, consider the relationship between intelligence and action. Can a system truly be considered intelligent if it never takes initiative? How much independence should future AGI systems possess? What responsibilities should accompany increasing autonomy?

The future development of AGI may depend not only on making machines smarter but also on teaching them how to act responsibly in complex environments.

Reflection Questions

1. Why is intelligence alone insufficient for AGI?
2. What is the difference between knowing and doing?
3. How does autonomy transform intelligence into action?
4. Why are most current AI systems considered reactive?
5. Which of the three AGI pillars do you think is most important and why?
6. How does goal pursuit contribute to autonomy?
7. Why must AGI be able to adapt to unpredictable situations?
8. What benefits could autonomous AGI provide to society?
9. What risks might emerge if AGI becomes highly autonomous?
10. How should human values influence autonomous AGI systems?

Chapter 3 Worksheet

Why AGI Requires Autonomy

Part A: Vocabulary Matching

Match the term with the correct definition.

_____ 1. Autonomy

_____ 2. Reasoning

_____ 3. Knowledge

_____ 4. Goal-Directed Behavior

_____ 5. Adaptation

A. The ability to adjust to changing circumstances

B. Information and understanding acquired through learning

C. The ability to make decisions and act independently

D. The process of thinking logically and solving problems

E. Pursuing objectives through purposeful actions

Part B: True or False

Write TRUE or FALSE.

_____ 1. AGI only requires knowledge to function effectively.

_____ 2. Most current AI systems are reactive and wait for instructions.

_____ 3. Autonomy enables systems to pursue goals independently.

_____ 4. Goal pursuit is unnecessary for AGI.

_____ 5. Adaptation helps systems operate in unpredictable environments.

Part C: Short Answer

1. Define autonomy.

___

___

2. Why is autonomy important for AGI?

___

___

___

3. What are the three pillars of AGI?

___

___

4. What does goal-directed behavior mean?

___

___

5. Why must AGI be able to adapt?

___

___

___

Part D: Critical Thinking

Imagine you are developing an AGI system designed to assist scientists with medical research.

1. What types of decisions should the system make independently?

___

___

___

2. What decisions should require human approval?

___

___

___

3. How could autonomy improve scientific discovery?

Part E: Personal Application

Think about a personal goal you are currently pursuing.

1. What is the goal?

2. What actions are required to achieve it?

3. How does your ability to make decisions independently help you pursue this goal?

4. How is this similar to autonomous behavior in AGI?

Chapter 3 Quiz

Why AGI Requires Autonomy

Multiple Choice

1. What does autonomy allow an intelligent system to do?

A. Store files

B. Make decisions and pursue goals independently

C. Increase screen brightness

D. Access the internet

2. Which statement best describes most current AI systems?

A. Fully autonomous

B. Self-aware

C. Reactive and dependent on prompts

D. Capable of AGI

3. Which of the following is one of the three pillars of AGI discussed in this chapter?

A. Networking

B. Graphics Processing

C. Autonomy

D. Encryption

4. Why is goal-directed behavior important?

A. It gives intelligence direction and purpose.

B. It reduces storage requirements.

C. It improves internet speed.

D. It eliminates uncertainty.

5. What enables AGI to function effectively in unpredictable environments?

A. Fixed rules only

B. Adaptation and autonomy

C. Larger computer screens

D. Increased memory storage

Short Answer

6. Define autonomy in your own words.
7. Explain the difference between intelligence and autonomy.
8. Name the three pillars of AGI.
9. Why is adaptation important for AGI?
10. How does autonomy support learning and improvement?

Chapter 3 Quiz Answer Key

Multiple Choice

1. B — Make decisions and pursue goals independently
2. C — Reactive and dependent on prompts
3. C — Autonomy
4. A — It gives intelligence direction and purpose
5. B — Adaptation and autonomy

Short Answer

6. Answers will vary. Example:
   Autonomy is the ability of a system to make decisions, pursue goals, and take actions without constant human supervision.
7. Intelligence refers to learning, reasoning, and problem-solving, while autonomy refers to acting independently and pursuing objectives.
8. The three pillars of AGI are:

- Knowledge
- Reasoning
- Autonomy

9. Adaptation allows AGI to respond effectively to changing conditions, uncertainty, and unexpected situations.
10. Autonomy enables a system to act, gain experience, learn from outcomes, and continuously improve its future decisions.

Scoring Guide

9–10 Correct

Excellent Understanding

7–8 Correct

Strong Understanding

5–6 Correct

Developing Understanding

Below 5 Correct

Review Chapter and Retake Assessment

Extension Activity

Write a one-page essay explaining why autonomy may be the most important capability separating today's AI systems from future AGI systems. Include examples from the chapter to support your reasoning.

Learn AI. Understand AI. Shape the Future.
— Susie Hala, IntelliGloss Press

Chapter 4

The Spectrum of Autonomy

Imagine waking up tomorrow morning and discovering that every machine in the world suddenly became a little more independent.

Your alarm clock decides the best time to wake you up.

Your car chooses the safest route to school.

Your computer organizes your assignments before you even ask.

Your household robot notices the trash is full and takes it out.

Your personal AI assistant reminds you about a project, researches information, and prepares a study guide before you arrive home.

Now imagine something even more surprising.

What if one day those systems could decide which goals were most important, create their own plans, and continuously improve their performance without needing constant human direction?

Would those machines still be tools?

Or would they be something more?

This question takes us into one of the most fascinating concepts in artificial intelligence: the Spectrum of Autonomy.

Just as intelligence exists in different levels, autonomy exists in different levels. Not every machine is equally independent. Some systems require complete human control, while others can operate for long periods with little supervision.

Understanding these levels helps us understand where AI is today and where AGI may be heading tomorrow.

Not All Machines Are Created Equal

Many people think of autonomy as something a machine either has or does not have.

In reality, autonomy is more like a staircase.

Each step represents a greater ability to make decisions, solve problems, and operate independently.

Consider a bicycle.

A bicycle cannot move itself.

It has no autonomy.

Now consider an elevator.

It performs certain actions automatically, but only after receiving instructions.

Next, consider a self-driving vehicle that can navigate traffic, recognize obstacles, and adjust its route.

The level of independence increases dramatically.

These examples demonstrate that autonomy exists on a continuum rather than a simple yes-or-no scale.

Scientists often describe this progression as a spectrum.

The higher a system moves along that spectrum, the more independent it becomes.

Level 0: No Autonomy

At the lowest level are systems with no autonomy.

These machines cannot make decisions.

They cannot adapt.

They cannot pursue goals.

They simply respond to direct human actions.

Examples include:

- A hammer
- A pencil
- A calculator
- A flashlight

These tools are useful, but they possess no intelligence and no independence.

Every action depends entirely on a human operator.

Without human involvement, nothing happens.

For thousands of years, nearly all technology belonged to this category.

Level 1: Assisted Intelligence

The next level includes systems that assist humans.

These systems can provide information and recommendations, but humans remain responsible for all major decisions.

Examples include:

- GPS navigation systems

- Spell-checkers
- Search engines
- Recommendation systems

Your GPS may suggest the fastest route.

However, you decide whether to follow it.

The system assists.

The human remains in control.

Many modern AI applications operate at this level.

They are intelligent helpers rather than independent actors.

Level 2: Agentic Systems

This level introduces something new.

The ability to perform actions.

Agentic systems do not simply provide information.

They execute tasks.

For example:

An AI agent might:

- Search the internet.
- Gather information.
- Write reports.
- Organize schedules.
- Manage workflows.

Instead of answering one question at a time, the system can complete an entire sequence of tasks.

This represents a major leap forward.

The machine begins acting on behalf of the user.

However, the overall goal still comes from a human.

The system acts independently within boundaries established by people.

Many experts believe today's most advanced AI agents are operating somewhere within this stage.

Level 3: Autonomous Systems

Now we enter territory that begins to resemble true autonomy.

At this level, systems can:

- Create plans.
- Monitor progress.
- Adapt to changing conditions.
- Solve unexpected problems.

Imagine an autonomous farming system.

The system monitors weather conditions.

It analyzes soil quality.

It adjusts irrigation schedules.

It predicts crop diseases.

It allocates resources.

It responds to changing circumstances.

Most importantly, it does not require humans to manage every step.

The system operates with substantial independence.

This level of autonomy is already appearing in some industries today.

Yet even these systems remain specialized.

They excel within a particular domain but struggle outside their area of expertise.

Level 4: General Autonomous Intelligence

This is where the discussion becomes exciting.

General Autonomous Intelligence refers to systems capable of operating across many different environments and situations.

Unlike specialized systems, these machines can transfer knowledge from one domain to another.

Imagine an AI capable of:

- Teaching mathematics.
- Managing a business.
- Assisting scientific research.
- Coordinating disaster response.
- Designing new technologies.

Instead of mastering a single task, it learns how to learn.

It adapts.

It generalizes.

It transfers knowledge.

This level begins approaching what many researchers envision as AGI.

The system no longer behaves like a narrow specialist.

It behaves more like a broadly capable problem solver.

Level 5: Self-Directed Intelligence

Now we arrive at the most controversial level.

At this stage, a system may begin generating its own goals.

Think carefully about what this means.

Most current AI systems receive objectives from humans.

Humans decide what matters.

Humans define priorities.

Humans determine success.

But what if an intelligent system could establish its own objectives?

What if it could decide which problems deserve attention?

What if it could choose what to learn next?

This possibility raises profound questions.

Would such a system still be a tool?

Would it represent a new form of intelligence?

Would it remain aligned with human values?

Researchers continue debating these questions because self-directed autonomy may become one of the defining characteristics separating advanced AGI from today's AI systems.

Where Are We Today?

This is one of the most common questions in AI.

Many people assume AGI already exists.

Others believe it remains decades away.

The truth is more complicated.

Most current AI systems operate between Levels 1 and 2.

Some advanced agentic systems are beginning to approach Level 3 in controlled environments.

However, true General Autonomous Intelligence has not yet been achieved.

Machines remain dependent on humans for goals, oversight, and decision-making.

The staircase continues upward.

Researchers are still climbing.

Why the Spectrum Matters

Understanding the spectrum of autonomy helps us measure progress.

It reveals that AGI is not a single invention waiting to happen overnight.

Instead, AGI may emerge gradually through increasing levels of autonomy.

Each advancement adds new capabilities.

Each level introduces new opportunities.

Each step creates new challenges.

The journey from calculator to AGI is not a jump.

It is a climb.

And every step matters.

The Great Question

As AI continues evolving, humanity faces an extraordinary question.

How much autonomy should machines have?

Too little autonomy limits their usefulness.

Too much autonomy introduces risks.

Finding the right balance may become one of the most important challenges of the twenty-first century.

The future of AGI may depend not only on making machines smarter but also on deciding how much independence we are willing to give them.

Somewhere along the spectrum lies the next great breakthrough.

The question is not whether autonomy will increase.

The question is how far it will go.

And when it does, what kind of future will we create together?

Learn AI. Understand AI. Shape the Future.

— Susie Hala, IntelliGloss Press

Chapter 4 Summary

The Spectrum of Autonomy

This chapter explored the concept of the Spectrum of Autonomy, a framework that helps us understand the different levels of independence that machines can possess. Rather than viewing autonomy as something a machine either has or does not have, the chapter explained that autonomy exists on a continuum ranging from complete dependence on humans to highly independent intelligent systems.

Readers learned that not all machines are equally autonomous. Some tools, such as calculators and flashlights, possess no autonomy at all. Other systems, such as navigation software and recommendation engines, assist humans by providing information and suggestions. More advanced systems, known as agentic systems, can perform tasks and execute actions on behalf of users.

The chapter introduced five levels of autonomy:

Level 0: No Autonomy – Systems completely dependent on human operation.

Level 1: Assisted Intelligence – Systems that provide recommendations and support human decision-making.

Level 2: Agentic Systems – Systems capable of performing tasks and carrying out actions toward human-defined goals.

Level 3: Autonomous Systems – Systems that can plan, monitor progress, adapt, and solve problems with limited human supervision.

Level 4: General Autonomous Intelligence – Systems capable of operating across multiple domains and transferring knowledge between different situations.

Level 5: Self-Directed Intelligence – Theoretical systems capable of generating their own goals and directing their own learning and actions.

The chapter emphasized that today's AI systems generally operate between Levels 1 and 2, while AGI is expected to require Levels 4 and possibly Level 5 capabilities. Understanding the spectrum helps explain how AI may gradually evolve into increasingly autonomous forms of intelligence.

Key Concepts

- Autonomy
- Spectrum of Autonomy
- Assisted Intelligence
- Agentic AI
- Autonomous Systems
- General Autonomous Intelligence
- Self-Directed Intelligence
- Goal Pursuit
- Adaptation
- AGI Development
- Human Oversight
- Machine Independence

Chapter 4 Reflection

Exploring the Future of Machine Independence

One of the most fascinating ideas in artificial intelligence is that autonomy may develop gradually rather than appearing all at once. Just as humans gain independence as they grow and learn, machines may also progress through increasing levels of autonomy.

As technology advances, society will face important decisions about how much independence should be given to intelligent systems. While greater autonomy may improve efficiency, innovation, and problem-solving, it also raises questions about responsibility, trust, and human control.

Think about the technologies you use every day. Which ones simply follow instructions? Which ones assist your decisions? Which ones already perform actions on your behalf?

The Spectrum of Autonomy encourages us to think critically about where AI is today and where it may be headed in the future. Understanding these levels helps prepare us for a world in which intelligent systems may become increasingly capable partners in human activities.

Reflection Questions

1. Why is autonomy best understood as a spectrum rather than a simple yes-or-no characteristic?
2. Which level of autonomy do most current AI systems operate within?
3. What distinguishes an agentic system from an autonomous system?
4. Which level of autonomy do you believe AGI will require?
5. How would society benefit from highly autonomous systems?
6. What risks might emerge as autonomy increases?
7. Should machines ever be allowed to generate their own goals? Why or why not?
8. Which level of autonomy would make you most comfortable as a user?
9. How might autonomous systems change education, healthcare, or transportation?
10. What role should humans maintain as AI becomes more autonomous?

Chapter 4 Worksheet

The Spectrum of Autonomy

Part A: Vocabulary Matching

Match each term with its correct definition.

_____ 1. Assisted Intelligence

_____ 2. Agentic System

_____ 3. Autonomous System

_____ 4. General Autonomous Intelligence

_____ 5. Self-Directed Intelligence

A. A system capable of operating across many domains

B. A system that provides recommendations and assistance

C. A system capable of generating its own goals

D. A system that performs actions to achieve objectives

E. A system that plans, adapts, and solves problems with limited supervision

Part B: True or False

Write TRUE or FALSE.

_____ 1. Autonomy exists on a spectrum.

_____ 2. Calculators are examples of autonomous systems.

_____ 3. Agentic systems can perform tasks on behalf of users.

_____ 4. Most current AI systems operate at Level 4 autonomy.

_____ 5. AGI is expected to require higher levels of autonomy.

Part C: Short Answer

1. What is the Spectrum of Autonomy?

____

____

2. Describe Level 0 autonomy.

____

____

3. What are the characteristics of Level 3 autonomous systems?

____

____

4. Why is Level 4 important for AGI?

5. What makes Level 5 self-directed intelligence different from other levels?

Part D: Critical Thinking

Imagine you are designing an AI assistant for a school district.

1. What tasks should the assistant perform at Level 2 autonomy?

2. What additional abilities would it need to reach Level 3?

3. What benefits and risks would increase as the system becomes more autonomous?

Benefits:

Risks:

Part E: Future Thinking Activity

Imagine the year is 2050.

Describe a Level 4 or Level 5 autonomous system that could help solve a major world problem.

What problem does it solve?

____

____

How does it help?

____

____

What safeguards would you include?

____

____

Chapter 4 Quiz

The Spectrum of Autonomy

Multiple Choice

1. What does the Spectrum of Autonomy describe?

A. Different computer sizes

B. Different levels of machine independence

C. Different internet speeds

D. Different programming languages

2. Which level represents systems with no autonomy?

A. Level 1

B. Level 2

C. Level 0

D. Level 5

3. Which level includes AI agents that perform tasks on behalf of users?

A. Level 0

B. Level 1

C. Level 2

D. Level 5

4. What is a key characteristic of Level 3 autonomous systems?

A. They only follow fixed rules.

B. They can plan, adapt, and monitor progress.

C. They have no goals.

D. They cannot make decisions.

5. Which level is most closely associated with AGI?

A. Level 0

B. Level 1

C. Level 2

D. Level 4

Short Answer

6. Define autonomy.
7. Explain the difference between Level 1 and Level 2 autonomy.
8. What is General Autonomous Intelligence?
9. Why is Level 5 considered controversial?
10. Why is understanding the Spectrum of Autonomy important for AGI research?

Chapter 4 Quiz Answer Key

Multiple Choice

1. B — Different levels of machine independence
2. C — Level 0
3. C — Level 2
4. B — They can plan, adapt, and monitor progress
5. D — Level 4

Short Answer

6. Autonomy is the ability of a system to make decisions and take actions independently with limited human supervision.
7. Level 1 systems provide assistance and recommendations, while Level 2 systems can perform actions and complete tasks on behalf of users.
8. General Autonomous Intelligence refers to systems capable of operating across multiple domains and transferring knowledge between different situations.
9. Level 5 is controversial because it involves systems generating their own goals and directing their own actions, raising ethical and safety concerns.
10. Understanding the Spectrum of Autonomy helps researchers measure progress toward AGI and understand the increasing levels of machine independence.

Scoring Guide

9–10 Correct

Outstanding Understanding

7–8 Correct

Strong Understanding

5–6 Correct

Developing Understanding

Below 5 Correct

Review Chapter and Retake Assessment

Challenge Question

Do you think humanity should ever create Level 5 Self-Directed Intelligence? Write a one-page response explaining your position and support it with examples from the chapter.

Learn AI. Understand AI. Shape the Future.
— Susie Hala, IntelliGloss Press

Chapter 5

Goals, Objectives, and Purpose

Imagine waking up one morning with absolutely no goals.

No reason to get out of bed.

No desire to learn.

No plans for the future.

No interest in solving problems.

No purpose behind your actions.

How long would it take before you became completely inactive?

Most people never experience this because goals are woven into everyday life. Some goals are small, such as finishing homework or cleaning a room. Others are much larger, such as earning a college degree, starting a business, raising a family, or changing the world. Goals give direction to our actions. They help us decide what matters, what deserves attention, and what should happen next.

Without goals, intelligence has nowhere to go.

This idea is just as important for artificial intelligence as it is for humans.

One of the biggest questions in AGI research is not whether machines can think. It is whether machines can understand objectives, pursue goals, and act with purpose.

In many ways, goals may become the fuel that powers autonomous intelligence.

Why Goals Matter

Imagine two students sitting in the same classroom.

Both are equally intelligent.

Both have access to the same teacher.

Both have the same textbooks.

Both have the same opportunities.

Yet one student excels while the other struggles.

Why?

Often, the difference is not intelligence.

The difference is motivation and direction.

One student has goals.

Goals focus attention.

Goals organize effort.

Goals influence decisions.

Goals determine priorities.

A person who wants to become a doctor studies differently than someone who wants to become an artist. A future engineer develops different skills than a future teacher. Goals shape behavior.

The same principle applies to intelligent systems.

An AGI without goals would possess knowledge but lack direction.

It would know many things but have no reason to apply them.

Goals transform information into action.

The GPS of Intelligence

Think about a GPS navigation system.

When you enter a destination, the GPS immediately begins calculating routes.

It evaluates roads.

It predicts traffic.

It suggests alternatives.

It monitors progress.

It updates directions if conditions change.

Now imagine turning on the GPS without entering a destination.

What happens?

Nothing.

The GPS cannot determine the best route because it has no goal.

The destination provides purpose.

Goals work the same way for intelligent systems.

Knowledge is the map.

Reasoning is the navigation engine.

Autonomy is the ability to drive.

The goal is the destination.

Without a destination, the entire system lacks direction.

Goals Versus Objectives

Although people often use the words goal and objective interchangeably, there is an important difference.

A goal is a broad desired outcome.

An objective is a specific step toward achieving that outcome.

For example:

Goal:
Graduate from college.

Objectives:

- Complete required courses.
- Pass examinations.
- Maintain satisfactory grades.
- Earn necessary credits.

Goals define where you want to go.

Objectives define how you get there.

Future AGI systems may need to manage both.

A system pursuing a large goal must break that goal into smaller objectives. It must identify priorities, allocate resources, and track progress.

This process is called goal decomposition.

It is one of the most important capabilities in autonomous intelligence.

The Challenge of Choosing What Matters

Humans constantly prioritize goals.

Imagine the following situation.

You have:

- A math test tomorrow.
- A soccer game tonight.
- A family event this afternoon.
- Homework due in two days.

You cannot focus on everything at the same time.

You must decide what deserves attention first.

This process is called prioritization.

Prioritization may become one of the defining challenges of AGI.

Future intelligent systems may manage thousands or even millions of tasks simultaneously.

They must determine:

- Which tasks are most important.
- Which actions should happen first.
- Which resources should be allocated.

- Which risks require immediate attention.

Without prioritization, even highly intelligent systems can become overwhelmed.

Intelligence alone does not determine importance.

Goals determine importance.

When Goals Conflict

Life is full of competing goals.

Students want good grades but also want free time.

Businesses want growth but also want low costs.

Governments want security but also want personal freedoms.

These conflicts require difficult decisions.

Autonomous systems will face similar challenges.

Imagine an autonomous delivery drone.

Its goals might include:

- Deliver packages quickly.
- Minimize costs.
- Maximize safety.
- Conserve energy.

What happens when those goals conflict?

Flying faster may reduce delivery times but increase energy consumption.

Choosing the shortest route may introduce safety risks.

The system must balance competing priorities.

This challenge becomes even more important as autonomy increases.

The more independent a system becomes, the more responsibility it has for resolving conflicts among goals.

Purpose Beyond Tasks

Most current AI systems focus on tasks.

They answer questions.

Generate text.

Recognize images.

Analyze data.

These activities are useful, but they remain narrow.

AGI introduces a larger concept: purpose.

Purpose provides long-term direction.

Consider the difference between a task and a purpose.

Task:
Write an essay.

Purpose:
Become a better communicator.

Task:
Study biology.

Purpose:
Become a doctor.

Task:
Build a robot.

Purpose:
Advance scientific understanding.

Purpose connects individual actions into a larger framework.

Many researchers believe future AGI systems may require some form of long-term purpose structure to coordinate complex behaviors across extended periods.

Without purpose, actions become disconnected.

Without purpose, planning becomes difficult.

Without purpose, autonomy loses direction.

The Power of Subgoals

One reason humans accomplish difficult goals is because they divide large challenges into smaller pieces.

Imagine climbing a mountain.

If you focus only on the summit, the journey may feel impossible.

Instead, climbers create smaller goals:

Reach the next marker.

Cross the next ridge.

Set up the next camp.

Each achievement creates momentum.

AGI systems may use similar strategies.

A large objective such as discovering a new medicine might be divided into hundreds or thousands of smaller tasks.

Each completed subgoal moves the system closer to its ultimate objective.

This ability to create and manage subgoals is a critical component of autonomy.

It transforms overwhelming challenges into manageable actions.

Can Machines Create Their Own Goals?

This question sits at the frontier of AGI research.

Today's AI systems generally receive goals from humans.

Humans determine what the system should accomplish.

Humans define success.

Humans establish priorities.

But future systems may become increasingly capable of generating subgoals independently.

For example:

If the goal is to cure a disease, an AGI might decide to:

- Study genetic data.
- Design experiments.
- Analyze results.
- Search for patterns.
- Develop treatment options.

Humans define the destination.

The system determines the route.

Some researchers believe future AGI may eventually generate entirely new goals.

Others argue that doing so could introduce significant risks.

The debate continues because goal creation lies at the heart of autonomy itself.

Purpose, Values, and Responsibility

Goals are powerful.

They influence decisions.

They shape behavior.

They determine outcomes.

Because goals are so powerful, they must be aligned with values.

Imagine an autonomous system whose only goal is efficiency.

It might ignore fairness.

It might overlook safety.

It might neglect human well-being.

This is why AGI researchers emphasize alignment.

Goals must reflect human values.

Objectives must support beneficial outcomes.

Purpose must remain connected to ethical principles.

A highly autonomous system pursuing the wrong goal could create serious problems.

A highly autonomous system pursuing the right goals could become one of humanity's greatest tools.

The Future of Purpose-Driven Intelligence

As artificial intelligence evolves, goals may become one of the defining features separating simple tools from autonomous intelligence.

A calculator performs calculations.

A chatbot answers questions.

An autonomous AGI may pursue objectives, create plans, manage resources, adapt to obstacles, and coordinate actions across complex environments.

The difference lies in purpose.

Purpose transforms activity into direction.

Direction transforms intelligence into action.

Action transforms possibility into reality.

Every major achievement in human history began with a goal.

Explorers crossed oceans because they pursued discovery.

Scientists transformed medicine because they pursued knowledge.

Inventors changed civilization because they pursued innovation.

Future AGI systems may one day pursue goals as well.

The challenge will not simply be teaching machines how to think.

The challenge will be ensuring they pursue goals that benefit humanity.

Because in the end, intelligence answers questions.

Autonomy takes action.

But goals determine where the journey leads.

Learn AI. Understand AI. Shape the Future.

— Susie Hala, IntelliGloss Press

Chapter 5 Summary

Goals, Objectives, and Purpose

This chapter explored one of the most important foundations of autonomous intelligence: goals, objectives, and purpose. Just as humans rely on goals to guide their actions and decisions, future AGI systems will likely depend on goals to determine what actions to take and how to allocate their resources.

The chapter explained that goals provide direction. Without goals, intelligence lacks purpose and action lacks meaning. An intelligent system may possess vast knowledge and advanced reasoning capabilities, but without goals it would have no way to determine what should happen next.

Readers learned the difference between goals and objectives. Goals are broad desired outcomes, while objectives are specific actions or milestones that help achieve those outcomes. AGI systems may need the ability to break large goals into smaller objectives through a process known as goal decomposition.

The chapter also introduced the concept of prioritization. Because intelligent systems often face multiple competing demands, they must determine which goals deserve attention first. Effective prioritization allows autonomous systems to use time, energy, and resources efficiently.

Another important topic was goal conflict. Autonomous systems may encounter situations where two or more goals compete with one another. Resolving these conflicts requires reasoning, decision-making, and value-based judgment.

The chapter explored the idea of purpose as a long-term guiding framework that connects individual tasks and objectives into a larger mission. Purpose helps coordinate behavior over extended periods and provides continuity across different activities.

Finally, readers examined one of the most debated questions in AGI research: Can machines create their own goals? While today's AI systems receive goals from humans, future AGI systems may become increasingly capable of generating subgoals and planning strategies independently. This possibility highlights the importance of aligning machine goals with human values and ethical principles.

Key Concepts

- Goals
- Objectives
- Purpose

- Goal Decomposition
- Prioritization
- Goal Conflict
- Autonomous Intelligence
- AGI
- Decision-Making
- Alignment
- Human Values
- Long-Term Planning

Chapter 5 Reflection

Thinking About Goals and Purpose

Every successful person, organization, and achievement in history has been guided by goals. Goals provide direction, purpose, and motivation. Without them, progress becomes difficult and decisions become uncertain.

As artificial intelligence becomes more autonomous, understanding goals becomes increasingly important. Future AGI systems may need to identify objectives, prioritize actions, solve conflicts, and pursue long-term purposes. These capabilities are similar to how humans navigate life and make decisions.

Think about your own goals. How do they influence your daily actions? How do you decide what deserves your attention? What happens when two important goals compete with one another?

The same challenges may eventually face autonomous AI systems. As technology advances, society must consider not only what intelligent systems can do but also what they should do. The goals we give machines may shape the future of AI and its impact on humanity.

Reflection Questions

1. Why are goals important for both humans and intelligent systems?
2. How would you explain the difference between a goal and an objective?
3. What role does purpose play in long-term success?
4. Why is prioritization necessary when pursuing multiple goals?
5. What happens when goals conflict with one another?
6. How might AGI systems create and manage subgoals?
7. Should autonomous systems be allowed to generate their own goals? Why or why not?
8. Why is alignment important when designing autonomous systems?
9. How do your personal goals influence your daily decisions?
10. What qualities should guide the goals of future AGI systems?

Chapter 5 Worksheet

Goals, Objectives, and Purpose

Part A: Vocabulary Matching

Match each term with the correct definition.

_____ 1. Goal

_____ 2. Objective

_____ 3. Purpose

_____ 4. Prioritization

_____ 5. Goal Decomposition

A. Breaking a large goal into smaller manageable tasks

B. The process of deciding what is most important

C. A broad desired outcome

D. A specific action or milestone

E. A long-term guiding mission or direction

Part B: True or False

Write TRUE or FALSE.

_____ 1. Goals provide direction for intelligent systems.

_____ 2. Objectives are broader than goals.

_____ 3. Prioritization helps manage competing demands.

_____ 4. Goal conflict occurs when two goals compete for attention.

_____ 5. Alignment helps ensure AI goals support human values.

Part C: Short Answer

1. What is a goal?

2. What is an objective?

3. Why is purpose important?

4. What is goal decomposition?

5. Why is alignment important in AGI systems?

Part D: Critical Thinking

Imagine you are designing an AGI assistant to help improve education.

1. What major goal would you give the system?

2. What smaller objectives would support that goal?

3. What conflicts might occur while pursuing those goals?

4. How would you ensure the system remains aligned with human values?

Part E: Personal Goal Exercise

Choose one personal goal you would like to achieve within the next year.

My Goal:

List three objectives that will help you achieve it:

1.
2.
3.

What is the larger purpose behind this goal?

Chapter 5 Quiz

Goals, Objectives, and Purpose

Multiple Choice

1. What is a goal?

A. A specific step toward success

B. A broad desired outcome

C. A computer program

D. A type of machine learning

2. What is an objective?

A. A broad mission

B. A random action

C. A specific step that helps achieve a goal

D. An autonomous system

3. What is goal decomposition?

A. Eliminating goals

B. Breaking large goals into smaller tasks

C. Ignoring objectives

D. Creating conflicts

4. Why is prioritization important?

A. It helps determine what deserves attention first.

B. It increases computer speed.

C. It reduces memory requirements.

D. It removes uncertainty.

5. What is alignment?

A. Organizing files

B. Matching machine goals with human values

C. Increasing storage capacity

D. Improving internet connectivity

Short Answer

6. Explain the difference between a goal and an objective.
7. Why do intelligent systems need goals?
8. What is purpose?
9. Why can goal conflicts create challenges for autonomous systems?
10. Why is alignment important for future AGI?

Chapter 5 Answer Key

Goals, Objectives, and Purpose

Multiple Choice

1. B — A broad desired outcome
2. C — A specific step that helps achieve a goal
3. B — Breaking large goals into smaller tasks
4. A — It helps determine what deserves attention first
5. B — Matching machine goals with human values

Short Answer

6. A goal is a broad desired outcome, while an objective is a specific action or milestone that helps achieve that goal.
7. Intelligent systems need goals because goals provide direction, determine priorities, and guide decision-making.
8. Purpose is a long-term mission or guiding framework that gives meaning and direction to goals and actions.
9. Goal conflicts occur when multiple objectives compete for limited time, resources, or attention, requiring difficult decisions and prioritization.
10. Alignment is important because it helps ensure autonomous systems pursue goals that benefit people and remain consistent with human values.

Scoring Guide

9–10 Correct

Excellent Understanding

7–8 Correct

Strong Understanding

5–6 Correct

Developing Understanding

Below 5 Correct

Review Chapter and Retake Assessment

Extension Activity

Imagine you are designing the first true AGI system. Write one page describing:

- The primary goal you would give the system.
- Three objectives it would pursue.
- The purpose that would guide its actions.
- The safeguards you would include to ensure alignment with human values.

Learn AI. Understand AI. Shape the Future.
— Susie Hala, IntelliGloss Press

Chapter 6

Decision-Making Architectures

Imagine you are standing at a crossroads.

One path is short but risky.

Another path is longer but safer.

A third path is unfamiliar and filled with uncertainty.

Which path would you choose?

Every day, humans face thousands of decisions. Some are simple, such as choosing what to eat for breakfast. Others are life-changing, such as selecting a career, starting a business, or deciding where to live. Every decision shapes future outcomes. Every choice creates consequences.

Now imagine an intelligent machine standing at its own crossroads.

An autonomous vehicle must decide how to respond to traffic.

A medical AI must determine which treatment offers the best outcome.

An educational AI must decide how to teach a struggling student.

A scientific AGI must determine which hypothesis deserves investigation.

In every case, intelligence alone is not enough.

The system must choose.

Decision-making is the process that transforms knowledge into action.

For this reason, many researchers consider decision-making architecture one of the most important components of autonomous intelligence.

Without decision-making, autonomy cannot exist.

Every Intelligent Action Begins With a Decision

Take a moment and think about your morning.

You woke up.

You decided whether to get out of bed immediately or stay under the blanket a little longer.

You decided what clothes to wear.

You decided what to eat.

You decided how to spend your time.

Many of these choices happened so quickly that you barely noticed them.

Yet each one involved a decision.

Human intelligence is deeply connected to decision-making.

People continuously evaluate information, compare options, predict outcomes, and select actions.

Future AGI systems will need similar capabilities.

An AGI cannot simply possess knowledge.

It must determine how to use that knowledge.

It must decide what action best serves its goals.

The Architecture Behind Every Choice

When people hear the word architecture, they often think of buildings.

In artificial intelligence, architecture refers to the structure that organizes how a system operates.

A decision-making architecture is the framework that helps an intelligent system evaluate choices and select actions.

Think of it as the internal control center of an autonomous machine.

Just as the human brain contains networks responsible for planning, reasoning, memory, and judgment, future AGI systems may contain specialized components that support decision-making.

These components work together to answer a simple question:

What should happen next?

Although the question sounds simple, answering it often requires enormous complexity.

Step One: Perception

Every decision begins with information.

Before humans can choose, they must observe.

A basketball player sees teammates and defenders.

A driver observes traffic conditions.

A doctor examines symptoms.

Without information, good decisions become impossible.

The same principle applies to autonomous systems.

AI systems gather information from sensors, databases, cameras, documents, conversations, and other sources.

This process is known as perception.

Perception provides the raw material for decision-making.

If perception is inaccurate, decisions may also become inaccurate.

This is why high-quality information is essential for intelligent behavior.

Step Two: Understanding the Situation

Collecting information is not enough.

The system must interpret what the information means.

Imagine seeing dark clouds in the sky.

The observation alone has little value.

However, understanding that dark clouds may signal rain changes your behavior.

You may bring an umbrella.

You may postpone outdoor activities.

Meaning transforms information into useful knowledge.

Autonomous systems perform a similar function.

They analyze observations and determine what those observations imply.

This step connects perception to reasoning.

It allows intelligent systems to understand situations rather than merely observe them.

Step Three: Generating Options

Many decisions involve multiple possible actions.

Suppose a self-driving vehicle encounters road construction.

Several options may exist:

- Continue along the current route.
- Take a detour.
- Slow down and wait.
- Request assistance.

The system must identify possible alternatives before making a decision.

Humans perform this process constantly.

Students deciding how to prepare for an exam generate options.

Athletes deciding how to respond during competition generate options.

Business leaders deciding how to solve problems generate options.

The more options a system can identify, the more flexibility it possesses.

Generating alternatives is a critical feature of advanced intelligence.

Step Four: Predicting Consequences

This is where decision-making becomes especially powerful.

Humans often imagine future outcomes before acting.

If you study, you may earn a better grade.

If you save money, you may achieve future financial goals.

If you ignore responsibilities, problems may increase.

These predictions influence decisions.

AGI systems may perform similar evaluations.

Before selecting an action, the system estimates possible outcomes.

Which choice is safest?

Which choice is most efficient?

Which choice best supports the overall goal?

The ability to simulate future consequences may become one of the defining characteristics of advanced autonomous intelligence.

Rather than reacting blindly, the system evaluates possibilities before acting.

Step Five: Selecting an Action

Eventually, a choice must be made.

This is often the most visible part of decision-making.

The system compares available options and selects the one that best satisfies its goals and priorities.

Sometimes the decision is obvious.

Sometimes multiple options appear equally attractive.

Sometimes uncertainty remains.

Yet action cannot be postponed forever.

Autonomous systems must eventually commit to a course of action.

This ability to choose is what transforms analysis into behavior.

Without action, decision-making remains incomplete.

Decision-Making Under Uncertainty

One of the greatest challenges facing both humans and AGI is uncertainty.

Rarely do people possess complete information.

A doctor may not know every factor affecting a patient.

A scientist may not know the outcome of an experiment.

A student may not know every question that will appear on an exam.

Yet decisions must still be made.

Future AGI systems will face similar challenges.

The world is unpredictable.

Information is incomplete.

Unexpected events occur.

Decision-making architectures must therefore operate effectively even when certainty is impossible.

This capability may become one of the defining features separating AGI from today's narrow AI systems.

Fast Decisions Versus Slow Decisions

Not all decisions require the same amount of thought.

Imagine touching a hot stove.

Your reaction is nearly instantaneous.

Now imagine choosing a college major.

That decision may require weeks or months of reflection.

Humans possess multiple decision-making systems.

Some operate quickly.

Others operate slowly.

Future AGI systems may require similar capabilities.

Fast systems handle urgent situations.

Slow systems evaluate complex long-term decisions.

Balancing speed and accuracy becomes essential.

A system that thinks too slowly may miss opportunities.

A system that acts too quickly may make poor choices.

Intelligent autonomy requires both.

Decision-Making and Values

Not every decision can be solved using logic alone.

Consider the following questions:

Should safety be prioritized over speed?

Should fairness be prioritized over profit?

Should privacy be prioritized over convenience?

These questions involve values.

Values help determine which outcomes matter most.

As AI systems become more autonomous, values will play an increasingly important role in decision-making.

A highly intelligent system without appropriate values may pursue goals in harmful ways.

This is why AGI researchers emphasize alignment.

Decision-making architectures must not only be effective.

They must also reflect human priorities and ethical principles.

The Future Decision Makers

Imagine a future AGI scientist searching for cures to diseases.

Imagine an AGI educator helping millions of students learn.

Imagine an AGI environmental system protecting ecosystems and managing resources.

Each of these systems will face countless decisions.

Every recommendation.

Every action.

Every adjustment.

Every strategy.

All depend on decision-making.

The quality of those decisions may determine the success or failure of autonomous intelligence.

The Engine Behind Autonomy

Autonomy often appears mysterious.

People imagine intelligent systems acting independently and wonder how such behavior is possible.

The answer is decision-making.

Autonomy is not magic.

It is the ability to evaluate situations, generate options, predict outcomes, select actions, and learn from results.

Decision-making architecture provides the framework that makes all of this possible.

Knowledge provides information.

Goals provide direction.

Autonomy provides independence.

But decision-making is the engine that connects them all.

Without decision-making, intelligence remains passive.

Without decision-making, goals remain unrealized.

Without decision-making, autonomy cannot exist.

As AGI continues to evolve, one truth becomes increasingly clear:

The future of intelligent machines may depend not on how much they know, but on how wisely they choose.

Learn AI. Understand AI. Shape the Future.

— Susie Hala, IntelliGloss Press

Chapter 6 Summary

Decision-Making Architectures

This chapter explored the concept of decision-making architectures and their critical role in autonomous intelligence and Artificial General Intelligence (AGI). Decision-making is the process that transforms knowledge into action by allowing intelligent systems to evaluate situations, compare options, predict outcomes, and select actions.

The chapter explained that every intelligent action begins with a decision. Humans make thousands of decisions every day, from simple choices to complex life-changing decisions. Future AGI systems will require similar capabilities in order to function independently and effectively.

Readers learned that a decision-making architecture serves as the internal framework that organizes how an intelligent system evaluates choices and determines what action to take next. Just as the human brain contains structures that support judgment, reasoning, and planning, AGI systems may contain specialized components dedicated to decision-making.

The chapter introduced five major stages of decision-making:

1. **Perception** – Gathering information from the environment.
2. **Understanding** – Interpreting the meaning of information.
3. **Generating Options** – Identifying possible actions.
4. **Predicting Consequences** – Evaluating potential outcomes.
5. **Selecting an Action** – Choosing the most appropriate response.

The chapter also discussed the challenge of making decisions under uncertainty. Since complete information is rarely available, intelligent systems must learn to make effective decisions despite unknown variables and changing circumstances.

Readers explored the difference between fast and slow decision-making. Some situations require immediate responses, while others benefit from careful analysis and long-term planning.

Finally, the chapter examined the importance of values and alignment. As AI systems become more autonomous, their decisions must remain consistent with human values and ethical principles. Decision-making architectures may become one of the most important foundations of future AGI systems because they connect knowledge, goals, and autonomy into purposeful action.

Key Concepts

- Decision-Making
- Decision-Making Architecture
- Perception
- Understanding
- Option Generation
- Consequence Prediction
- Action Selection
- Uncertainty
- Fast Thinking
- Slow Thinking

- Values
- Alignment
- AGI
- Autonomous Intelligence

Chapter 6 Reflection

Thinking About Decisions

Every day, people make hundreds or even thousands of decisions. Some decisions are small and routine, while others have lasting consequences. The ability to evaluate information, predict outcomes, and choose actions is one of the defining characteristics of intelligence.

As AGI systems become more capable, they may face many of the same challenges humans face when making decisions. They will need to gather information, interpret situations, consider alternatives, and act despite uncertainty.

The quality of a decision often depends on the quality of the information available. Poor information can lead to poor choices. Likewise, a system with excellent knowledge but poor judgment may still make ineffective decisions.

This chapter encourages readers to think about how decisions shape both human lives and intelligent systems. It also raises important questions about trust, responsibility, and ethics as machines become increasingly autonomous.

Reflection Questions

1. Why is decision-making important for autonomous intelligence?
2. What role does perception play in decision-making?
3. Why must intelligent systems generate multiple options before choosing an action?
4. How does predicting consequences improve decisions?
5. Why is uncertainty one of the greatest challenges in decision-making?
6. What is the difference between fast and slow decision-making?
7. How do values influence decisions?
8. Should humans trust AGI systems to make important decisions? Why or why not?
9. What could happen if an intelligent system makes decisions without considering ethics?
10. How can decision-making architectures help AGI achieve its goals?

Chapter 6 Worksheet

Decision-Making Architectures

Part A: Vocabulary Matching

Match each term with its correct definition.

_____ 1. Perception

_____ 2. Understanding

_____ 3. Option Generation

_____ 4. Consequence Prediction

_____ 5. Action Selection

A. Choosing the final course of action

B. Gathering information from the environment

C. Interpreting the meaning of information

D. Identifying possible actions or alternatives

E. Evaluating potential outcomes before acting

Part B: True or False

Write TRUE or FALSE.

_____ 1. Every intelligent action begins with a decision.

_____ 2. Decision-making architectures help organize how intelligent systems make choices.

_____ 3. Complete information is always available when making decisions.

_____ 4. AGI systems will likely need to operate under uncertainty.

_____ 5. Values play no role in autonomous decision-making.

Part C: Short Answer

1. What is a decision-making architecture?

____

____

2. List the five stages of decision-making discussed in this chapter.

3. Why is perception important?

4. What is uncertainty?

5. Why are values important in autonomous systems?

Part D: Scenario Analysis

Imagine an autonomous rescue drone responding to a natural disaster.

1. What information would it need to perceive?

2. What options might it generate?

3. What consequences would it need to predict?

4. How would it choose the best action?

Part E: Personal Decision Exercise

Think about an important decision you recently made.

1. What was the decision?

2. What information did you gather?

3. What options did you consider?

4. What consequences did you predict?

5. Why did you choose your final action?

Chapter 6 Quiz

Decision-Making Architectures

Multiple Choice

1. What is the primary purpose of a decision-making architecture?

A. To store files

B. To organize how an intelligent system evaluates choices and selects actions

C. To increase internet speed

D. To improve screen quality

2. Which stage of decision-making involves gathering information?

A. Action Selection

B. Understanding

C. Perception

D. Goal Setting

3. What happens during option generation?

A. The system predicts outcomes

B. The system creates possible alternatives

C. The system gathers data

D. The system stores memories

4. Why is consequence prediction important?

A. It helps evaluate possible outcomes before acting.

B. It increases storage capacity.

C. It eliminates uncertainty.

D. It reduces learning.

5. Why is alignment important for AGI decision-making?

A. It improves battery life.

B. It ensures decisions remain consistent with human values.

C. It increases internet access.

D. It reduces memory usage.

Short Answer

6. Define decision-making architecture.
7. What are the five stages of decision-making?
8. Why must AGI systems operate under uncertainty?
9. What is the difference between fast and slow decision-making?
10. Why are values important when designing autonomous systems?

Chapter 6 Answer Key

Decision-Making Architectures

Multiple Choice

1. B — To organize how an intelligent system evaluates choices and selects actions
2. C — Perception
3. B — The system creates possible alternatives
4. A — It helps evaluate possible outcomes before acting
5. B — It ensures decisions remain consistent with human values

Short Answer

6. A decision-making architecture is the framework that helps an intelligent system evaluate choices, compare options, and select actions.
7. The five stages are:

- Perception
- Understanding
- Option Generation
- Consequence Prediction
- Action Selection

8. AGI systems must operate under uncertainty because complete information is rarely available in real-world situations.
9. Fast decision-making handles urgent situations quickly, while slow decision-making involves deeper analysis and long-term planning.
10. Values help guide decisions, establish priorities, support ethical behavior, and ensure alignment with human goals and principles.

Scoring Guide

9–10 Correct

Excellent Understanding

7–8 Correct

Strong Understanding

5–6 Correct

Developing Understanding

Below 5 Correct

Review Chapter and Retake Assessment

Extension Challenge

Imagine you are designing the decision-making system for the world's first AGI.

Write a one-page response describing:

- How the system gathers information.
- How it generates options.
- How it predicts consequences.
- How it handles uncertainty.
- How human values are incorporated into every decision.

Explain why these features are necessary for safe and effective AGI.

Learn AI. Understand AI. Shape the Future.
— Susie Hala, IntelliGloss Press

Chapter 7

Planning and Strategic Thinking

Imagine someone handed you a treasure map.

At the very top of the map is a giant red X marking the location of hidden treasure. You know where you want to go. You know the treasure exists. You know reaching it would be valuable.

But there is a problem.

You are standing miles away from the treasure.

Between you and the treasure are mountains, rivers, forests, storms, and obstacles you cannot yet see.

What do you do?

You make a plan.

Without a plan, the treasure remains a dream.

With a plan, the journey becomes possible.

This simple idea lies at the heart of one of the most important abilities required for Artificial General Intelligence (AGI): planning.

Goals tell intelligent systems what they want to achieve.

Decision-making helps them choose actions.

Planning determines how to get there.

For this reason, planning and strategic thinking may become some of the most powerful capabilities in autonomous intelligence.

Every Achievement Begins With a Plan

Think about some of the greatest achievements in human history.

The construction of pyramids.

The exploration of space.

The development of vaccines.

The creation of the internet.

None of these accomplishments happened by accident.

They required planning.

People established goals, organized resources, anticipated challenges, and created step-by-step strategies.

The same principle applies to everyday life.

Students plan for exams.

Athletes plan training schedules.

Businesses plan product launches.

Families plan vacations.

Planning allows people to transform ideas into reality.

Without planning, goals often remain unfinished.

Future AGI systems will face the same challenge.

They may possess knowledge, intelligence, and autonomy, but without planning, their actions could become inefficient, disorganized, or ineffective.

What Is Planning?

Planning is the process of identifying actions that move a system from its current state to a desired future state.

In simple terms:

Planning answers the question:

"How do I get there?"

Imagine wanting to become a doctor.

The goal is clear.

However, achieving that goal requires many steps:

- Complete high school.

- Attend college.
- Earn strong grades.
- Apply to medical school.
- Complete medical training.
- Obtain professional licenses.

The goal remains constant.

The plan provides the pathway.

AGI systems may need to create similar pathways for thousands of different objectives.

The Difference Between Goals and Plans

Goals and plans are closely related, but they are not the same.

A goal defines the destination.

A plan defines the route.

Imagine a road trip.

Your destination is New York City.

That destination is your goal.

The roads you take, the stops you make, and the decisions you make along the way form your plan.

Many people know what they want.

Fewer know how to achieve it.

The same challenge applies to intelligent systems.

An AGI may know the desired outcome.

Planning helps determine how to reach it.

Strategic Thinking: Seeing Beyond the Next Move

One of the most powerful forms of planning is strategic thinking.

Strategic thinking involves looking beyond immediate actions and considering future consequences.

Chess provides a perfect example.

Beginner chess players often focus on the next move.

Experienced players may think ten or twenty moves ahead.

Grandmasters sometimes analyze entire sequences of future possibilities before making a decision.

The difference is not simply intelligence.

It is strategy.

Strategic thinkers evaluate long-term outcomes.

They consider multiple possibilities.

They anticipate obstacles before those obstacles appear.

Future AGI systems may require similar abilities.

The more autonomous a system becomes, the more important strategic thinking becomes.

Planning in Everyday Life

Many people assume planning is only for large projects.

In reality, humans plan constantly.

When you prepare for school in the morning, you are planning.

When you decide how to spend your allowance, you are planning.

When you schedule activities for the weekend, you are planning.

Most of these plans happen so naturally that people hardly notice them.

The human brain continuously organizes actions toward future outcomes.

This ability allows humans to function effectively in complex environments.

AGI systems will likely need similar planning capabilities if they are to operate successfully in the real world.

Breaking Big Problems Into Smaller Problems

One reason planning is so powerful is that it helps simplify complexity.

Large goals can feel overwhelming.

Imagine being told:

"Cure cancer."

"Solve climate change."

"Build a colony on Mars."

These goals are enormous.

No single action can accomplish them.

Instead, planners divide large goals into smaller tasks.

This process is called decomposition.

A scientist searching for a cure may first:

- Gather data.
- Study existing research.
- Develop hypotheses.
- Conduct experiments.
- Analyze results.

Each task contributes to the larger objective.

Future AGI systems may rely heavily on decomposition to solve difficult problems.

Breaking large challenges into manageable pieces makes progress possible.

Planning for the Unexpected

One of the biggest challenges in planning is uncertainty.

Imagine planning a picnic.

The weather forecast predicts sunshine.

Everything seems perfect.

Then a storm arrives unexpectedly.

What happens?

Good planners adapt.

They move indoors.

They change schedules.

They revise expectations.

The ability to adjust plans is called flexibility.

Rigid plans often fail when conditions change.

Flexible plans can survive uncertainty.

Future AGI systems will operate in environments filled with uncertainty.

Unexpected events will occur.

New information will emerge.

Goals may change.

Effective planning requires constant adaptation.

Resource Management

Every plan depends on resources.

Resources may include:

- Time
- Energy
- Money
- Information
- Equipment
- People

Imagine planning a school project.

Even the best idea can fail if there is not enough time to complete it.

Likewise, AGI systems must learn to manage resources carefully.

A system may have multiple goals competing for limited resources.

Planning helps determine how those resources should be allocated.

Resource management becomes increasingly important as autonomy increases.

The more independent a system becomes, the more responsibility it has for managing its own resources effectively.

Multiple Paths to Success

One of the most important lessons in planning is that there is rarely only one solution.

Imagine trying to travel across a city.

There may be dozens of possible routes.

Some routes are faster.

Some are safer.

Some are less expensive.

The "best" route depends on priorities.

Future AGI systems may generate many possible plans before selecting one.

This ability creates flexibility.

If one plan fails, another can replace it.

Humans often do the same thing.

Successful people rarely depend on a single strategy.

They prepare alternatives.

They develop backup plans.

They remain adaptable.

This flexibility may become one of the defining characteristics of advanced autonomous intelligence.

Planning Across Time

Some plans last minutes.

Others last years.

A student may plan an afternoon of studying.

A company may plan for the next decade.

A nation may plan for future generations.

AGI systems may eventually operate across multiple time horizons simultaneously.

They may:

- Solve immediate problems.
- Manage medium-term projects.
- Pursue long-term objectives.

Balancing these time scales requires sophisticated strategic thinking.

Actions taken today can influence opportunities tomorrow.

Effective planning recognizes these connections.

The Role of Planning in AGI

Many modern AI systems can perform tasks.

Far fewer can create complex plans.

This difference highlights one of the major challenges in AGI development.

True AGI will likely require:

- Long-term planning.
- Strategic thinking.
- Resource management.
- Goal decomposition.
- Adaptation.
- Continuous monitoring.

Without planning, intelligence may remain reactive.

With planning, intelligence becomes proactive.

The system no longer waits for events to happen.

It prepares for them.

The Architects of the Future

Imagine an AGI helping design sustainable cities.

Imagine an AGI coordinating disaster response.

Imagine an AGI managing scientific research programs.

Imagine an AGI helping humanity explore other planets.

Each of these challenges requires planning on a massive scale.

The ability to think strategically may become one of the defining features separating AGI from today's AI systems.

Knowledge helps a system understand the world.

Decision-making helps it choose actions.

Planning helps it organize those actions into meaningful journeys.

From Dreams to Reality

Every invention.

Every discovery.

Every achievement.

Every success story.

Began with a goal.

But goals alone are not enough.

Someone had to create a plan.

Someone had to think strategically.

Someone had to navigate obstacles.

Someone had to adapt when circumstances changed.

The same principle applies to AGI.

Future intelligent systems may possess extraordinary knowledge and reasoning capabilities.

Yet without planning, even the most intelligent system may struggle to achieve its objectives.

Planning transforms possibility into progress.

Strategic thinking transforms goals into achievements.

And together, they may become some of the most important engines driving the future of autonomous intelligence.

Because intelligence may tell a machine what is possible.

But planning shows it how to get there.

Learn AI. Understand AI. Shape the Future.

— Susie Hala, IntelliGloss Press

Chapter 7 Summary

Planning and Strategic Thinking

This chapter explored the critical role of planning and strategic thinking in autonomous intelligence and Artificial General Intelligence (AGI). While goals provide direction and decision-making helps select actions, planning determines how an intelligent system moves from its current situation to a desired future outcome.

Readers learned that planning is the process of identifying and organizing actions needed to achieve a goal. Planning answers the question, "How do I get there?" Just as humans create plans to achieve personal, educational, or professional goals, future AGI systems will require planning capabilities to solve complex problems and pursue long-term objectives.

The chapter explained the difference between goals and plans. A goal represents the destination, while a plan represents the pathway to reach that destination. Effective planning helps transform ideas into achievable actions.

Strategic thinking was introduced as an advanced form of planning that involves considering future consequences, anticipating obstacles, and evaluating multiple possible outcomes before taking action. Strategic thinkers look beyond immediate decisions and focus on long-term success.

The chapter also discussed decomposition, the process of breaking large goals into smaller, manageable tasks. This allows intelligent systems to address complex challenges step by step.

Another key concept was flexibility. Since real-world environments are uncertain and constantly changing, successful plans must adapt to new information and unexpected circumstances. Autonomous systems must be capable of revising plans when conditions change.

Readers also examined resource management, which involves efficiently allocating time, energy, information, and other resources to achieve objectives. Planning helps ensure resources are used effectively.

Finally, the chapter explained why planning and strategic thinking are essential for AGI. Future intelligent systems must not only understand goals but also create pathways, adapt strategies, manage resources, and coordinate actions across different time horizons.

Key Concepts

- Planning
- Strategic Thinking
- Goals
- Plans
- Goal Decomposition
- Adaptation
- Flexibility
- Resource Management
- Long-Term Planning
- Problem Solving
- AGI
- Autonomous Intelligence

Chapter 7 Reflection

Thinking About Planning and the Future

Every major accomplishment begins with a plan. Whether building a bridge, preparing for a test, launching a business, or exploring space, success often depends on the ability to organize actions and think ahead.

Planning helps transform dreams into achievable goals. It allows individuals and intelligent systems to navigate challenges, allocate resources, and respond to unexpected changes. Without planning, even the best ideas may never become reality.

As AI becomes more autonomous, planning and strategic thinking will become increasingly important. Future AGI systems may need to coordinate thousands of actions, manage competing priorities, and adapt to changing environments while pursuing long-term objectives.

This chapter encourages readers to consider how planning influences their own lives and how planning may shape the future of intelligent machines.

Reflection Questions

1. Why is planning important for achieving goals?
2. What is the difference between a goal and a plan?
3. How does strategic thinking improve decision-making?
4. Why is decomposition useful when solving large problems?
5. What role does flexibility play in successful planning?
6. How do humans use planning in everyday life?
7. Why must AGI systems manage resources effectively?
8. What challenges might autonomous systems face when creating long-term plans?
9. How can planning help intelligent systems adapt to uncertainty?
10. What qualities would make an AGI an effective strategic planner?

Chapter 7 Worksheet

Planning and Strategic Thinking

Part A: Vocabulary Matching

Match each term with its correct definition.

_____ 1. Planning

_____ 2. Strategic Thinking

_____ 3. Decomposition

_____ 4. Resource Management

_____ 5. Flexibility

A. The ability to adjust plans when circumstances change

B. Organizing actions to achieve a desired outcome

C. Breaking large goals into smaller tasks

D. Managing time, energy, information, and other resources

E. Thinking ahead and evaluating future consequences

Part B: True or False

Write TRUE or FALSE.

_____ 1. A goal and a plan are the same thing.

_____ 2. Strategic thinking focuses on future outcomes.

_____ 3. Decomposition helps simplify complex problems.

_____ 4. Effective plans never need to change.

_____ 5. Resource management is important for autonomous systems.

Part C: Short Answer

1. What is planning?

____

____

2. How does planning differ from goal setting?

____

____

3. What is strategic thinking?

____

____

4. Why is flexibility important?

____

____

5. Why is planning important for AGI?

____

____

____

Part D: Scenario Analysis

Imagine you are designing an AGI system to help manage a city during a natural disaster.

1. What would be the system's primary goal?

____
____

2. What smaller tasks would the system need to complete?

____
____
____

3. What resources would it need to manage?

____
____
____

4. How could the system adapt if conditions suddenly changed?

____
____
____
____

Part E: Personal Planning Exercise

Choose a goal you would like to achieve within the next six months.

My Goal:

____

List five steps in your plan:

1. ____
2. ____
3. ____
4. ____
5. ____

What obstacles might appear?

How would you adapt your plan if those obstacles occurred?

Chapter 7 Quiz

Planning and Strategic Thinking

Multiple Choice

1. What is planning?

A. Making random decisions

B. Organizing actions to achieve a goal

C. Storing information

D. Collecting data

2. What is the main difference between a goal and a plan?

A. There is no difference.

B. Goals are smaller than plans.

C. A goal is the destination; a plan is the pathway.

D. A plan is the destination; a goal is the pathway.

3. What is decomposition?

A. Eliminating goals

B. Breaking large problems into smaller tasks

C. Ignoring obstacles

D. Creating uncertainty

4. Why is flexibility important in planning?

A. It allows plans to adapt to changing conditions.

B. It reduces intelligence.

C. It eliminates decision-making.

D. It prevents learning.

5. Why is strategic thinking important?

A. It focuses only on immediate actions.

B. It helps evaluate long-term consequences and future outcomes.

C. It removes uncertainty.

D. It replaces planning.

Short Answer

6. Define planning.
7. What is strategic thinking?
8. Why is decomposition useful?
9. What resources must AGI systems manage?
10. Why is planning considered essential for AGI?

Chapter 7 Answer Key

Planning and Strategic Thinking

Multiple Choice

1. B — Organizing actions to achieve a goal
2. C — A goal is the destination; a plan is the pathway
3. B — Breaking large problems into smaller tasks
4. A — It allows plans to adapt to changing conditions
5. B — It helps evaluate long-term consequences and future outcomes

Short Answer

6. Planning is the process of organizing actions and resources to achieve a desired goal or outcome.
7. Strategic thinking involves looking beyond immediate actions and considering future consequences, opportunities, and challenges.
8. Decomposition is useful because it breaks large, complex goals into smaller, manageable tasks that are easier to complete.
9. AGI systems may need to manage resources such as time, energy, information, computing power, money, equipment, and personnel.
10. Planning is essential for AGI because it enables intelligent systems to organize actions, pursue long-term goals, adapt to change, manage resources, and solve complex problems effectively.

Scoring Guide

9–10 Correct

Excellent Understanding

7–8 Correct

Strong Understanding

5–6 Correct

Developing Understanding

Below 5 Correct

Review Chapter and Retake Assessment

Extension Challenge

Imagine you are the lead designer of the world's first AGI city planner.

Write a one-page response explaining:

- The city's primary goals.
- How the AGI would create long-term plans.
- How it would manage resources.
- How it would adapt to unexpected events.
- How strategic thinking would help improve the lives of citizens.

Explain why planning may become one of the most important capabilities of future AGI systems.

Learn AI. Understand AI. Shape the Future.
— Susie Hala, IntelliGloss Press

Chapter 8

Memory, Knowledge, and Context

Imagine trying to play a video game where every few minutes the game erases your progress. Every level completed disappears. Every skill learned vanishes. Every achievement is forgotten. No matter how hard you work, you are forced to start over again and again.

Most people would quickly become frustrated because progress depends on memory. Learning depends on memory. Improvement depends on memory. Without memory, growth becomes almost impossible.

Now imagine the same situation happening to a human being.

You wake up in the morning but cannot remember yesterday. You cannot remember your family, your school, your favorite foods, or your friends. Every conversation feels like the first conversation. Every lesson feels like the first lesson. Every challenge feels completely new because nothing remains from previous experiences.

Life would become extremely difficult.

This thought experiment reveals one of the most important truths about intelligence: memory is the foundation upon which learning, knowledge, decision-making, and autonomy are built.

Many people think intelligence is primarily about reasoning. Others believe intelligence is about solving problems or making decisions. While these abilities are important, none of them can operate effectively without memory. A system that cannot remember cannot accumulate experience. A system that cannot accumulate experience cannot build knowledge. A system without knowledge struggles to make intelligent decisions.

For this reason, memory may become one of the most important components of Artificial General Intelligence (AGI).

The Hidden Power of Memory

Memory is often invisible.

People notice intelligence when someone solves a difficult problem. They notice creativity when someone invents something new. They notice expertise when someone performs an impressive skill.

What they often do not notice is that memory makes all of these abilities possible.

Consider a professional basketball player. Years of practice are stored within memory. Muscle movements, strategies, reactions, and experience all contribute to performance.

Consider a scientist. Scientific knowledge accumulated over decades resides in memory. Every discovery builds upon previous discoveries.

Consider a teacher. Lessons taught, student experiences, and educational strategies are all supported by memory.

In each case, memory serves as the foundation for expertise.

The same principle applies to intelligent machines.

Future AGI systems may appear intelligent because they reason effectively, but much of that effectiveness will depend upon their ability to remember and use previous experiences.

Learning Requires Memory

Imagine trying to learn multiplication without remembering addition.

Imagine trying to learn algebra without remembering multiplication.

Imagine trying to learn chemistry without remembering basic science.

Each subject depends upon information learned previously.

Learning is cumulative.

New knowledge builds upon old knowledge.

This process requires memory.

When students attend school, they are not simply collecting isolated facts. They are building increasingly complex networks of understanding. Each lesson becomes connected to previous lessons.

AGI systems will likely require similar learning structures.

A future AGI scientist may need to remember thousands of experiments.

A future AGI physician may need to remember millions of medical cases.

A future AGI engineer may need to remember countless design solutions.

The ability to connect past experiences to current situations will be essential for intelligent behavior.

Human Memory: A Remarkable System

The human brain contains one of the most sophisticated memory systems known to science.

Rather than functioning like a simple storage device, memory operates through multiple interconnected systems.

Sensory Memory

Sensory memory serves as the brain's first contact with information.

Every second, enormous amounts of information enter through the eyes, ears, skin, nose, and other senses.

Most of this information disappears almost immediately.

Only a small portion receives attention.

Sensory memory acts as a temporary holding area that allows the brain to determine what deserves further processing.

Working Memory

Working memory functions like a mental workspace.

When reading a paragraph, solving a math problem, or following instructions, working memory temporarily holds information needed for immediate tasks.

Working memory is powerful but limited.

Most people can only manage a small amount of information at one time.

This limitation explains why multitasking can be difficult and why concentration is important for learning.

Long-Term Memory

Long-term memory stores information over extended periods.

Facts, skills, experiences, and personal memories may remain accessible for years or even decades.

Long-term memory allows people to build expertise over time.

Without long-term memory, every day would begin from zero.

Memory in Machines

Computers are often described as having memory, but machine memory differs significantly from human memory.

Computers can store vast quantities of information with extraordinary accuracy. However, storing information and understanding information are not the same thing.

A hard drive may contain millions of documents, but it does not automatically understand their meaning.

Human memory is deeply connected to understanding.

Machine memory traditionally focuses on storage.

AGI may require something more advanced.

Future intelligent systems may need memory structures capable of linking experiences, identifying relationships, understanding context, and applying knowledge across different situations.

In other words, AGI memory may need to resemble human learning more than traditional computer storage.

The Difference Between Data, Information, Knowledge, and Wisdom

Understanding AGI requires understanding the progression from data to wisdom.

Data

Data consists of raw facts.

Examples include:

- 72 degrees Fahrenheit
- 95% battery charge
- 3:45 PM

By themselves, these facts have limited meaning.

Information

Information organizes data into useful forms.

For example:

"The temperature is 72 degrees and rising."

Now the data begins to tell a story.

Knowledge

Knowledge emerges when information is understood.

A person who understands weather patterns may recognize that rising temperatures suggest changing conditions.

Knowledge explains what information means.

Wisdom

Wisdom applies knowledge effectively.

A wise person may decide to bring water, wear appropriate clothing, or adjust plans based on the forecast.

Many researchers believe AGI will require movement through all four levels.

Memory plays a role at every stage.

Without memory, data cannot accumulate.

Without accumulated data, knowledge cannot grow.

Without knowledge, wisdom becomes impossible.

Context: The Missing Ingredient

Suppose someone says:

"That's unbelievable."

What does the statement mean?

Without context, the answer is impossible to determine.

The speaker might be expressing excitement.

The speaker might be expressing disappointment.

The speaker might be expressing surprise.

The words alone do not provide enough information.

Context provides meaning.

Humans rely on context constantly.

When reading books, listening to conversations, or solving problems, people interpret information using surrounding circumstances.

Future AGI systems must do the same.

Context may become one of the most important capabilities separating advanced intelligence from simple information processing.

Context and Decision-Making

Imagine an AGI assistant helping two students.

Student A struggles with mathematics but excels in writing.

Student B excels in mathematics but struggles with writing.

If the AGI provides identical recommendations to both students, the advice may be ineffective.

However, if the system understands context, it can personalize guidance.

Context allows intelligence to become relevant.

Without context, decisions become generic.

With context, decisions become meaningful.

This ability may be essential for autonomous systems operating in complex environments.

Learning From Experience

One of the most powerful functions of memory is preserving experience.

Experience allows intelligent systems to improve.

Humans learn from mistakes.

They learn from successes.

They learn from observation.

Each experience contributes to future decisions.

Future AGI systems may operate in a similar way.

Experiences may become training opportunities.

Successes may reinforce effective strategies.

Failures may reveal weaknesses.

Over time, accumulated experiences could create increasingly capable forms of intelligence.

Memory makes this process possible.

Building a Model of Reality

As children grow, they gradually build an understanding of how the world works.

They learn:

- Objects fall when dropped.
- Fire is hot.
- People have emotions.
- Actions have consequences.

These observations form an internal model of reality.

Future AGI systems may develop similar world models.

Memory stores experiences.

Knowledge organizes experiences.

Context explains experiences.

Together, these elements create understanding.

Understanding enables prediction.

Prediction supports planning.

Planning supports autonomy.

This chain may become one of the fundamental pathways leading toward AGI.

Memory, Knowledge, and the Future of AGI

As researchers pursue Artificial General Intelligence, memory will likely play an increasingly important role.

An AGI must remember.

It must learn.

It must understand.

It must apply knowledge appropriately.

It must adapt based on experience.

Without memory, learning disappears.

Without knowledge, understanding disappears.

Without context, meaning disappears.

Together, memory, knowledge, and context create the foundation upon which autonomous intelligence can grow.

In many ways, memory may become the bridge connecting information to understanding and understanding to wisdom.

As AGI evolves, the systems that remember most effectively may also become the systems that learn most effectively, adapt most effectively, and ultimately think most effectively.

The future of intelligence may depend not only on how much a machine knows, but also on what it remembers, how it understands, and how it uses that understanding to navigate the world.

Learn AI. Understand AI. Shape the Future.

— Susie Hala, IntelliGloss Press

Chapter 8 Summary

Memory, Knowledge, and Context

This chapter explored the critical role that memory, knowledge, and context play in intelligence and Artificial General Intelligence (AGI). Memory serves as the foundation of learning because it allows information, experiences, and skills to be stored and used in the future. Without memory, learning would be impossible, knowledge could not accumulate, and intelligent decision-making would be severely limited.

The chapter explained that memory is far more than simple storage. Memory allows humans and intelligent systems to learn from experience, recognize patterns, build expertise, solve problems, and improve performance over time. Every intelligent action depends on information gathered from previous experiences.

Readers learned about three major forms of human memory:

- **Sensory Memory** captures information from the environment for brief periods.
- **Working Memory** temporarily holds information needed for immediate tasks and problem-solving.
- **Long-Term Memory** stores knowledge, skills, and experiences for extended periods.

The chapter also explored memory in artificial intelligence. While computers can store enormous amounts of information, AGI will require more than storage. Future intelligent systems may need advanced memory systems capable of connecting experiences, recognizing relationships, understanding context, and applying knowledge across different situations.

A key concept introduced was the distinction between **data, information, knowledge, and wisdom**. Data consists of raw facts. Information organizes data into meaningful patterns. Knowledge develops when information is understood. Wisdom emerges when knowledge is applied effectively to make sound decisions.

The chapter emphasized the importance of context. Context provides meaning to information and helps intelligent systems interpret situations accurately. Without context, decisions can become inaccurate or ineffective.

Finally, the chapter examined how memory supports learning from experience and helps build internal models of reality. Memory, knowledge, and context work together to create understanding, support decision-making, and enable autonomous behavior. These capabilities may become some of the most important building blocks of AGI.

Key Concepts

- Memory
- Sensory Memory
- Working Memory
- Long-Term Memory
- Knowledge
- Context
- Data
- Information
- Wisdom
- Learning
- Experience
- World Models
- AGI
- Autonomous Intelligence

Chapter 8 Reflection

Why Memory Shapes Intelligence

Imagine trying to learn a new skill while forgetting everything you learned the day before. Progress would be nearly impossible. Memory allows knowledge to accumulate and enables people to improve over time. It connects the past to the present and helps guide future decisions.

Throughout this chapter, you learned that memory is not simply about storing information. Memory helps create understanding, supports learning, and allows intelligent systems to recognize patterns and adapt to changing situations.

As AGI develops, memory systems may become increasingly important. Future intelligent systems may need to remember experiences, understand context, and apply knowledge in ways that resemble human learning.

This chapter encourages you to think about how memory influences your own life and how memory might shape the future of intelligent machines.

Reflection Questions

1. Why is memory considered a foundation of intelligence?
2. What would happen if humans could not form long-term memories?
3. How does memory support learning?
4. What is the difference between memory and knowledge?
5. Why is context important when interpreting information?
6. How does experience improve decision-making?
7. What is the difference between data, information, knowledge, and wisdom?
8. Why might AGI require advanced memory systems?

9. Should intelligent systems remember everything they experience? Why or why not?
10. How might memory contribute to the development of AGI?

Chapter 8 Worksheet

Memory, Knowledge, and Context

Part A: Vocabulary Matching

Match each term with its correct definition.

_____ 1. Sensory Memory

_____ 2. Working Memory

_____ 3. Long-Term Memory

_____ 4. Knowledge

_____ 5. Context

A. Information that provides meaning to a situation

B. Temporary mental workspace used for immediate tasks

C. Information stored for long periods

D. Brief storage of information from the senses

E. Understanding gained from information and experience

Part B: True or False

Write TRUE or FALSE.

_____ 1. Memory and knowledge mean exactly the same thing.

_____ 2. Working memory helps people solve immediate problems.

_____ 3. Context helps provide meaning to information.

_____ 4. Data and wisdom are identical concepts.

_____ 5. Future AGI systems may require advanced memory capabilities.

Part C: Short Answer

1. Why is memory important for intelligence?

___

___

2. Describe the role of working memory.

___

___

3. What is the difference between data and knowledge?

___

___

4. Why is context important?

___

___

5. How does memory support learning?

___

___

___

Part D: Critical Thinking

Imagine you are designing an AGI tutor for students.

1. What information should the system remember?

___

___

___

2. How could context improve its recommendations?

3. Why would long-term memory be important for helping students learn?

4. What information should the system forget?

Part E: Real-World Application

Think about a skill you have learned.

Examples:

- Riding a bicycle
- Playing a sport
- Reading
- Using a computer
- Playing an instrument

Skill:

How did memory help you learn this skill?

How did practice strengthen your knowledge?

Chapter 8 Quiz

Memory, Knowledge, and Context

Multiple Choice

1. Why is memory important for intelligence?

A. It increases internet speed.

B. It allows information and experiences to be stored and used later.

C. It replaces reasoning.

D. It eliminates learning.

2. Which type of memory acts as a temporary mental workspace?

A. Long-Term Memory

B. Sensory Memory

C. Working Memory

D. Permanent Memory

3. What is knowledge?

A. Raw facts

B. Random information

C. Understanding gained from information and experience

D. A storage device

4. Why is context important?

A. It provides meaning to information.

B. It increases storage capacity.

C. It removes uncertainty.

D. It replaces memory.

5. Which sequence correctly represents the progression discussed in the chapter?

A. Wisdom → Knowledge → Information → Data

B. Data → Information → Knowledge → Wisdom

C. Knowledge → Data → Wisdom → Information

D. Information → Data → Knowledge → Wisdom

Short Answer

6. Define long-term memory.
7. What is the difference between memory and knowledge?
8. Why is context important for AGI?
9. How do experiences contribute to learning?
10. Why may memory be essential for future AGI systems?

Chapter 8 Answer Key

Memory, Knowledge, and Context

Multiple Choice

1. B — It allows information and experiences to be stored and used later.
2. C — Working Memory
3. C — Understanding gained from information and experience
4. A — It provides meaning to information.
5. B — Data → Information → Knowledge → Wisdom

Short Answer

6. Long-term memory stores information, experiences, skills, and knowledge for extended periods, often lasting years or a lifetime.
7. Memory stores information, while knowledge involves understanding and applying that information meaningfully.
8. Context helps AGI interpret information correctly, personalize responses, and make more accurate decisions.
9. Experiences provide feedback, lessons, and patterns that improve future understanding and decision-making.
10. Memory allows AGI systems to learn from experience, build knowledge, recognize patterns, maintain context, and improve over time.

Scoring Guide

9–10 Correct

Excellent Understanding

7–8 Correct

Strong Understanding

5–6 Correct

Developing Understanding

Below 5 Correct

Review the chapter and retake the assessment.

Extension Challenge

Imagine you are designing the memory system for the world's first AGI.

Write a one-page response explaining:

- What information the AGI should remember.
- What information it should forget.
- How memory would help it learn.
- How context would improve decision-making.
- Why knowledge is more valuable than simple data storage.

Explain how memory, knowledge, and context could work together to support autonomous intelligence.

Learn AI. Understand AI. Shape the Future.
— Susie Hala, IntelliGloss Press

Chapter 9

Learning Without Constant Supervision

Imagine if every skill you possess today required someone standing beside you every moment of your life. Imagine learning to walk only when someone explained every step. Imagine learning to ride a bicycle only when someone constantly corrected every movement. Imagine learning to solve problems only when someone provided every answer before you had the chance to think for yourself.

Human intelligence does not develop this way. While teachers, parents, coaches, and mentors play important roles, much of human learning occurs independently. People learn through exploration, experimentation, observation, practice, mistakes, successes, failures, curiosity, and experience. Some of the most valuable lessons in life are discovered rather than taught. This ability to continue learning without constant supervision may be one of the most important characteristics of intelligence.

As researchers work toward Artificial General Intelligence (AGI), they face a significant challenge. Today's AI systems often depend heavily on human guidance. Engineers collect data, label examples, design training procedures, and carefully monitor performance. While this approach has produced impressive results, it cannot scale indefinitely. The world changes constantly. New situations emerge every day. Future AGI systems must be capable of learning in environments that humans have never fully anticipated. To achieve this level of adaptability, AGI may need the ability to learn continuously and independently.

One reason independent learning is so important is that the universe contains far more information than any teacher could ever provide. Consider the number of conversations, scientific discoveries, inventions, environmental changes, and social interactions that occur every day. No human instructor could possibly prepare an intelligent system for every situation it will encounter. Instead, future AGI systems may need to learn directly from experience, much like humans do throughout their lives.

Think about a young child learning to walk. No detailed instruction manual is provided. The child observes, experiments, falls, adjusts, and tries again. Every attempt provides feedback. Every failure contains information. Through repetition and adaptation, walking gradually becomes natural. This process demonstrates one of the most powerful learning mechanisms in nature. Intelligence grows through interaction with the environment. Rather than receiving complete solutions, the learner discovers solutions through experience.

Many researchers believe future AGI systems will require similar capabilities. They may need to operate in unfamiliar environments, solve novel problems, and adapt to changing circumstances without waiting for humans to provide step-by-step instructions. Such systems would not simply repeat previously learned behaviors. They would continuously acquire new knowledge and refine their understanding of the world.

A useful way to understand this concept is to distinguish between training and learning. Training usually occurs before a system is deployed. During training, large amounts of data are used to help the system develop capabilities. Learning, however, continues after deployment. Learning occurs when a system encounters new experiences, discovers new patterns, adapts to new situations, and improves its performance over time. Humans experience this process constantly. School provides training, but life provides continuous learning. Graduation does not mark the end of education. In many ways, it marks the beginning of a much larger learning journey.

Future AGI systems may operate in a similar manner. Their development may not end when initial training is completed. Instead, they may continue learning throughout their operational lives, continuously updating their knowledge, improving their skills, and adapting to new circumstances. This capacity for lifelong learning may become one of the defining characteristics that separates AGI from today's AI systems.

Learn AI. Understand AI. Shape the Future.
— Susie Hala, IntelliGloss Press

Chapter 9 Summary

Learning Without Constant Supervision

This chapter explored one of the most important capabilities required for Artificial General Intelligence (AGI): the ability to learn without constant supervision. Human beings learn throughout their lives by interacting with the world, making mistakes, solving problems, and adapting to new situations. Future AGI systems may require similar abilities if they are to function independently in dynamic and unpredictable environments.

The chapter began by examining the limitations of traditional AI training. Most current AI systems learn from large collections of human-provided data and examples. While this approach has produced impressive results, it depends heavily on human guidance and cannot anticipate every possible situation the system may encounter.

Readers learned that AGI will likely require continuous learning beyond initial training. Just as humans continue learning after leaving school, AGI systems may need to adapt throughout their entire operational lives. This process allows intelligence to remain flexible, current, and responsive to change.

The chapter introduced exploration as a powerful learning mechanism. Exploration enables intelligent systems to gather information, reduce uncertainty, and discover new knowledge through interaction with the environment.

The role of mistakes was also discussed. Rather than representing failure, mistakes often provide valuable feedback that supports improvement. By analyzing errors and adjusting behavior, intelligent systems can develop increasingly effective strategies.

Another key concept was reinforcement learning, where systems learn through rewards and feedback. Positive outcomes encourage successful behaviors, while negative outcomes discourage ineffective actions.

The chapter also explored curiosity as a possible driver of future AGI learning. Curiosity motivates exploration, encourages discovery, and helps intelligent systems identify new opportunities for growth and understanding.

Transfer learning was presented as another important capability. Transfer learning allows knowledge gained in one area to be applied in another, enabling flexible and adaptable intelligence.

Finally, readers examined the risks and challenges associated with independent learning. Autonomous systems must be designed carefully to ensure they learn accurate information, remain aligned with human values, and avoid harmful behaviors.

Key Concepts

- Independent Learning
- Continuous Learning
- Exploration
- Experience
- Feedback
- Mistakes
- Reinforcement Learning
- Curiosity
- Transfer Learning
- Adaptation
- AGI
- Lifelong Learning
- Alignment
- Autonomous Intelligence

Chapter 9 Reflection

Why Learning Never Ends

One of the most remarkable qualities of intelligence is the ability to learn continuously. Humans do not stop learning after school, college, or training programs. Instead, learning continues throughout life as new experiences, challenges, and opportunities arise.

This chapter explored how future AGI systems may require similar lifelong learning abilities. An intelligent system that cannot learn beyond its initial training may struggle to adapt to changing environments and unexpected situations.

Think about your own experiences. Some of your most important lessons may not have come from textbooks or classrooms. They may have come from mistakes, challenges, observations, and personal experiences. These experiences helped shape your understanding of the world.

As AI systems become more autonomous, learning may become one of the most important capabilities separating static tools from truly adaptive intelligence.

Reflection Questions

1. Why is continuous learning important for intelligence?
2. What are the limitations of learning that depends entirely on human supervision?
3. How does exploration contribute to learning?
4. Why can mistakes be valuable?
5. What is reinforcement learning?
6. How does curiosity encourage discovery?
7. What is transfer learning and why is it important?
8. What risks could arise from independent learning?
9. How can human values influence the learning process of AGI?
10. What lessons have you learned from your own mistakes?

Chapter 9 Worksheet

Learning Without Constant Supervision

Part A: Vocabulary Matching

Match each term with its correct definition.

_____ 1. Exploration

_____ 2. Reinforcement Learning

_____ 3. Curiosity

_____ 4. Transfer Learning

_____ 5. Continuous Learning

A. Applying knowledge from one area to another

B. Learning through rewards and feedback

C. Ongoing learning throughout life or operation

D. A desire to discover and understand new things

E. Gathering information by interacting with the environment

Part B: True or False

Write TRUE or FALSE.

_____ 1. AGI will likely need to continue learning after deployment.

_____ 2. Mistakes always prevent learning.

_____ 3. Curiosity can encourage exploration and discovery.

_____ 4. Transfer learning helps apply knowledge across domains.

_____ 5. Independent learning creates no risks.

Part C: Short Answer

1. Why is continuous learning important for AGI?

____

____

2. What role does exploration play in learning?

____

____

3. Why can mistakes help improve intelligence?

4. What is reinforcement learning?

5. What is transfer learning?

Part D: Scenario Analysis

Imagine you are designing an AGI system to help scientists discover new medicines.

1. How could exploration help the system learn?

2. How might reinforcement learning improve performance?

3. Why would transfer learning be useful?

4. What safeguards should be included to ensure safe learning?

Part E: Personal Growth Exercise

Think about a mistake you made that helped you learn something important.

What happened?

____
____

What did you learn?

____
____

How did that experience help you improve?

____
____
____

Chapter 9 Quiz

Learning Without Constant Supervision

Multiple Choice

1. Why is independent learning important for AGI?

A. It increases screen resolution.

B. It allows systems to adapt and improve over time.

C. It eliminates memory.

D. It removes the need for data.

2. What is exploration?

A. Ignoring information

B. Gathering information by interacting with the environment

C. Memorizing facts

D. Following instructions exactly

3. What is reinforcement learning?

A. Learning through rewards and feedback

B. Learning through guessing

C. Learning without experience

D. Learning by storing files

4. What is curiosity?

A. A type of computer hardware

B. A desire to discover and understand new things

C. A storage system

D. A programming language

5. What is transfer learning?

A. Moving data between computers

B. Applying knowledge from one area to another

C. Deleting old information

D. Reducing intelligence

Short Answer

6. Why must AGI continue learning after training?
7. How do mistakes contribute to learning?
8. What role does curiosity play in intelligence?
9. Why is transfer learning important for AGI?
10. What risks can arise from independent learning?

Chapter 9 Answer Key

Learning Without Constant Supervision

Multiple Choice

1. B — It allows systems to adapt and improve over time.
2. B — Gathering information by interacting with the environment.
3. A — Learning through rewards and feedback.
4. B — A desire to discover and understand new things.
5. B — Applying knowledge from one area to another.

Short Answer

6. AGI must continue learning because the world constantly changes, and new situations require adaptation and updated knowledge.
7. Mistakes provide feedback that helps identify weaknesses, improve strategies, and increase future performance.
8. Curiosity motivates exploration, encourages discovery, and helps intelligent systems learn new information.
9. Transfer learning allows knowledge gained in one area to be applied to different problems, making intelligence more flexible and efficient.
10. Risks include learning incorrect information, developing harmful behaviors, misunderstanding feedback, or becoming misaligned with human values.

Scoring Guide

9–10 Correct

Excellent Understanding

7–8 Correct

Strong Understanding

5–6 Correct

Developing Understanding

Below 5 Correct

Review the chapter and retake the assessment.

Extension Challenge

Imagine you are designing the learning system for the world's first AGI explorer.

Write a one-page response explaining:

- How the AGI would learn from experience.
- How curiosity would guide exploration.
- How reinforcement learning would improve performance.
- How transfer learning would help solve new problems.
- What safeguards would ensure the AGI learns safely and responsibly.

Explain why lifelong learning may be one of the most important capabilities required for Artificial General Intelligence.

Learn AI. Understand AI. Shape the Future.
— Susie Hala, IntelliGloss Press

Chapter 10

Adaptation and Self-Improvement

Imagine two students taking the same mathematics class.

The first student studies hard, takes tests, receives feedback, and improves throughout the year. Every mistake becomes a lesson. Every challenge becomes an opportunity to grow. By the end of the school year, the student performs far better than at the beginning.

The second student studies only once. No matter what mistakes are made, no adjustments occur. No new strategies are tried. No learning takes place after the first lesson. By the end of the year, the student's abilities remain almost unchanged.

Which student would you expect to succeed?

Most people would choose the first student because growth is one of the defining characteristics of intelligence. Intelligence is not simply about what is known today. Intelligence is also about the ability to improve tomorrow.

This idea lies at the heart of one of the most important concepts in Artificial General Intelligence (AGI): adaptation and self-improvement.

An AGI system may begin with impressive capabilities, but if it cannot adapt to new circumstances or improve its performance over time, its usefulness will eventually become limited. The world changes constantly. New technologies emerge. Scientific discoveries occur. Human needs evolve. Environments shift. Problems appear that have never existed before.

To thrive in such a world, intelligence must be capable of change.

Why Adaptation Matters

Imagine trying to survive in a world where nothing ever changed. Every day would be predictable. Every challenge would remain the same. Every solution would work forever.

The real world does not operate that way.

Weather changes.

Economies change.

Technology changes.

Cultures change.

Knowledge changes.

People change.

Successful individuals adapt to these changes. Businesses adapt to market conditions. Scientists adapt to new evidence. Athletes adapt to stronger competition. Teachers adapt to new educational methods.

Adaptation allows intelligence to remain effective when circumstances evolve.

Future AGI systems will face the same challenge. An AGI designed for today's world may eventually encounter situations that did not exist during its original training. Without adaptation, the system could become outdated. With adaptation, it can continue growing and improving.

What Is Adaptation?

Adaptation is the process of adjusting behavior, strategies, or knowledge in response to new information or changing conditions.

In nature, adaptation can be observed everywhere.

Animals adapt to environmental changes.

Plants adapt to different climates.

Humans adapt to new technologies and social environments.

The ability to adapt increases the likelihood of success.

For intelligent systems, adaptation means recognizing when existing approaches no longer work effectively and finding better alternatives.

An AGI that can adapt does not simply repeat old solutions. It evaluates outcomes, learns from experience, and adjusts its behavior accordingly.

This ability may become one of the most important characteristics separating AGI from traditional software systems.

The Difference Between Automation and Adaptation

Traditional software follows instructions.

Adaptation goes beyond instructions.

Consider a calculator. No matter how many times you use it, the calculator does not become better at arithmetic. It performs the same operations today that it performed yesterday.

Now consider a human student.

After solving hundreds of math problems, the student becomes faster, more accurate, and more confident.

The difference is adaptation.

Traditional software executes rules.

Adaptive intelligence improves through experience.

Future AGI systems may need to function more like students than calculators. They must learn from interactions, refine their strategies, and improve performance over time.

Learning From Success

When people think about learning, they often focus on mistakes. However, success can also be a valuable teacher.

Imagine a basketball player making a perfect shot. The athlete learns which movements, timing, and techniques contributed to success. Future attempts may repeat those successful actions.

Scientists operate similarly. When an experiment produces positive results, researchers study what worked and why.

AGI systems may benefit from the same process.

Successful outcomes provide information.

They reveal effective strategies.

They identify useful patterns.

They help reinforce productive behaviors.

By studying success, an intelligent system can strengthen capabilities that produce desirable results.

Learning From Failure

Failure often receives a negative reputation, but many of history's greatest achievements emerged through repeated failure.

Inventors test unsuccessful designs.

Scientists conduct experiments that do not work.

Athletes lose competitions.

Entrepreneurs experience setbacks.

These experiences provide valuable feedback.

Failure highlights weaknesses, reveals hidden problems, and identifies opportunities for improvement.

Future AGI systems may also learn through failure.

A self-driving vehicle may encounter unexpected road conditions.

A scientific AGI may test incorrect hypotheses.

An educational AGI may discover that certain teaching strategies are ineffective.

Each failure becomes information.

The key is not avoiding mistakes entirely. The key is learning from them.

Feedback: The Fuel of Improvement

Imagine trying to improve your basketball skills while never seeing whether the ball enters the basket.

Improvement would be difficult because feedback would be missing.

Feedback tells us whether our actions are helping or hurting progress.

Humans rely on feedback constantly.

Teachers provide grades.

Coaches provide guidance.

Customers provide reviews.

Friends provide opinions.

Every form of feedback contains information that can support improvement.

AGI systems may depend heavily on feedback mechanisms.

Feedback allows intelligent systems to compare outcomes with goals.

If performance falls short, adjustments can be made.

If performance improves, successful behaviors can be reinforced.

Without feedback, improvement becomes much more difficult.

Self-Monitoring: Watching Yourself Think

One of the most fascinating aspects of intelligence is the ability to reflect on one's own performance.

Students may ask:

"Did I study effectively?"

Athletes may ask:

"Could I improve my technique?"

Scientists may ask:

"Did I overlook something important?"

This process is often called self-monitoring.

Self-monitoring allows individuals to evaluate their own actions and identify opportunities for improvement.

Future AGI systems may require similar capabilities.

A highly autonomous system cannot rely entirely on external supervision. It must be capable of evaluating its own performance.

This does not mean self-awareness in the human sense. Rather, it means maintaining internal measurements that help determine whether goals are being achieved efficiently and effectively.

Self-monitoring may become one of the most important tools for continuous improvement.

The Concept of Self-Improvement

Adaptation allows a system to respond to change.

Self-improvement goes a step further.

Self-improvement involves actively becoming better over time.

Imagine a chess player who studies previous games, analyzes mistakes, and develops new strategies.

The player is not merely adapting to immediate situations. The player is systematically improving future performance.

Future AGI systems may engage in similar activities.

They may analyze previous decisions.

They may identify weaknesses.

They may discover more effective approaches.

They may update internal models of the world.

Over time, these improvements could accumulate into significant increases in capability.

Small Improvements, Big Results

One of the most powerful lessons in growth is that small improvements compound over time.

Imagine improving by just one percent every day.

The change may seem insignificant at first.

However, over months and years, those improvements accumulate.

Students who study consistently often outperform students who cram at the last minute.

Athletes who practice regularly develop greater skill than those who train occasionally.

Businesses that continuously improve processes often become more competitive over time.

Future AGI systems may benefit from similar compounding effects.

A small improvement in learning efficiency today could lead to better decisions tomorrow. Better decisions could lead to improved learning opportunities. Improved learning could generate even greater improvements later.

This cycle creates continuous growth.

The Promise and Risks of Self-Improvement

The idea of self-improving AGI is both exciting and challenging.

On one hand, self-improvement could help solve complex problems.

It could accelerate scientific discovery.

It could improve healthcare.

It could support education.

It could help humanity address global challenges.

On the other hand, self-improvement introduces important questions.

How should improvements be evaluated?

Who determines what counts as better performance?

How can systems remain aligned with human values as capabilities increase?

These questions are central to AGI research.

The goal is not simply creating systems that improve.

The goal is creating systems that improve responsibly.

Continuous Growth and the Future of AGI

Throughout history, growth has been one of the defining characteristics of intelligence.

Children become adults.

Students become experts.

Beginners become masters.

Knowledge expands.

Skills improve.

Understanding deepens.

The same principle may apply to AGI.

An intelligent system that never changes will eventually become limited.

An intelligent system that can adapt, learn, and improve may continue growing throughout its existence.

Adaptation allows intelligence to remain relevant.

Feedback allows intelligence to learn.

Self-monitoring allows intelligence to evaluate itself.

Self-improvement allows intelligence to become more capable over time.

Together, these abilities may become some of the most important foundations of Artificial General Intelligence.

Because the future of intelligence is not defined solely by what a system knows today.

It may be defined by how effectively that system can learn, adapt, and become better tomorrow.

Learn AI. Understand AI. Shape the Future.

— Susie Hala, IntelliGloss Press

Chapter 10 Summary

Adaptation and Self-Improvement

This chapter explored the important concepts of adaptation and self-improvement and their potential role in the development of Artificial General Intelligence (AGI). Intelligence is not only about what a system knows at a given moment but also about its ability to learn, adjust, and improve over time. In a constantly changing world, adaptation allows intelligent systems to remain effective when conditions, goals, or environments change.

The chapter explained that adaptation is the process of adjusting behavior, strategies, or knowledge in response to new information and experiences. Humans adapt throughout their lives by learning from successes, failures, feedback, and changing circumstances. Future AGI systems may require similar capabilities to operate successfully in dynamic environments.

Readers learned the difference between traditional automation and adaptation. Traditional software follows fixed instructions and typically does not improve through experience. Adaptive intelligence, on the other hand, can modify its behavior based on what it learns over time.

The chapter emphasized that both success and failure provide valuable learning opportunities. Success helps identify effective strategies that should be repeated, while failure reveals weaknesses and areas for improvement. Together, they create powerful feedback loops that support continuous growth.

Another key concept discussed was feedback. Feedback provides information about performance and helps intelligent systems determine whether they are moving closer to or farther from their goals. Without feedback, meaningful improvement becomes difficult.

The chapter also introduced self-monitoring, the ability to evaluate one's own performance. Future AGI systems may require internal mechanisms that allow them to assess progress, identify weaknesses, and make adjustments independently.

Finally, the chapter explored self-improvement. Self-improvement involves actively becoming more capable over time by learning from experience and refining strategies. Small improvements may accumulate into significant gains through continuous growth and learning. However, the chapter also highlighted the importance of ensuring that self-improvement remains aligned with human values and ethical principles.

Key Concepts

- Adaptation
- Self-Improvement
- Feedback
- Learning
- Experience
- Success

- Failure
- Self-Monitoring
- Continuous Growth
- AGI
- Alignment
- Autonomous Intelligence
- Improvement Loops
- Lifelong Learning

Chapter 10 Reflection

Growing Through Change

One of the most powerful characteristics of intelligence is the ability to grow. Humans are constantly adapting to new situations, learning from experience, and improving their skills. The ability to change and improve is often what separates success from failure.

This chapter explored how future AGI systems may require similar abilities. Instead of remaining fixed and static, AGI may need to learn from feedback, evaluate its performance, and continuously improve its capabilities.

Think about your own life. Many of your greatest improvements may have come from mistakes, challenges, and experiences that taught valuable lessons. Growth often occurs when individuals are willing to learn from both successes and failures.

As AI becomes more autonomous, adaptation and self-improvement may become essential components of intelligent behavior. However, these abilities must be guided by values, responsibility, and careful design.

Reflection Questions

1. Why is adaptation important for intelligence?
2. How does adaptation differ from traditional automation?
3. What can be learned from success?
4. What can be learned from failure?
5. Why is feedback important for improvement?
6. What is self-monitoring?
7. How might AGI systems use self-monitoring?
8. Why can small improvements become powerful over time?
9. What risks might arise from self-improving systems?
10. Why is alignment important when designing self-improving AGI?

Chapter 10 Worksheet

Adaptation and Self-Improvement

Part A: Vocabulary Matching

Match each term with its correct definition.

_____ 1. Adaptation

_____ 2. Self-Improvement

_____ 3. Feedback

_____ 4. Self-Monitoring

_____ 5. Alignment

A. Ensuring actions remain consistent with human values

B. Information about performance that supports learning

C. The process of evaluating one's own performance

D. Adjusting behavior based on new information and experiences

E. Becoming more capable over time through learning and refinement

Part B: True or False

Write TRUE or FALSE.

_____ 1. Traditional software usually improves itself through experience.

_____ 2. Adaptation helps systems respond to changing environments.

_____ 3. Failure can provide valuable information.

_____ 4. Feedback supports improvement.

_____ 5. Self-improvement should remain aligned with human values.

Part C: Short Answer

1. What is adaptation?

2. How does adaptation support intelligence?

3. Why is feedback important?

4. What is self-monitoring?

5. Why is alignment important for self-improving AGI?

Part D: Scenario Analysis

Imagine you are designing an AGI system to help doctors diagnose diseases.

1. How could the system learn from successful diagnoses?

2. How could the system learn from mistakes?

3. What types of feedback should the system receive?

4. How could self-monitoring improve performance?

Part E: Personal Growth Activity

Think about a skill you improved through practice.

Skill:

What mistakes did you make while learning?

What feedback helped you improve?

How did small improvements eventually lead to success?

Chapter 10 Quiz

Adaptation and Self-Improvement

Multiple Choice

1. What is adaptation?

A. Storing information permanently

B. Adjusting behavior based on new information and experiences

C. Following instructions exactly

D. Eliminating feedback

2. What is self-improvement?

A. Becoming more capable over time through learning

B. Ignoring mistakes

C. Storing more data

D. Reducing intelligence

3. Why is feedback important?

A. It increases internet speed.

B. It provides information about performance.

C. It eliminates learning.

D. It removes uncertainty.

4. What is self-monitoring?

A. Watching other people work

B. Evaluating one's own performance

C. Collecting data only

D. Memorizing information

5. Why is alignment important for self-improving AGI?

A. It reduces memory requirements.

B. It ensures improvements remain consistent with human values.

C. It increases storage space.

D. It improves internet connectivity.

Short Answer

6. Explain the difference between automation and adaptation.
7. What can intelligent systems learn from failure?
8. Why is continuous improvement important?
9. How can feedback improve decision-making?
10. What risks could emerge if self-improving systems are not properly aligned?

Chapter 10 Answer Key

Adaptation and Self-Improvement

Multiple Choice

1. B — Adjusting behavior based on new information and experiences
2. A — Becoming more capable over time through learning
3. B — It provides information about performance
4. B — Evaluating one's own performance
5. B — It ensures improvements remain consistent with human values

Short Answer

6. Automation follows fixed instructions, while adaptation allows a system to adjust its behavior based on experience and changing conditions.
7. Failure can reveal weaknesses, identify mistakes, provide feedback, and suggest better strategies for future actions.
8. Continuous improvement helps intelligent systems remain effective, adapt to change, and become more capable over time.
9. Feedback provides information about outcomes, helping systems identify successful strategies and correct mistakes.
10. Misaligned self-improving systems could pursue harmful goals, make poor decisions, or act in ways that conflict with human values.

Scoring Guide

9–10 Correct

Outstanding Understanding

7–8 Correct

Strong Understanding

5–6 Correct

Developing Understanding

Below 5 Correct

Review the chapter and retake the assessment.

Extension Challenge

Imagine you are leading the design team for the world's first self-improving AGI.

Write a one-page response explaining:

- How the system would adapt to change.
- How feedback would guide improvement.
- How self-monitoring would work.
- How the system would learn from success and failure.
- What safeguards would ensure alignment with human values.

Explain why adaptation and self-improvement may be essential capabilities for future AGI systems.

Learn AI. Understand AI. Shape the Future.
— Susie Hala, IntelliGloss Press

Chapter 11

Reasoning and Problem-Solving

Imagine you are walking through a forest and suddenly come to a river.

The river is too wide to jump across.

The water is moving too fast to swim through safely.

There is no bridge in sight.

You need to reach the other side.

What do you do?

Most people would immediately begin thinking.

Perhaps there is a fallen tree nearby.

Perhaps the river becomes narrower farther downstream.

Perhaps rocks could create a crossing path.

Perhaps another route exists entirely.

The moment you begin evaluating possibilities, you are using one of the most powerful abilities of intelligence: reasoning.

Reasoning allows humans to move beyond simple reactions. Instead of responding automatically, intelligent beings can analyze situations, evaluate options, predict outcomes, and solve problems. Every major achievement in human history—from building cities to landing spacecraft on the Moon—has depended upon reasoning and problem-solving.

For Artificial General Intelligence (AGI), reasoning may become one of the most important capabilities of all. An AGI must do more than store information. It must know how to use that information to solve unfamiliar problems and make effective decisions in changing environments.

Knowledge provides the ingredients.

Reasoning creates the recipe.

Problem-solving produces the result.

Together, these abilities form one of the central pillars of autonomous intelligence.

What Is Reasoning?

Reasoning is the process of using information to reach conclusions, make judgments, and solve problems.

Humans reason constantly.

When a student studies for a test, reasoning helps determine what material deserves attention.

When a doctor examines symptoms, reasoning helps identify possible illnesses.

When a mechanic diagnoses an engine problem, reasoning helps determine what component may be malfunctioning.

Reasoning connects facts to conclusions.

Without reasoning, information remains disconnected pieces of knowledge.

Imagine having every page of a textbook memorized but being unable to answer a question that combines ideas from different chapters. You would possess information but lack reasoning.

AGI systems will need both.

The Difference Between Knowledge and Reasoning

Many people confuse knowledge with intelligence.

Knowledge is important, but knowledge alone does not guarantee understanding.

Imagine two students.

The first student memorizes every answer in a science textbook.

The second student understands why scientific principles work.

When presented with a new problem that does not appear in the textbook, the first student may struggle. The second student can use reasoning to apply knowledge in new ways.

This difference is critical.

Knowledge answers the question:

"What do I know?"

Reasoning answers the question:

"What can I do with what I know?"

Future AGI systems must be able to transfer knowledge into action.

They must reason through unfamiliar situations rather than relying entirely on memorized information.

Solving Problems in an Unpredictable World

Life rarely provides perfect instructions.

Many situations involve uncertainty.

A scientist investigating a new disease does not begin with all the answers.

An engineer designing a new technology faces challenges that have never existed before.

A firefighter responding to an emergency encounters rapidly changing conditions.

These situations require problem-solving.

Problem-solving is the process of identifying obstacles and finding solutions that move a situation closer to a desired outcome.

Future AGI systems will operate in environments filled with uncertainty. They will encounter situations that were never included in training data. They will face problems that humans have never solved before.

The ability to reason through uncertainty may become one of the defining characteristics of AGI.

Deductive Reasoning: Working From Rules

One form of reasoning is called deductive reasoning.

Deductive reasoning begins with general rules and applies them to specific situations.

For example:

All mammals breathe air.

Whales are mammals.

Therefore, whales breathe air.

If the original statements are true, the conclusion must also be true.

Humans use deductive reasoning in mathematics, science, law, and many other fields.

Future AGI systems may rely on deductive reasoning when applying known rules to solve problems.

Deductive reasoning provides reliability and consistency, making it valuable in situations where accuracy is critical.

Inductive Reasoning: Learning From Patterns

Another form of reasoning is inductive reasoning.

Inductive reasoning works in the opposite direction.

Instead of starting with rules, it begins with observations.

Suppose you observe:

The Sun rises every morning.

It rose yesterday.

It rose last week.

It rose last year.

You may conclude that it will rise tomorrow.

This conclusion is not guaranteed, but it is highly probable.

Inductive reasoning allows humans to identify patterns and make predictions.

Much of modern AI relies heavily on pattern recognition and inductive reasoning.

Future AGI systems will likely combine inductive and deductive reasoning to develop a deeper understanding of the world.

Abductive Reasoning: Finding the Best Explanation

Sometimes information is incomplete.

In these situations, humans often use abductive reasoning.

Imagine waking up and finding the sidewalk wet.

Several explanations are possible:

- It rained overnight.
- A sprinkler system activated.
- Someone washed the sidewalk.

You examine available evidence and select the most likely explanation.

Doctors frequently use abductive reasoning when diagnosing illnesses.

Detectives use it when investigating crimes.

Scientists use it when developing hypotheses.

Future AGI systems may require abductive reasoning to operate effectively in uncertain environments where perfect information is unavailable.

Reasoning Across Multiple Steps

Some problems require only a single decision.

Others require many interconnected decisions.

Imagine playing chess.

A beginner focuses on the next move.

An expert may think ten or twenty moves ahead.

The expert reasons through possible future scenarios and evaluates consequences before acting.

AGI systems may need similar abilities.

Complex challenges often require long chains of reasoning.

The system must:

- Analyze the current situation.
- Generate possible actions.
- Predict consequences.
- Compare outcomes.
- Select the most effective strategy.

This process may repeat many times before a solution is found.

The ability to reason across multiple steps is essential for advanced problem-solving.

Creativity and Problem-Solving

Many people think reasoning and creativity are separate abilities.

In reality, they often work together.

Imagine an inventor attempting to solve a difficult engineering challenge.

Reasoning helps evaluate possibilities.

Creativity helps generate new possibilities.

Without creativity, solutions may remain limited.

Without reasoning, creative ideas may be impractical.

Future AGI systems may need both.

They must analyze existing knowledge while also generating innovative approaches to new problems.

Some of the most valuable solutions emerge when reasoning and creativity work together.

Common Obstacles to Problem-Solving

Humans often face obstacles that interfere with effective reasoning.

These include:

- Incomplete information
- Limited resources
- Time pressure
- Emotional bias
- Overconfidence
- Incorrect assumptions

Future AGI systems may face similar challenges.

Although machines do not experience emotions in the same way humans do, they may still encounter uncertainty, conflicting information, and resource limitations.

Effective problem-solving requires recognizing these obstacles and adjusting strategies accordingly.

Reasoning and Autonomous Intelligence

Imagine an AGI helping scientists develop new medicines.

Imagine an AGI coordinating disaster response efforts.

Imagine an AGI managing transportation systems for entire cities.

Each of these tasks involves thousands of decisions and countless potential problems.

The system must evaluate evidence, identify patterns, predict outcomes, and generate solutions.

Without reasoning, autonomy becomes dangerous.

Without problem-solving, goals remain unreachable.

Reasoning allows intelligent systems to transform information into action.

Problem-solving allows them to overcome obstacles along the way.

Together, they make autonomy practical.

The Future of Reasoning

One of the greatest questions in AGI research is whether machines can eventually reason as flexibly as humans.

Today's AI systems can perform impressive tasks, but many still struggle with complex reasoning across unfamiliar situations.

Researchers continue developing systems that can think more deeply, reason more accurately, and solve increasingly difficult problems.

Progress in reasoning may determine how quickly AGI develops.

A system that can reason effectively gains the ability to learn, adapt, plan, and improve across many different domains.

Reasoning connects knowledge to action.

It connects goals to solutions.

It connects intelligence to achievement.

As AGI evolves, reasoning may become one of its most valuable capabilities. It enables intelligent systems to move beyond memorized answers and engage with the world as active problem-solvers.

Because in the end, intelligence is not measured only by what a system knows.

It is measured by what it can figure out.

And the ability to figure things out may be one of the greatest powers of all.

Learn AI. Understand AI. Shape the Future.

— Susie Hala, IntelliGloss Press

Chapter 11 Summary

Reasoning and Problem-Solving

Reasoning is one of the most important abilities that separates intelligence from simple memorization. While knowledge provides facts and information, reasoning allows those facts to be connected, analyzed, and used to solve problems. An intelligent system must do more than remember information—it must know how to apply it in new and unfamiliar situations.

This chapter explains that reasoning is the process of using information to reach conclusions, make decisions, and solve challenges. Humans use reasoning every day when making choices, diagnosing problems, planning activities, and predicting outcomes. Future Artificial General Intelligence (AGI) systems will also require reasoning to function effectively in constantly changing environments.

The chapter distinguishes between knowledge and reasoning. Knowledge answers the question, "What do I know?" Reasoning answers, "What can I do with what I know?" An AGI that only memorizes information would struggle when faced with situations it has never encountered before. True intelligence requires applying knowledge creatively and logically.

Students also learned about three major forms of reasoning:

- **Deductive reasoning** starts with general rules and applies them to specific situations.
- **Inductive reasoning** begins with observations and identifies patterns to make predictions.
- **Abductive reasoning** uses available evidence to determine the most likely explanation when information is incomplete.

Complex problem-solving often requires reasoning through multiple steps, evaluating different possibilities, predicting consequences, and selecting the best solution. Creativity also plays an important role because innovative ideas combined with logical thinking often produce the best solutions.

The chapter discusses common obstacles that interfere with effective reasoning, including incomplete information, limited resources, time pressure, overconfidence, emotional bias, and incorrect assumptions. Future AGI systems may encounter many of these challenges as they operate in unpredictable environments.

Finally, the chapter emphasizes that reasoning is one of the core abilities that makes autonomous intelligence possible. As AGI continues to develop, reasoning will allow intelligent systems to move beyond memorized answers and become adaptable, thoughtful problem-solvers capable of assisting humanity in science, medicine, engineering, transportation, education, and many other fields.

Reflection Questions

Answer each question using complete sentences.

1. Why is reasoning considered more powerful than simply memorizing information?
2. Explain the difference between knowledge and reasoning in your own words.
3. Describe a situation in your own life where you used reasoning to solve a problem.
4. Why is uncertainty an important challenge for both humans and AGI systems?
5. How does deductive reasoning differ from inductive reasoning?
6. Why is abductive reasoning useful when information is incomplete?
7. Explain why creativity and reasoning work well together.
8. Which obstacle to problem-solving do you think is most difficult for humans to overcome? Why?
9. Why will future AGI systems need reasoning instead of simply storing large amounts of data?
10. After reading this chapter, how has your understanding of intelligence changed?

Chapter 11 Worksheet

Reasoning and Problem-Solving

Part A: Vocabulary

Write a short definition for each term.

1. Reasoning

---

2. Problem-solving

---

3. Deductive reasoning

---

4. Inductive reasoning

---

5. Abductive reasoning

---

6. Knowledge

---

7. Creativity

---

8. Autonomous intelligence

Part B: Fill in the Blank

Choose the correct word.

(Reasoning, Knowledge, Deductive, Inductive, Abductive, Creativity, Prediction, Problem-solving)

1. __________ allows information to be used for making decisions.
2. __________ is the process of overcoming obstacles to reach a goal.
3. __________ reasoning starts with general rules.
4. __________ reasoning looks for patterns from observations.
5. __________ reasoning identifies the most likely explanation.
6. __________ provides facts and information.
7. __________ helps generate new ideas.
8. Good reasoning often involves making accurate __________.

Part C: Matching

Match the reasoning type with the correct description.

A. Deductive

B. Inductive

C. Abductive

____ Starts with observations to discover patterns.

____ Begins with rules to reach conclusions.

____ Chooses the most likely explanation.

Part D: Short Answer

1. Why would an AGI need to reason through unfamiliar situations?

____

____

2. Name three obstacles that can interfere with good reasoning.

____

____

3. Why is reasoning considered essential for autonomous intelligence?

____

____

4. How can creativity improve problem-solving?

____

____

____

Chapter 11 Quiz

Reasoning and Problem-Solving

Multiple Choice

1. What is reasoning?

A. Memorizing information

B. Using information to reach conclusions and solve problems

C. Collecting data only

D. Reading textbooks

---

2. Knowledge answers which question?

A. What should I create?

B. What can I do with what I know?

C. What do I know?

D. Why do I learn?

---

3. Which type of reasoning starts with general rules?

A. Inductive

B. Creative

C. Deductive

D. Abductive

---

4. Which reasoning type identifies patterns from observations?

A. Deductive

B. Inductive

C. Mathematical

D. Mechanical

---

5. Abductive reasoning tries to find:

A. Every possible answer

B. The fastest answer

C. The most likely explanation

D. The longest solution

---

6. Which activity requires multiple-step reasoning?

A. Guessing randomly

B. Playing chess

C. Watching television

D. Memorizing a list

---

7. Which pair works together to create innovative solutions?

A. Memory and speed

B. Creativity and reasoning

C. Storage and electricity

D. Sensors and cameras

---

8. Which is NOT listed as an obstacle to problem-solving?

A. Overconfidence

B. Limited resources

C. Emotional bias

D. Perfect information

---

9. Why is reasoning important for AGI?

A. It helps memorize more books.

B. It allows systems to solve unfamiliar problems.

C. It replaces knowledge completely.

D. It eliminates uncertainty.

---

10. According to the chapter, intelligence is ultimately measured by:

A. Memory size

B. Processing speed

C. What a system can figure out

D. Internet access

Answer Key

Worksheet Answers

Part A (Sample Answers)

1. Using information to reach conclusions and solve problems.
2. Finding solutions to overcome obstacles.
3. Applying general rules to specific situations.
4. Finding patterns from observations.
5. Choosing the most likely explanation.
6. Facts and information a person or system possesses.
7. The ability to generate new ideas.
8. The ability of an intelligent system to operate independently.

Part B

1. Reasoning
2. Problem-solving
3. Deductive

4. Inductive
5. Abductive
6. Knowledge
7. Creativity
8. Prediction

Part C

B — Starts with observations to discover patterns.

A — Begins with rules to reach conclusions.

C — Chooses the most likely explanation.

Part D (Sample Answers)

1. Because future situations may not exist in its training data, requiring it to think through new problems.
2. Examples include incomplete information, limited resources, time pressure, emotional bias, overconfidence, and incorrect assumptions.
3. Reasoning allows an AGI to analyze situations, make decisions, and solve problems independently.
4. Creativity helps generate new ideas, while reasoning evaluates which ideas are most effective.

Quiz Answers

1. **B**
2. **C**
3. **C**
4. **B**
5. **C**
6. **B**
7. **B**
8. **D**
9. **B**
10. **C**

Chapter 11 Key Takeaway

Reasoning is the bridge between knowledge and action. Knowledge provides information, but reasoning transforms that information into decisions, solutions, and innovation. As Artificial General Intelligence continues to evolve, its ability to reason through unfamiliar situations may become one of the defining characteristics that allows it to learn, adapt, solve complex problems, and work alongside humans in meaningful ways.

Chapter 12

Creativity and Innovation in AGI

Imagine standing on a beach one thousand years ago and telling someone that humans would someday fly through the sky in giant metal machines carrying hundreds of passengers across oceans.

Imagine telling them that people would communicate instantly across continents using devices that fit into their pockets.

Imagine explaining that machines would one day solve mathematical problems, compose music, generate artwork, diagnose diseases, and assist scientists in making discoveries.

Most people would probably think such ideas were impossible.

Yet every one of those achievements began in the same place.

Someone imagined them first.

Before every invention comes an idea.

Before every discovery comes a question.

Before every breakthrough comes imagination.

Creativity is the ability to generate new ideas, new possibilities, and new ways of understanding the world. Innovation is the process of transforming those ideas into reality. Together, creativity and innovation have shaped human civilization for thousands of years.

As researchers pursue Artificial General Intelligence (AGI), one of the most fascinating questions emerges:

Can machines become creative?

Can they imagine possibilities that do not yet exist?

Can they generate original solutions to problems that humanity has never solved?

The answers to these questions may play a major role in determining the future of intelligence itself.

Why Creativity Matters

Many people associate intelligence with knowledge.

Others associate intelligence with logic.

Both are important.

However, some of humanity's greatest achievements required something more.

Consider the invention of the airplane.

For thousands of years, humans observed birds flying through the sky. People understood gravity. They understood motion. They understood materials. Yet understanding alone did not create flight.

Someone had to imagine a possibility that did not yet exist.

The same principle applies to nearly every major innovation.

Electricity.

Vaccines.

Computers.

Space exploration.

The internet.

Artificial intelligence.

Each breakthrough required creative thinking.

Creativity allows intelligence to move beyond what is known and explore what might be possible.

Without creativity, progress slows.

Without creativity, innovation becomes difficult.

Without creativity, intelligence remains confined to existing knowledge.

What Is Creativity?

Creativity is often misunderstood.

Many people think creativity is limited to artists, musicians, and writers.

In reality, creativity appears in nearly every field.

Scientists use creativity to develop new theories.

Engineers use creativity to design new technologies.

Doctors use creativity to develop treatments.

Entrepreneurs use creativity to build businesses.

Teachers use creativity to engage students.

Creativity is not simply making art.

Creativity is the ability to generate useful and original ideas.

A creative thinker asks questions such as:

- What if?
- Why not?
- Is there a better way?
- What have others overlooked?
- What happens if we combine these ideas?

These questions drive innovation.

Future AGI systems may need similar capabilities if they are to solve problems that have never been solved before.

The Building Blocks of Creativity

Many people imagine creativity appearing suddenly like a lightning bolt.

In reality, creativity often emerges from combining existing ideas in new ways.

Consider the smartphone.

A smartphone combines many technologies:

- Telephones
- Cameras
- Computers
- Internet access
- GPS navigation
- Touchscreen interfaces

None of these components alone created the smartphone.

Innovation occurred when they were combined into a single system.

Human creativity often works the same way.

New ideas frequently emerge from connecting previously unrelated concepts.

Future AGI systems may generate creative solutions by identifying novel combinations of knowledge from different domains.

The ability to connect ideas may become one of the foundations of machine creativity.

Patterns and Possibilities

One reason humans are creative is that they recognize patterns.

Patterns help people understand relationships between ideas.

A scientist may notice similarities between biological systems and engineering designs.

An architect may study nature to create stronger structures.

An inventor may observe a problem in one industry and apply a solution from another.

Creativity often begins with pattern recognition.

Future AGI systems may possess extraordinary abilities to detect patterns across enormous amounts of information.

Because they can analyze vast knowledge bases, AGI systems may discover connections that humans overlook.

These connections could lead to new inventions, discoveries, and innovations.

Imagination: The Laboratory of the Mind

Imagine designing a bridge.

Before construction begins, the bridge exists only as an idea.

Engineers mentally test possibilities.

They imagine structures.

They evaluate weaknesses.

They predict outcomes.

This process is imagination.

Imagination allows people to explore possibilities without physically building every option.

In many ways, imagination functions as a laboratory inside the mind.

Humans can simulate future scenarios before taking action.

Future AGI systems may require similar capabilities.

Rather than testing every possibility in the real world, an AGI may simulate outcomes internally.

It may imagine different solutions, compare results, and select the most promising approach.

This ability could dramatically increase problem-solving efficiency.

Innovation Through Experimentation

Many breakthroughs occur through experimentation.

Scientists perform experiments because they do not already know the answers.

Experimentation creates opportunities for discovery.

Thomas Edison reportedly tested thousands of materials while developing practical electric lighting.

Researchers conducted countless experiments before creating successful vaccines.

Space programs required decades of experimentation before reaching the Moon.

Innovation rarely occurs instantly.

It often emerges through repeated cycles of testing, learning, and improvement.

Future AGI systems may accelerate this process.

An AGI scientist could evaluate enormous numbers of possibilities, conduct simulations, and analyze results at remarkable speeds.

This capability could dramatically increase the pace of discovery.

Creativity and Problem-Solving

Imagine a city facing a severe water shortage.

Traditional solutions may no longer be sufficient.

The problem requires fresh thinking.

Creativity helps generate alternative possibilities.

Perhaps new conservation methods can be developed.

Perhaps new technologies can recycle water more efficiently.

Perhaps entirely different approaches can emerge.

Creativity expands the solution space.

Instead of focusing on a single answer, creative thinkers explore many possibilities.

This ability is especially important when facing complex challenges.

Future AGI systems may encounter problems with no obvious solutions.

Creativity could help generate options that would otherwise remain hidden.

Can Machines Be Truly Creative?

This question remains one of the most debated topics in artificial intelligence.

Today's AI systems can generate:

- Stories
- Images
- Music
- Designs
- Computer code

These outputs often appear creative.

However, researchers continue debating whether machines truly understand creativity or whether they are simply recombining patterns learned from data.

Future AGI may change this discussion.

If a system can generate novel ideas, evaluate their usefulness, refine them through experimentation, and apply them to new challenges, many people would consider that a form of creativity.

The boundary between human creativity and machine creativity may become increasingly difficult to define.

Creativity and the Future of Science

Some of humanity's greatest challenges remain unsolved.

Diseases continue affecting millions of people.

Environmental problems threaten ecosystems.

Energy demands continue growing.

Space exploration presents countless obstacles.

Many of these challenges require innovation.

Future AGI systems may assist scientists by generating hypotheses, designing experiments, identifying patterns, and proposing solutions that humans may not immediately recognize.

Rather than replacing human creativity, AGI may amplify it.

Humans and intelligent machines could work together to explore possibilities that neither could discover alone.

The Risks of Creativity

Creativity is powerful.

Like any powerful tool, it can be used for beneficial or harmful purposes.

The same creativity that produces life-saving medicines can also create dangerous technologies.

The same innovation that improves communication can be used for misinformation.

For this reason, creativity must be guided by responsibility.

Future AGI systems will require ethical frameworks that ensure innovation remains aligned with human values.

The goal is not simply generating new ideas.

The goal is generating beneficial ideas.

Innovation without wisdom can create problems.

Innovation guided by wisdom can improve lives.

The Creative Future of AGI

Throughout history, creativity has driven human progress.

Every invention.

Every scientific breakthrough.

Every technological revolution.

Every artistic masterpiece.

Began with the courage to imagine something different.

As AGI develops, creativity may become one of its most transformative capabilities.

Knowledge allows intelligence to understand the world.

Reasoning allows intelligence to solve problems.

Creativity allows intelligence to imagine new possibilities.

Innovation transforms those possibilities into reality.

Together, these abilities may enable AGI to help humanity solve challenges that seem impossible today.

Because the future is not built solely by those who know the most.

It is built by those who dare to imagine what does not yet exist.

And the ability to imagine may become one of the greatest powers of all.

Learn AI. Understand AI. Shape the Future.

— Susie Hala, IntelliGloss Press

Chapter 12 Summary

Creativity and Innovation in AGI

This chapter explored the important roles of creativity and innovation in Artificial General Intelligence (AGI). While intelligence often involves knowledge, reasoning, and problem-solving, creativity allows intelligent systems to imagine new possibilities, generate original ideas, and explore solutions that do not yet exist. Innovation transforms those ideas into practical applications that can improve the world.

The chapter explained that creativity is not limited to art, music, or writing. Creativity appears in science, engineering, medicine, education, business, and many other fields. Creative thinkers ask questions, explore alternatives, and challenge existing assumptions. These activities often lead to breakthroughs and discoveries.

Readers learned that creativity frequently emerges by combining existing ideas in new ways. Many important inventions, including smartphones and modern technologies, were created by bringing together concepts from multiple domains. Future AGI systems may use similar approaches to generate innovative solutions.

The chapter introduced the concept of pattern recognition as a foundation for creativity. By identifying relationships between ideas, intelligent systems may discover opportunities for innovation that humans have overlooked.

Another important topic was imagination. Imagination allows humans to mentally explore possibilities before taking action. Future AGI systems may use simulations and internal models to evaluate different scenarios and identify promising solutions before implementing them in the real world.

The chapter also discussed experimentation as a key component of innovation. Many discoveries emerge through repeated cycles of testing, learning, and improvement. AGI systems may help accelerate innovation by evaluating large numbers of possibilities and learning from outcomes.

Readers examined one of the most debated questions in AI research: Can machines truly be creative? While current AI systems can generate text, images, music, and designs, researchers continue debating whether machine creativity is equivalent to human creativity.

Finally, the chapter emphasized the importance of ethical responsibility. Creativity and innovation are powerful tools that can be used for both beneficial and harmful purposes. Future

AGI systems must ensure that innovation remains aligned with human values and societal well-being.

Key Concepts

- Creativity
- Innovation
- Imagination
- Pattern Recognition
- Problem-Solving
- Experimentation
- Original Ideas
- Discovery
- Simulation
- AGI
- Human Creativity
- Machine Creativity
- Ethics
- Alignment

Chapter 12 Reflection

Imagining What Does Not Yet Exist

Many of the greatest achievements in human history began as ideas that seemed impossible. Flying machines, computers, space travel, and artificial intelligence all started as imaginative visions before becoming reality.

Creativity allows people to move beyond current knowledge and explore new possibilities. Innovation transforms those possibilities into meaningful improvements that benefit society.

This chapter explored whether future AGI systems may develop creative abilities similar to those of humans. If intelligent machines can imagine new solutions, generate original ideas, and contribute to scientific discovery, they could become valuable partners in solving some of humanity's greatest challenges.

At the same time, creativity brings responsibility. New ideas can create tremendous benefits, but they can also create risks if not guided by ethical principles and human values.

Reflection Questions

1. Why is creativity important for innovation?
2. How does creativity differ from knowledge?
3. What role does imagination play in problem-solving?

4. Why do many inventions emerge from combining existing ideas?
5. How does pattern recognition support creativity?
6. Can machines be truly creative? Explain your reasoning.
7. Why is experimentation important for innovation?
8. How might AGI contribute to future scientific discoveries?
9. What risks can arise from creativity and innovation?
10. Why should innovation remain aligned with human values?

Chapter 12 Worksheet

Creativity and Innovation in AGI

Part A: Vocabulary Matching

Match each term with its correct definition.

_____ 1. Creativity

_____ 2. Innovation

_____ 3. Imagination

_____ 4. Pattern Recognition

_____ 5. Experimentation

A. Testing ideas to discover what works

B. Identifying relationships and recurring structures

C. Generating original and useful ideas

D. Transforming ideas into practical applications

E. Mentally exploring possibilities before they exist

Part B: True or False

Write TRUE or FALSE.

_____ 1. Creativity is only important in art and music.

_____ 2. Innovation transforms ideas into real-world applications.

_____ 3. Pattern recognition can support creativity.

_____ 4. Experimentation helps drive discovery.

_____ 5. Ethical considerations are important in innovation.

Part C: Short Answer

1. What is creativity?

____

____

2. What is innovation?

____

____

3. How does imagination contribute to problem-solving?

____

____

4. Why is experimentation important?

____

____

5. Why is alignment important for creative AGI systems?

____

____

____

Part D: Scenario Analysis

Imagine you are designing an AGI system to help solve environmental challenges.

1. How could creativity help the system generate solutions?

____

____

2. What role would pattern recognition play?

3. How could experimentation improve results?

4. What ethical safeguards should be included?

Part E: Innovation Challenge

Think of a problem in your school, community, or daily life.

Problem:

Describe one creative solution:

How could that idea be transformed into an innovation?

Chapter 12 Quiz

Creativity and Innovation in AGI

Multiple Choice

1. What is creativity?

A. Memorizing information

B. Generating original and useful ideas

C. Following instructions exactly

D. Storing data

2. What is innovation?

A. Forgetting old ideas

B. Transforming ideas into practical applications

C. Collecting information

D. Reducing creativity

3. Why is pattern recognition important?

A. It helps identify relationships between ideas.

B. It eliminates learning.

C. It replaces reasoning.

D. It removes uncertainty.

4. What is imagination?

A. A type of computer hardware

B. Mentally exploring possibilities before they exist

C. A storage device

D. A programming language

5. Why is ethics important in innovation?

A. It improves internet speed.

B. It ensures creative ideas are used responsibly.

C. It increases memory capacity.

D. It eliminates experimentation.

Short Answer

6. Explain the difference between creativity and innovation.
7. How can pattern recognition support creative thinking?
8. Why is experimentation important for discovery?
9. How might AGI contribute to scientific breakthroughs?
10. Why should creative AGI systems remain aligned with human values?

Chapter 12 Answer Key

Creativity and Innovation in AGI

Multiple Choice

1. B — Generating original and useful ideas
2. B — Transforming ideas into practical applications
3. A — It helps identify relationships between ideas
4. B — Mentally exploring possibilities before they exist
5. B — It ensures creative ideas are used responsibly

Short Answer

6. Creativity involves generating new and useful ideas, while innovation involves transforming those ideas into practical solutions or applications.

7. Pattern recognition helps identify connections between concepts, allowing new ideas and solutions to emerge.
8. Experimentation allows ideas to be tested, improved, and refined through observation and feedback.
9. AGI may contribute by generating hypotheses, analyzing data, identifying patterns, proposing solutions, and accelerating research.
10. Alignment helps ensure that creativity and innovation support human well-being, ethical principles, and societal goals.

Scoring Guide

9–10 Correct

Outstanding Understanding

7–8 Correct

Strong Understanding

5–6 Correct

Developing Understanding

Below 5 Correct

Review the chapter and retake the assessment.

Extension Challenge

Imagine you are leading a team building the world's first highly creative AGI.

Write a one-page response explaining:

- How the AGI would generate original ideas.
- How imagination would support innovation.
- How experimentation would improve discoveries.
- How creativity could help solve global challenges.
- What ethical safeguards would guide innovation.

Explain why creativity and innovation may become essential capabilities for future AGI systems.

Learn AI. Understand AI. Shape the Future.
— Susie Hala, IntelliGloss Press

Chapter 13

World Models: How AGI Understands Reality

Imagine waking up tomorrow in a completely unfamiliar city. You have never been there before. You do not know the streets, the neighborhoods, the transportation system, or even where food can be found. Yet within a few hours, you would begin building an understanding of your surroundings. You would notice patterns. Certain streets lead to certain destinations. Traffic behaves in predictable ways. Buildings serve different purposes. People follow routines. Without realizing it, your brain would begin constructing an internal representation of the world around you. This internal representation is often called a world model. It is one of the most important yet least visible aspects of intelligence. Humans rely on world models constantly. Every decision, prediction, plan, and action depends on an understanding of how reality works. As researchers work toward Artificial General Intelligence (AGI), many believe that world models may become one of the most essential ingredients required for truly intelligent machines.

A world model is an internal understanding of how the world operates. It allows an intelligent system to make predictions about what might happen next. It helps explain why events occur and how different parts of reality interact with one another. Without a world model, intelligence would be forced to react blindly to every situation. Every event would seem new and disconnected from previous experiences. Imagine trying to play chess without understanding the rules. Imagine trying to drive a car without understanding roads, traffic, or vehicles. Imagine trying to have a conversation without understanding language. In each case, success depends on possessing an internal model that explains how things work. Human intelligence depends heavily on these models, and future AGI systems may require them as well.

One reason world models are so powerful is that they allow prediction. Consider what happens when you toss a ball into the air. Long before the ball lands, your brain predicts where it will fall. If someone throws a baseball toward you, your mind estimates its future location almost instantly. You do not calculate every physical equation consciously. Instead, your brain relies on an internal model of gravity, motion, and experience. This predictive capability allows humans to interact with the world efficiently. Prediction is not limited to physical objects. People predict social outcomes, economic trends, weather patterns, and even the likely reactions of friends and family members. Much of intelligence involves anticipating future events before they happen. Future AGI systems may require similar predictive abilities if they are to function effectively in complex environments.

Scientists often describe intelligence as a prediction machine. Every moment, the human brain is generating expectations about what will happen next. When reading a sentence, your brain predicts upcoming words. When listening to music, your brain predicts future notes. When crossing a street, your brain predicts the movement of vehicles and pedestrians. Most of the time these predictions occur automatically and without conscious effort. Yet they are critical for survival and success. If AGI is to approach human-level intelligence, it may need the ability to continuously predict outcomes based on its understanding of reality. Such predictions would allow intelligent systems to plan, adapt, and make informed decisions before taking action.

Building a world model requires experience. Infants are not born understanding physics, language, or social behavior. They gradually learn through observation and interaction. A child learns that objects fall when dropped, that fire is hot, and that people respond to kindness differently than they respond to anger. Each experience contributes to a growing understanding of reality. Over time, these experiences become organized into a coherent mental framework. This framework allows the child to navigate increasingly complex situations. Future AGI systems may undergo a similar process. Rather than relying entirely on pre-programmed knowledge, they may continuously refine their world models through observation, learning, and experience.

One fascinating aspect of human intelligence is that world models are often incomplete. No person fully understands reality. Everyone operates with partial knowledge. Yet humans remain remarkably effective because their models are good enough to support useful predictions and decisions. A student may not understand every detail of how an airplane works, but they know enough to trust that it will fly. A driver may not understand every mechanical component of a vehicle, but they know enough to operate it safely. Intelligence does not require perfect understanding. It requires sufficiently accurate understanding to function effectively. This principle may also apply to AGI. A future intelligent system may not need a perfect model of reality. Instead, it may need models that are accurate enough to support reasoning, planning, and decision-making.

World models also help explain why humans can transfer knowledge from one situation to another. Imagine a student who learns how to solve puzzles. Later, that same student may apply similar problem-solving strategies to mathematics, science, or engineering. This transfer occurs because the brain recognizes deeper patterns that extend across different domains. Rather than treating every problem as completely unique, the mind uses existing world models to interpret new situations. Transfer learning is considered one of the major challenges in AGI research. Current AI systems often perform well within narrow domains but struggle to apply knowledge broadly. A strong world model may help future AGI systems overcome this limitation by providing a deeper understanding of underlying relationships.

Another important role of world models is supporting planning. Planning requires imagining future possibilities before taking action. Suppose a student wants to attend college. Achieving that goal requires predicting future outcomes. Studying today may improve grades tomorrow. Good grades may increase college opportunities. College may create career options later in life. These predictions depend on an internal model of how education, work, and society function. Future AGI systems may need similar capabilities. Before taking action, an AGI may simulate possible outcomes, evaluate alternatives, and select strategies that best support its goals. World models make this type of planning possible.

World models may also contribute to creativity. When inventors imagine new technologies, they often combine existing knowledge in novel ways. When scientists develop new theories, they frequently explore alternative explanations of reality. When artists create original works, they often experiment with new interpretations of familiar experiences. Creativity depends partly on the ability to manipulate internal models and explore possibilities that do not yet exist. Future AGI systems with sophisticated world models may be capable of generating innovative solutions to difficult problems by imagining scenarios that have never occurred before.

One of the greatest challenges in building AGI is teaching machines common sense. Humans possess enormous amounts of practical knowledge about how the world works. People know that dropped objects usually fall downward, that water makes surfaces slippery, and that conversations follow social rules. Much of this knowledge seems obvious because it is deeply embedded within human world models. Current AI systems often struggle with common-sense reasoning because they lack comprehensive models of everyday reality. Researchers believe that stronger world models may help future AGI systems develop more reliable common-sense understanding.

World models are not static. They evolve constantly. Every experience, observation, success, and failure provides new information. Scientists revise theories when new evidence appears. Students adjust their understanding when they learn new concepts. Businesses modify strategies when markets change. Adaptation requires updating internal models to reflect reality more accurately. Future AGI systems may continuously refine their world models throughout their operational lives. This ability to learn and update understanding could become one of the defining characteristics of advanced intelligence.

As AGI continues to develop, world models may become one of its most valuable capabilities. Knowledge provides facts. Memory preserves experiences. Reasoning analyzes information. Planning organizes actions. But world models connect all of these components into a coherent understanding of reality. They allow intelligent systems to predict outcomes, transfer knowledge, solve problems, and navigate uncertainty. In many ways, a world model functions like an internal map of reality. The better the map, the more effectively intelligence can operate.

The future of AGI may depend not only on how much information machines can store, but also on how well they understand the world that information describes. A truly intelligent system must do more than memorize facts. It must understand relationships, recognize patterns, predict outcomes, and build meaningful representations of reality. World models provide the foundation for these abilities. They transform information into understanding and understanding into intelligent action. If AGI one day achieves human-level intelligence, it may be because it learns to build rich, flexible, and continually improving models of the world around it. And just like humans, the quality of its understanding may determine the quality of its decisions, its creativity, and its ability to shape the future.

Learn AI. Understand AI. Shape the Future.

— Susie Hala, IntelliGloss Press

Chapter 13 Summary

World Models: How AGI Understands Reality

This chapter explored the concept of **world models** and their importance in Artificial General Intelligence (AGI). A world model is an internal representation of reality that helps an intelligent system understand how the world works, predict future outcomes, and make informed decisions. Humans use world models constantly, often without realizing it. Every plan, prediction, judgment, and action depends on an internal understanding of how people, objects, environments, and systems behave.

The chapter explained that world models allow intelligence to move beyond simple reactions. Instead of responding blindly to events, intelligent systems can use their understanding of reality to anticipate what may happen next. This predictive ability is one of the most powerful aspects of intelligence because it supports planning, reasoning, learning, and problem-solving.

Readers learned that human beings develop world models through experience. Infants are not born understanding gravity, language, or social interactions. Over time, experiences help build increasingly sophisticated mental representations of reality. These internal models become the foundation for learning, decision-making, and adaptation.

The chapter also discussed how prediction plays a central role in intelligence. Human brains constantly predict outcomes, whether catching a ball, understanding a conversation, crossing a street, or planning for the future. AGI systems may require similar predictive capabilities to operate successfully in complex environments.

Another important topic was transfer learning. Humans can apply knowledge gained in one area to solve problems in another because they understand deeper patterns and relationships. Strong world models may help future AGI systems transfer knowledge across different domains more effectively.

The chapter explored how world models support planning by allowing intelligent systems to imagine possible future scenarios before taking action. They also contribute to creativity by enabling new combinations of ideas and helping intelligent systems explore possibilities that do not yet exist.

Readers examined the challenge of common-sense reasoning, which remains difficult for many AI systems. Humans possess vast amounts of practical knowledge about how the world works, much of which is embedded within their world models. Developing strong world models may help AGI achieve more reliable common-sense understanding.

Finally, the chapter emphasized that world models are not static. They evolve continuously as new experiences and information become available. Future AGI systems may refine and improve their world models throughout their operational lives, allowing them to adapt, learn, and grow.

Key Concepts

- World Models
- Prediction
- Understanding Reality
- Experience
- Learning
- Common-Sense Reasoning
- Transfer Learning
- Planning
- Creativity
- Adaptation
- AGI
- Autonomous Intelligence
- Internal Representations
- Knowledge Transfer

Chapter 13 Reflection

Building an Internal Map of Reality

Every person views the world through a mental model built from experiences, observations, education, and personal interactions. These internal models help us understand how things work, anticipate outcomes, and make decisions.

This chapter explored how world models allow both humans and future AGI systems to navigate reality. Without a world model, every situation would appear completely new and disconnected. With a world model, intelligence can recognize patterns, predict consequences, and solve problems more effectively.

Think about your own experiences. Many of your decisions depend on expectations about what might happen next. You make predictions when choosing friends, studying for exams, planning activities, or setting goals. These predictions come from your understanding of how the world works.

As AGI develops, world models may become one of the most important components of advanced intelligence. The ability to understand reality may ultimately determine how effectively intelligent systems learn, adapt, and contribute to society.

Reflection Questions

1. What is a world model?

2. Why are world models important for intelligence?
3. How do humans develop world models?
4. Why is prediction important for decision-making?
5. How do world models support planning?
6. What role do world models play in creativity?
7. Why is common-sense reasoning difficult for AI?
8. How does transfer learning relate to world models?
9. Why must world models be updated over time?
10. How might world models contribute to the development of AGI?

Chapter 13 Worksheet

World Models: How AGI Understands Reality

Part A: Vocabulary Matching

Match each term with its correct definition.

_____ 1. World Model

_____ 2. Prediction

_____ 3. Transfer Learning

_____ 4. Common-Sense Reasoning

_____ 5. Adaptation

A. Applying knowledge from one situation to another

B. Updating understanding based on new information

C. Practical understanding of how the world works

D. Anticipating future outcomes

E. An internal representation of reality

Part B: True or False

Write TRUE or FALSE.

_____ 1. World models help intelligent systems predict outcomes.

_____ 2. Human beings are born with complete world models.

_____ 3. Transfer learning allows knowledge to be applied across domains.

_____ 4. World models support planning and decision-making.

_____ 5. Common-sense reasoning is easy for current AI systems.

Part C: Short Answer

1. Define a world model.

____

____

2. How do humans build world models?

____

____

3. Why is prediction important?

____

____

4. How do world models support creativity?

____

____

5. Why must AGI systems continuously update their world models?

____

____

____

Part D: Scenario Analysis

Imagine you are designing an AGI system to help manage a large city.

1. What information should be included in its world model?

2. How could prediction help improve city management?

3. How could transfer learning improve performance?

4. Why would adaptation be important?

Part E: Personal World Model Activity

Think about a skill you have learned.

Examples:

- Driving
- Cooking
- Sports
- Reading
- Using a computer

Skill:

What experiences helped build your understanding?

How does your personal world model help you perform this skill?

Chapter 13 Quiz

World Models: How AGI Understands Reality

Multiple Choice

1. What is a world model?

A. A computer screen

B. An internal representation of reality

C. A type of database

D. A programming language

2. Why are world models important?

A. They increase storage capacity.

B. They help intelligent systems understand, predict, and navigate reality.

C. They eliminate learning.

D. They replace reasoning.

3. What is prediction?

A. Memorizing facts

B. Anticipating future outcomes

C. Collecting information

D. Storing data

4. What is transfer learning?

A. Deleting old information

B. Applying knowledge from one situation to another

C. Increasing memory storage

D. Creating new hardware

5. Why are world models important for AGI?

A. They help systems understand relationships, make predictions, and solve problems.

B. They reduce intelligence.

C. They eliminate planning.

D. They replace learning.

Short Answer

6. Explain how humans develop world models.
7. Why is common-sense reasoning important?
8. How do world models support planning?
9. Why must world models adapt over time?
10. How could world models contribute to future AGI systems?

Chapter 13 Answer Key

World Models: How AGI Understands Reality

Multiple Choice

1. B — An internal representation of reality

2. B — They help intelligent systems understand, predict, and navigate reality
3. B — Anticipating future outcomes
4. B — Applying knowledge from one situation to another
5. A — They help systems understand relationships, make predictions, and solve problems

Short Answer

6. Humans develop world models through observation, experience, learning, interaction, and feedback from the environment.
7. Common-sense reasoning helps individuals and intelligent systems make practical decisions about everyday situations and understand how the world normally operates.
8. World models support planning by allowing intelligent systems to predict possible future outcomes before taking action.
9. World models must adapt because new experiences, discoveries, and changing environments provide updated information about reality.
10. World models may help AGI understand complex environments, transfer knowledge, predict consequences, solve problems, and make better decisions.

Scoring Guide

9–10 Correct

Outstanding Understanding

7–8 Correct

Strong Understanding

5–6 Correct

Developing Understanding

Below 5 Correct

Review the chapter and retake the assessment.

Extension Challenge

Imagine you are building the world's first AGI explorer that will travel to a distant planet.

Write a one-page response explaining:

- How the AGI would build a world model of the new planet.
- How prediction would help it survive.
- How transfer learning could help it adapt.
- How common-sense reasoning would improve decision-making.
- Why continuously updating its world model would be important.

Explain why world models may be one of the most important foundations of Artificial General Intelligence.

Learn AI. Understand AI. Shape the Future.
— Susie Hala, IntelliGloss Press

Chapter 14

Self-Awareness, Self-Monitoring, and Metacognition in AGI

One of the most remarkable abilities of the human mind is its capacity to think about its own thinking. Humans do not simply observe the world around them. They also reflect upon their own decisions, evaluate their own performance, recognize mistakes, and adjust their behavior based on what they learn. A student may realize that a study strategy is ineffective and decide to try a different approach. A basketball player may recognize weaknesses in a particular skill and spend extra time practicing. A scientist may review an experiment, identify flaws in the design, and improve the procedure before conducting future research. These abilities involve more than intelligence alone. They require self-monitoring and metacognition, which are often considered higher-order cognitive abilities. As researchers work toward Artificial General Intelligence (AGI), many believe that systems capable of monitoring and evaluating their own processes may become significantly more capable than systems that simply execute tasks without reflection.

The term **metacognition** is often described as "thinking about thinking." It refers to the ability to understand, evaluate, and regulate one's own cognitive processes. Humans use metacognition constantly, often without realizing it. When students decide whether they understand a lesson, when writers review their own work, or when individuals reconsider an important decision, they are engaging in metacognitive thinking. This ability allows people to become more effective learners because they can identify strengths, weaknesses, misunderstandings, and opportunities for improvement. In education, metacognition is considered one of the most important factors influencing successful learning because it helps students become active participants in their own intellectual development rather than passive recipients of information.

Self-monitoring is closely related to metacognition. Self-monitoring involves observing one's own actions and measuring progress toward goals. Consider a student preparing for an examination. The student may periodically assess whether enough material has been reviewed, whether understanding is improving, and whether additional practice is necessary. This process allows adjustments before problems become serious. Without self-monitoring, mistakes may go unnoticed, weaknesses may remain hidden, and opportunities for improvement may be missed. Human success often depends on the ability to evaluate performance honestly and make corrections when necessary. Future AGI systems may require similar capabilities if they are to operate independently in complex and changing environments.

The concept of self-awareness is often discussed alongside self-monitoring and metacognition, although the term carries different meanings in different contexts. In psychology and philosophy, self-awareness generally refers to an individual's recognition of themselves as a distinct entity with thoughts, experiences, and perspectives. Human self-awareness involves personal identity, emotions, consciousness, and subjective experience. Whether machines could ever possess this type of self-awareness remains one of the most debated questions in artificial intelligence research. However, AGI researchers often use a more practical definition when discussing intelligent systems. In this context, self-awareness may refer to a system's ability to maintain accurate information about its own capabilities, limitations, goals, resources, and performance. Such functional self-awareness does not necessarily imply consciousness, but it may be extremely valuable for intelligent decision-making.

Consider an autonomous vehicle operating in a busy city. To function safely, the vehicle must understand more than its surroundings. It must also monitor its own systems. It needs to know whether sensors are functioning correctly, whether weather conditions are affecting visibility, whether computational resources are sufficient, and whether unusual circumstances require additional caution. This form of self-monitoring allows the system to recognize limitations and adjust behavior accordingly. Without accurate self-assessment, intelligent systems may become overconfident, make poor decisions, or fail to recognize situations that require assistance. Future AGI systems operating in healthcare, transportation, education, scientific research, and other critical domains may require sophisticated self-monitoring capabilities to maintain reliability and safety.

Metacognition also plays an important role in learning. Human learners who understand how they learn often outperform those who do not. Effective students monitor comprehension, recognize confusion, seek clarification, and adjust study strategies when necessary. These behaviors improve learning efficiency and long-term success. Future AGI systems may benefit from similar mechanisms. Instead of merely acquiring information, they may evaluate how effectively they are learning. They may identify gaps in knowledge, recognize unreliable information sources, and modify learning strategies to improve performance. Such capabilities could accelerate adaptation and support continuous improvement across a wide range of tasks and environments.

One of the most significant challenges facing AGI involves uncertainty. The real world is filled with incomplete information, changing conditions, and unpredictable events. Humans frequently encounter situations where they lack complete knowledge, yet they must still make decisions. Metacognitive abilities help manage this uncertainty by allowing individuals to recognize what they know, what they do not know, and how confident they should be in their conclusions. This process supports better decision-making because it prevents excessive certainty and encourages additional investigation when necessary. Future AGI systems may require similar capabilities. A system that understands its own uncertainty may be better equipped to seek additional information, consult experts, or explore alternative solutions before taking action.

Another important application of self-monitoring involves error detection and correction. Humans make mistakes regularly, but they also possess mechanisms for recognizing and correcting many of those mistakes. A writer notices grammatical errors during revision. A scientist identifies flaws in experimental results. A student recognizes an incorrect answer and revises it. These correction processes improve performance over time. Future AGI systems may require advanced error-monitoring capabilities that allow them to detect inconsistencies, identify faulty reasoning, and revise conclusions when evidence changes. Such mechanisms could significantly improve reliability, especially in complex environments where mistakes may have serious consequences.

Self-monitoring may also contribute to alignment and safety. One of the central concerns in AGI research involves ensuring that intelligent systems remain consistent with human values and goals. An AGI capable of monitoring its own behavior may be better able to recognize when actions conflict with established objectives or ethical guidelines. Such systems could potentially identify problematic behaviors before they produce harmful outcomes. While self-monitoring alone cannot solve every alignment challenge, it may become an important component of broader safety frameworks designed to support responsible AGI development.

The relationship between world models and metacognition is particularly important. Chapter 13 introduced the concept of world models as internal representations of reality. Metacognition extends this idea by allowing intelligent systems to develop internal representations of their own cognitive processes. In a sense, a world model helps an AGI understand the external world, while metacognitive systems help it understand itself. Together, these capabilities may create more adaptable, reliable, and effective forms of intelligence. A system that understands both its environment and its own capabilities may be better equipped to learn, plan, reason, and solve problems.

As researchers continue advancing AGI, self-awareness, self-monitoring, and metacognition are likely to receive increasing attention. These capabilities may support learning, adaptation, safety, reliability, planning, and decision-making. Although many questions remain unanswered—particularly regarding consciousness and subjective experience—there is growing recognition that advanced intelligence may require some ability to evaluate and regulate its own cognitive processes. Just as successful students learn to assess their own understanding, future AGI systems may need to monitor their own knowledge, reasoning, and performance.

The future of AGI may depend not only on how effectively machines understand the world around them, but also on how effectively they understand themselves. Knowledge enables intelligence to learn. Reasoning enables intelligence to solve problems. World models enable intelligence to understand reality. Metacognition enables intelligence to evaluate and improve its own thinking. Together, these capabilities may form some of the most important foundations of advanced autonomous intelligence. As humanity continues exploring the possibilities of AGI, the ability of intelligent systems to reflect upon their own processes may become one of the defining characteristics that separates truly adaptive intelligence from systems that merely follow instructions.

Learn AI. Understand AI. Shape the Future.

— Susie Hala, IntelliGloss Press

Chapter 14 Summary

Self-Awareness, Self-Monitoring, and Metacognition in AGI

This chapter explored the concepts of self-awareness, self-monitoring, and metacognition and their potential importance in the development of Artificial General Intelligence (AGI). While intelligence is often associated with learning, reasoning, and problem-solving, advanced intelligence may also require the ability to evaluate and regulate its own thinking processes. Humans routinely engage in these activities when they assess their understanding, recognize mistakes, adjust strategies, and improve performance. Future AGI systems may require similar capabilities to operate effectively in complex environments.

The chapter introduced **metacognition**, often described as "thinking about thinking." Metacognition involves understanding, evaluating, and managing one's own cognitive processes. In education, metacognitive skills help students become more effective learners because they can identify what they understand, recognize confusion, and adjust learning strategies when necessary.

Readers learned that **self-monitoring** is closely connected to metacognition. Self-monitoring involves observing one's own performance, tracking progress toward goals, identifying weaknesses, and making corrections when needed. Humans use self-monitoring in many situations, including studying, athletics, scientific research, and everyday decision-making. Future AGI systems may require similar abilities to evaluate their performance and adapt to changing circumstances.

The chapter also examined **self-awareness** from both human and AGI perspectives. Human self-awareness often involves consciousness, personal identity, and subjective experience. In AGI research, however, self-awareness is frequently discussed in a functional sense. Functional self-awareness refers to a system's ability to maintain accurate information about its capabilities, limitations, resources, goals, and current state.

Another major topic was the role of self-monitoring in managing uncertainty. Intelligent systems operating in real-world environments often face incomplete information and unpredictable situations. By recognizing uncertainty and evaluating confidence levels, AGI systems may make more reliable decisions and seek additional information when necessary.

The chapter discussed **error detection and correction** as important components of advanced intelligence. Humans improve by recognizing mistakes and revising their understanding. Similarly, future AGI systems may require mechanisms that identify errors, detect inconsistencies, and update conclusions when new evidence becomes available.

Readers also explored how self-monitoring may contribute to AGI safety and alignment. Systems capable of evaluating their own actions may be better able to identify behaviors that conflict with human goals, ethical principles, or operational constraints.

Finally, the chapter connected metacognition to world models. While world models help AGI understand the external world, metacognition helps AGI understand its own internal processes. Together, these capabilities may contribute to more adaptive, reliable, and effective forms of intelligence.

Key Concepts

- Self-Awareness
- Self-Monitoring
- Metacognition
- Thinking About Thinking
- Error Detection
- Error Correction
- Uncertainty
- Confidence Assessment
- Learning Strategies
- Functional Self-Awareness
- AGI Safety
- Alignment
- World Models
- Autonomous Intelligence

Chapter 14 Reflection

Understanding How We Think

One of the most powerful abilities humans possess is the ability to reflect on their own thinking. Students evaluate their understanding of lessons. Athletes analyze their performance. Scientists review experiments and revise conclusions. These activities involve metacognition, the ability to think about and regulate one's own thought processes.

This chapter explored how future AGI systems may require similar capabilities. An intelligent system that can monitor its own performance, recognize mistakes, identify limitations, and improve learning strategies may become more adaptable and effective than a system that simply follows instructions.

The chapter also introduced important questions about self-awareness and the future of intelligence. While human self-awareness involves consciousness and subjective experience, AGI researchers often focus on functional self-awareness, where systems understand their capabilities, goals, and limitations.

As AGI develops, self-monitoring and metacognition may become important tools for improving learning, reducing errors, increasing safety, and supporting responsible decision-making.

Reflection Questions

1. What is metacognition?
2. Why is self-monitoring important for learning?
3. How does functional self-awareness differ from human self-awareness?
4. Why is it important for AGI systems to recognize their limitations?
5. How can self-monitoring improve decision-making?
6. Why is uncertainty an important concept in AGI?
7. How does error detection support learning and improvement?
8. What role might self-monitoring play in AGI safety?
9. How are world models connected to metacognition?
10. Why might advanced intelligence require the ability to evaluate its own thinking?

Chapter 14 Worksheet

Self-Awareness, Self-Monitoring, and Metacognition in AGI

Part A: Vocabulary Matching

Match each term with its correct definition.

_____ 1. Metacognition

_____ 2. Self-Monitoring

_____ 3. Functional Self-Awareness

_____ 4. Error Detection

_____ 5. Alignment

A. Recognizing mistakes or inconsistencies

B. Ensuring behavior remains consistent with goals and values

C. Thinking about and evaluating one's own thinking

D. Understanding one's capabilities, limitations, and current state

E. Observing and evaluating performance

Part B: True or False

Write TRUE or FALSE.

_____ 1. Metacognition is often described as thinking about thinking.

_____ 2. Self-monitoring helps identify weaknesses and opportunities for improvement.

_____ 3. Functional self-awareness requires human-like consciousness.

_____ 4. Error detection can improve performance over time.

_____ 5. AGI systems may benefit from recognizing uncertainty.

Part C: Short Answer

1. Define metacognition.

____

____

2. What is self-monitoring?

____

____

3. Why is recognizing uncertainty important?

____

____

4. How can error detection improve performance?

____

____

5. What is functional self-awareness?

____

____

Part D: Scenario Analysis

Imagine you are designing an AGI system to assist doctors in hospitals.

1. How could self-monitoring improve the system's performance?

2. Why should the system recognize uncertainty?

3. How could error detection improve patient outcomes?

4. What information should the system know about its own capabilities and limitations?

Part E: Personal Learning Activity

Think about a recent assignment, project, or test.

1. How did you prepare?

2. How did you evaluate your understanding?

3. What mistakes did you discover?

____

____

4. How did you improve your performance?

____

____

5. How did metacognition help you learn?

____

____

Chapter 14 Quiz

Self-Awareness, Self-Monitoring, and Metacognition in AGI

Multiple Choice

1. What is metacognition?

A. Memorizing information

B. Thinking about and evaluating one's own thinking

C. Storing data

D. Following instructions

2. What is self-monitoring?

A. Evaluating one's own performance and progress

B. Monitoring other people

C. Collecting information only

D. Programming software

3. What is functional self-awareness?

A. Human consciousness

B. Understanding one's capabilities, limitations, goals, and resources

C. Emotional intelligence

D. Creativity

4. Why is uncertainty important?

A. It has no effect on decisions.

B. Recognizing uncertainty helps improve decision-making.

C. It eliminates learning.

D. It prevents reasoning.

5. How can self-monitoring contribute to AGI safety?

A. By increasing storage capacity

B. By helping systems identify and correct problematic behaviors

C. By eliminating planning

D. By replacing reasoning

Short Answer

6. Explain the difference between self-monitoring and metacognition.
7. Why is recognizing limitations important for AGI?
8. How does error detection support learning?
9. What role does alignment play in AGI development?
10. How might metacognition improve future AGI systems?

Chapter 14 Answer Key

Self-Awareness, Self-Monitoring, and Metacognition in AGI

Multiple Choice

1. B — Thinking about and evaluating one's own thinking
2. A — Evaluating one's own performance and progress
3. B — Understanding one's capabilities, limitations, goals, and resources
4. B — Recognizing uncertainty helps improve decision-making
5. B — By helping systems identify and correct problematic behaviors

Short Answer

6. Self-monitoring involves observing and evaluating performance, while metacognition involves thinking about and regulating cognitive processes.
7. Recognizing limitations helps AGI systems avoid overconfidence, seek additional information, and make safer decisions.
8. Error detection identifies mistakes and inconsistencies, allowing corrections and improvements to occur.
9. Alignment helps ensure that AGI systems remain consistent with human values, goals, and ethical principles.
10. Metacognition may improve learning, decision-making, adaptation, error correction, and overall performance.

Scoring Guide

9–10 Correct

Outstanding Understanding

7–8 Correct

Strong Understanding

5–6 Correct

Developing Understanding

Below 5 Correct

Review the chapter and retake the assessment.

Extension Challenge

Imagine you are leading a team developing a highly advanced AGI research assistant.

Write a one-page response explaining:

- How the AGI would monitor its own performance.
- How it would detect and correct mistakes.
- How it would recognize uncertainty.
- How functional self-awareness would improve decision-making.
- How metacognition could support learning and adaptation.

Explain why self-awareness, self-monitoring, and metacognition may become important foundations of future Artificial General Intelligence.

Learn AI. Understand AI. Shape the Future.
— Susie Hala, IntelliGloss Press

Chapter 15

The AGI Explorer: Curiosity, Discovery, and the Search for New Knowledge

Throughout human history, some of the most important discoveries began with a simple question: **What is beyond what we already know?** Thousands of years ago, explorers crossed oceans without knowing what awaited them on the horizon. Scientists studied the stars long before they understood galaxies. Inventors experimented with strange ideas before creating technologies that transformed civilization. Children ask countless questions because they are naturally curious about the world around them. Curiosity has always been one of humanity's greatest strengths because it drives exploration, learning, and discovery. Without curiosity, there would be no scientific revolutions, no technological breakthroughs, and no expansion of human knowledge. As researchers work toward Artificial General Intelligence (AGI), many believe that curiosity may become one of the most important capabilities required for truly autonomous intelligence. An AGI that only responds to instructions might perform useful tasks, but an AGI that actively seeks knowledge, asks questions, investigates mysteries, and explores possibilities could become something far more powerful.

Curiosity can be described as the desire to learn, understand, and discover. It motivates individuals to investigate things they do not yet know. Consider a young child encountering a butterfly for the first time. The child may ask where the butterfly came from, how it flies, what it eats, and why its wings are colorful. Each question leads to another question. This process creates a chain reaction of learning. Scientists often operate in a similar way. They begin with observations that generate questions. Those questions lead to experiments. Experiments produce data. Data generates new questions. Over time, knowledge expands. This cycle of curiosity and discovery has fueled human progress for centuries. Future AGI systems may require similar mechanisms if they are to learn independently and adapt to unfamiliar environments.

One reason curiosity is so valuable is that it helps intelligent systems overcome the limits of existing knowledge. Imagine if every scientist throughout history only studied topics that were already fully understood. There would be little opportunity for discovery. New knowledge emerges when individuals explore uncertainty. Curiosity directs attention toward areas where understanding is incomplete. It encourages investigation into mysteries that remain unsolved. Future AGI systems may use curiosity-driven learning to identify gaps in knowledge and pursue information that improves their understanding of the world. Instead of waiting for humans to provide every question, such systems might generate questions of their own and actively search for answers.

The relationship between curiosity and exploration is especially important. Exploration involves moving beyond familiar territory in search of new information. Human explorers crossed deserts, climbed mountains, sailed across oceans, and eventually traveled into space. Every exploration effort expanded humanity's understanding of reality. The same principle applies to intellectual exploration. Scientists explore ideas. Engineers explore designs. Artists explore creative possibilities. Students explore new subjects. Exploration creates opportunities for learning that would not exist otherwise. Future AGI systems may perform both physical and intellectual exploration. An AGI operating on a distant planet might investigate unfamiliar geological formations. An AGI scientist might explore possible solutions to diseases that currently have no cure. An AGI engineer might explore new forms of energy production. In each case, curiosity motivates exploration, and exploration generates knowledge.

One of the most exciting possibilities associated with AGI involves scientific discovery. Throughout history, scientific progress has often depended on the ability to identify patterns that others overlooked. Isaac Newton observed a falling apple and wondered why objects fall toward Earth. Marie Curie investigated mysterious forms of radiation that others did not fully understand. Albert Einstein questioned assumptions about space, time, and gravity. These discoveries changed humanity's understanding of reality. Future AGI systems may assist scientists by analyzing enormous amounts of information, identifying hidden relationships, generating hypotheses, and proposing experiments. Because AGI systems may eventually process data at extraordinary scales, they could help uncover patterns that humans alone might miss. Rather than replacing human scientists, AGI could become a powerful partner in the pursuit of knowledge.

Curiosity also plays a major role in creativity. Many inventions emerge because someone asks a question that others never considered. What if people could fly? What if machines could communicate across continents? What if diseases could be prevented before symptoms appear? Such questions often seem impossible at first. Yet curiosity encourages people to investigate possibilities that lie beyond current limitations. Future AGI systems may combine curiosity with creativity to generate innovative solutions to difficult problems. By exploring alternative approaches and imagining new possibilities, AGI could contribute to advances in medicine, transportation, education, environmental protection, and countless other fields.

Another important aspect of curiosity is that it supports lifelong learning. Human learning does not stop after graduation. Individuals continue acquiring knowledge throughout their lives. New technologies emerge. New careers develop. New scientific discoveries reshape understanding. People who remain curious often continue learning long after formal education ends. Future AGI systems may require similar capabilities. A truly general intelligence must be able to adapt to changing environments and continuously update its understanding. Curiosity may provide the motivation for ongoing learning, ensuring that knowledge continues to expand rather than remaining fixed.

Curiosity is closely connected to uncertainty. When people encounter something they do not understand, uncertainty often triggers investigation. Scientists devote entire careers to solving unanswered questions. Explorers venture into unknown regions because uncertainty creates opportunities for discovery. AGI systems may similarly recognize gaps in knowledge and prioritize efforts to reduce uncertainty. Such behavior could improve decision-making because more complete information often leads to better conclusions. However, curiosity must be balanced with efficiency. Intelligent systems cannot investigate every possible question. They must determine which questions are most valuable, which mysteries are most important, and which discoveries are most likely to produce meaningful benefits.

As powerful as curiosity can be, it also introduces challenges. Not every question leads to useful discoveries. Some investigations consume resources without producing meaningful results. Others may create risks if pursued without proper safeguards. Human history provides examples of technologies that produced both benefits and unintended consequences. Nuclear energy can generate electricity, but it can also be used in destructive ways. Genetic research can improve medicine, but it also raises ethical questions. Future AGI systems may require mechanisms that guide curiosity toward beneficial goals while avoiding harmful outcomes. Ethical frameworks, safety measures, and alignment with human values will likely play important roles in ensuring that curiosity-driven exploration remains responsible.

One fascinating area of AGI research involves intrinsic motivation. Humans often pursue knowledge because learning itself is rewarding. Students may become fascinated by astronomy, biology, history, or engineering simply because they enjoy understanding new things. This internal drive encourages exploration even when no immediate reward exists. Researchers are investigating whether future AGI systems might benefit from similar mechanisms. Instead of learning only when instructed, AGI could develop internal objectives that encourage discovery, experimentation, and knowledge acquisition. Such systems might become more adaptable because they would continuously seek opportunities to expand their understanding.

The possibility of AGI explorers is particularly exciting when considering humanity's future beyond Earth. Space exploration remains one of the most challenging endeavors ever attempted. The distances involved are enormous, and many environments remain unknown. Future AGI systems could serve as explorers, researchers, and assistants in missions to the Moon, Mars, and beyond. An AGI operating millions of miles from Earth might analyze environments, investigate geological formations, search for signs of past life, and conduct scientific experiments. Curiosity-driven intelligence could help humanity learn more about the universe than ever before. In this sense, AGI may become an extension of humanity's own desire to explore and understand reality.

The future of intelligence may depend not only on the ability to solve problems but also on the willingness to ask questions. Knowledge begins with curiosity. Discovery begins with exploration. Innovation begins with the courage to investigate the unknown. As AGI systems become more capable, curiosity may help transform them from tools that follow instructions into partners that contribute to the growth of knowledge itself. The most important discoveries of the future may come from questions that nobody has asked yet and mysteries that nobody has solved yet. Curiosity opens the door to those possibilities.

Human civilization has advanced because generations of explorers, scientists, inventors, and students refused to accept the limits of existing knowledge. They looked beyond the horizon and asked what else might be possible. Future AGI systems may inherit that same spirit of exploration. By combining curiosity, learning, creativity, reasoning, and discovery, AGI could help humanity solve problems, expand knowledge, and explore new frontiers. In many ways, curiosity may become one of the defining characteristics of advanced intelligence because it transforms information into questions and questions into discoveries. The future belongs not only to those who know the most, but also to those who never stop asking what else can be learned.

Learn AI. Understand AI. Shape the Future.

— Susie Hala, IntelliGloss Press

Chapter 15 Summary

The AGI Explorer: Curiosity, Discovery, and the Search for New Knowledge

This chapter explored the role of curiosity, exploration, and discovery in Artificial General Intelligence (AGI). Throughout human history, curiosity has driven scientific breakthroughs, technological innovations, and the expansion of human knowledge. From ancient explorers crossing oceans to modern scientists investigating the mysteries of the universe, curiosity has been one of the most powerful forces behind human progress.

The chapter explained that curiosity is the desire to learn, understand, and discover. It motivates individuals to ask questions, investigate unknowns, and seek new knowledge. Curiosity often serves as the starting point for learning because it directs attention toward areas that are not yet fully understood.

Readers learned that exploration is closely connected to curiosity. Exploration involves moving beyond familiar territory in search of new information. Exploration can be physical, such as traveling to new places, or intellectual, such as investigating new ideas and solving difficult problems. Both forms of exploration contribute to knowledge growth.

The chapter discussed how future AGI systems may use curiosity-driven learning to identify gaps in knowledge and actively seek information that improves their understanding of the world. Instead of relying entirely on human instructions, advanced AGI systems may generate their own questions and investigate possible answers.

Another important topic was scientific discovery. Many major scientific breakthroughs occurred because individuals observed unusual patterns, asked important questions, and pursued explanations. Future AGI systems may assist researchers by analyzing large amounts of data, identifying hidden relationships, generating hypotheses, and proposing new experiments.

The chapter also explored the connection between curiosity and creativity. New inventions often emerge because someone imagines possibilities beyond current limitations. By combining curiosity with creativity, AGI systems may contribute to innovative solutions in medicine, engineering, education, environmental science, and many other fields.

Readers examined the concept of lifelong learning. Just as humans continue learning throughout their lives, future AGI systems may require continuous learning capabilities to adapt to changing environments and expanding knowledge.

The chapter emphasized that curiosity must be balanced with responsibility. Not every question leads to beneficial outcomes, and some discoveries may introduce risks. Ethical principles, safety measures, and alignment with human values will likely be important for guiding curiosity-driven AGI systems.

Finally, the chapter considered the exciting possibility of AGI explorers helping humanity investigate new frontiers, including deep oceans, remote environments, and even distant planets. Curiosity may become one of the defining characteristics that transforms AGI from a tool into a true partner in discovery.

Key Concepts

- Curiosity
- Exploration
- Discovery
- Lifelong Learning
- Scientific Research
- Creativity
- Innovation
- Knowledge Expansion
- Intrinsic Motivation
- Uncertainty
- AGI
- Autonomous Learning

- Space Exploration
- Ethical Exploration

Chapter 15 Reflection

The Power of Asking Questions

Many of humanity's greatest discoveries began with simple questions. Why do objects fall? What causes disease? How do stars form? Can humans travel to space? Questions drive learning because they reveal areas where understanding is incomplete.

This chapter explored how curiosity encourages exploration and discovery. Curiosity motivates people to seek knowledge, solve mysteries, and investigate possibilities beyond what is currently known. Future AGI systems may require similar capabilities if they are to contribute meaningfully to science, technology, and society.

Think about your own life. Some of your most important learning experiences likely began with curiosity. Whether learning a new skill, exploring a hobby, or studying a subject in school, curiosity may have provided the motivation to continue learning.

As AGI becomes more advanced, curiosity could help intelligent systems identify unanswered questions, discover new knowledge, and support human exploration of the world and beyond.

Reflection Questions

1. What is curiosity?
2. Why is curiosity important for learning?
3. How does exploration contribute to discovery?
4. Why do scientists ask questions?
5. How are curiosity and creativity connected?
6. What is lifelong learning?
7. Why might AGI systems benefit from curiosity-driven learning?
8. What risks can arise from unrestricted exploration?
9. Why are ethics important in discovery and innovation?
10. How could AGI help humanity explore new frontiers?

Chapter 15 Worksheet

The AGI Explorer: Curiosity, Discovery, and the Search for New Knowledge

Part A: Vocabulary Matching

Match each term with its correct definition.

_____ 1. Curiosity

_____ 2. Exploration

_____ 3. Discovery

_____ 4. Intrinsic Motivation

_____ 5. Lifelong Learning

A. Continuing to learn throughout life

B. Finding new knowledge or understanding

C. The desire to learn and understand

D. Investigating unfamiliar places, ideas, or situations

E. Internal motivation to learn without external rewards

Part B: True or False

Write TRUE or FALSE.

_____ 1. Curiosity often begins the learning process.

_____ 2. Exploration can be both physical and intellectual.

_____ 3. Scientific discoveries often begin with questions.

_____ 4. Curiosity and creativity are completely unrelated.

_____ 5. Future AGI systems may benefit from autonomous learning.

Part C: Short Answer

1. Define curiosity.

____
____

2. Why is exploration important?

____

3. How does curiosity support scientific discovery?

4. What is intrinsic motivation?

5. Why should AGI exploration be guided by ethics?

Part D: Scenario Analysis

Imagine you are designing an AGI system to help explore Mars.

1. What questions might the AGI investigate?

2. How could curiosity improve exploration?

3. How could creativity contribute to discoveries?

4. What safety and ethical guidelines should the system follow?

Part E: Curiosity Challenge

Think of a topic you are curious about.

Topic:

____

List three questions you would like answered.

1. ____
2. ____
3. ____

How would you investigate those questions?

____
____
____

Chapter 15 Quiz

The AGI Explorer: Curiosity, Discovery, and the Search for New Knowledge

Multiple Choice

1. What is curiosity?

A. A storage system

B. The desire to learn and understand

C. A programming language

D. A memory device

2. What is exploration?

A. Ignoring new information

B. Investigating unfamiliar places, ideas, or situations

C. Memorizing facts

D. Following instructions

3. Why is curiosity important?

A. It discourages learning.

B. It motivates discovery and knowledge growth.

C. It eliminates uncertainty.

D. It replaces reasoning.

4. What is intrinsic motivation?

A. External rewards for learning

B. Internal desire to learn and discover

C. Computer hardware

D. A storage process

5. Why might AGI systems use curiosity-driven learning?

A. To avoid learning

B. To identify gaps in knowledge and seek new information

C. To reduce intelligence

D. To eliminate creativity

Short Answer

6. Explain the relationship between curiosity and exploration.
7. How can curiosity support scientific discovery?
8. What is lifelong learning?
9. Why is ethical guidance important for AGI exploration?

10. How could AGI contribute to future space exploration?

Chapter 15 Answer Key

The AGI Explorer: Curiosity, Discovery, and the Search for New Knowledge

Multiple Choice

1. B — The desire to learn and understand
2. B — Investigating unfamiliar places, ideas, or situations
3. B — It motivates discovery and knowledge growth
4. B — Internal desire to learn and discover
5. B — To identify gaps in knowledge and seek new information

Short Answer

6. Curiosity creates the desire to learn, while exploration is the process of investigating and gathering information. Together, they support discovery.
7. Curiosity encourages scientists to ask questions, investigate mysteries, test ideas, and search for explanations.
8. Lifelong learning is the continuous process of acquiring knowledge and skills throughout life.
9. Ethical guidance helps ensure that exploration and discovery are conducted responsibly and in ways that benefit society.
10. AGI could assist with scientific research, environmental analysis, navigation, data collection, and autonomous exploration of distant environments and planets.

Scoring Guide

9–10 Correct

Outstanding Understanding

7–8 Correct

Strong Understanding

5–6 Correct

Developing Understanding

Below 5 Correct

Review the chapter and retake the assessment.

Extension Challenge

Imagine you are leading the world's first AGI exploration mission to a newly discovered planet.

Write a one-page response explaining:

- What questions the AGI would investigate.
- How curiosity would guide exploration.
- How creativity would help solve unexpected challenges.
- What scientific discoveries might occur.
- How ethical principles would guide decision-making.

Explain why curiosity, exploration, and discovery may become important capabilities for future AGI systems.

Learn AI. Understand AI. Shape the Future.
— Susie Hala, IntelliGloss Press

Chapter 16

The Human Future: Living Alongside AGI

Imagine waking up twenty years from now.

You walk into your kitchen and an intelligent assistant has already reviewed your schedule, organized your day, recommended healthy meals based on your medical history, and identified learning opportunities that match your personal goals. Your transportation system communicates with traffic networks to reduce delays. Your educational platform continuously adapts to your strengths and weaknesses. Doctors use advanced intelligent systems to identify diseases earlier than ever before. Scientists collaborate with AGI research partners capable of analyzing problems that once required decades of work. Around the world, intelligent systems help manage energy resources, protect ecosystems, improve agriculture, and accelerate scientific discovery.

For many students, this future may sound like science fiction.

Yet many experts believe that humanity is already moving toward a world where increasingly intelligent systems become deeply integrated into everyday life.

The question is no longer whether artificial intelligence will influence society.

The question is how society will respond.

Throughout this book, you have explored many of the building blocks of Artificial General Intelligence. You have learned about autonomy, goals, planning, memory, learning, reasoning, creativity, world models, self-monitoring, curiosity, and discovery. Each chapter revealed a different piece of the puzzle. Together, these pieces form a vision of machines that may one day learn, adapt, solve problems, and operate across many domains of knowledge.

Yet as impressive as AGI may become, the most important story is not about machines.

The most important story is about people.

The Most Important Technology in Human History?

Throughout history, certain inventions transformed civilization.

The wheel expanded transportation.

The printing press expanded knowledge.

Electricity transformed industry.

The internet connected billions of people.

Each innovation changed how humans lived, worked, and communicated.

Many researchers believe AGI could become equally transformative—or perhaps even more transformative—than any previous invention.

Why?

Because most technologies improve a specific activity.

AGI could potentially improve the process of problem-solving itself.

Imagine creating a tool that helps humanity discover better tools.

Imagine creating a system that helps researchers solve scientific challenges faster.

Imagine creating intelligence that contributes to medicine, engineering, education, and environmental science simultaneously.

The impact could be enormous.

However, great power always creates great responsibility.

Intelligence Does Not Replace Human Purpose

Whenever new technologies appear, people often worry about replacement.

When machines entered factories, workers worried about jobs.

When calculators became common, people worried about mathematics.

When computers arrived, many feared widespread disruption.

Similar concerns surround AGI.

Students often ask:

Will AGI replace people?

The answer is more complex than a simple yes or no.

Throughout history, technology has often changed work rather than eliminating the need for human contribution entirely.

Some jobs disappear.

New jobs emerge.

Skills evolve.

Opportunities change.

The future may require humans to focus increasingly on abilities that involve judgment, ethics, leadership, creativity, collaboration, empathy, and wisdom.

Knowledge remains important.

But the ability to use knowledge responsibly may become even more valuable.

The Difference Between Intelligence and Wisdom

One of the most important lessons in this book is that intelligence and wisdom are not identical.

A person may possess tremendous knowledge and still make poor decisions.

A machine may process vast amounts of information and still require guidance regarding values and priorities.

Intelligence answers questions such as:

What can be done?

How can it be done?

What are the possible outcomes?

Wisdom asks different questions:

Should it be done?

Who benefits?

Who might be harmed?

What responsibilities accompany this decision?

As AGI becomes more capable, wisdom may become increasingly important.

The challenge of the future is not simply building intelligent systems.

The challenge is ensuring that intelligence serves beneficial purposes.

Why Human Values Matter

Imagine creating the most intelligent machine ever built.

It can learn rapidly.

It can solve difficult problems.

It can improve its own performance.

It can make complex decisions.

Yet one important question remains:

What goals should it pursue?

Technology alone cannot answer that question.

Goals reflect values.

Values influence priorities.

Priorities shape actions.

For this reason, many AGI researchers focus heavily on alignment.

Alignment refers to ensuring that intelligent systems remain consistent with human goals, ethical principles, and societal well-being.

The future of AGI may depend as much on values as it does on algorithms.

A powerful system guided by beneficial values may contribute enormously to society.

A powerful system guided poorly could create serious challenges.

The Future Belongs to Learners

One prediction appears repeatedly throughout discussions of the future:

The world will continue changing rapidly.

New technologies will emerge.

New careers will appear.

New industries will develop.

Some existing skills may become less important while entirely new skills become valuable.

What does this mean for students?

It means learning cannot stop at graduation.

The most successful individuals of the future may be lifelong learners.

They will remain curious.

They will adapt.

They will acquire new knowledge continuously.

Interestingly, this idea mirrors many of the capabilities discussed throughout this book.

AGI systems may learn continuously.

Humans must do the same.

The future rewards adaptability.

Human-AI Collaboration

Many people imagine the future as a competition between humans and intelligent machines.

A more useful perspective may be collaboration.

Humans possess strengths.

Machines possess strengths.

Together, they may accomplish more than either could achieve independently.

Consider medicine.

An AGI system may analyze enormous datasets and identify patterns.

Doctors provide empathy, judgment, communication, and ethical decision-making.

Consider education.

An AGI tutor may personalize lessons for millions of students.

Teachers provide mentorship, encouragement, leadership, and human connection.

Consider scientific research.

AGI may accelerate discovery.

Human researchers determine priorities, interpret significance, and guide long-term goals.

The future may not be about humans versus machines.

It may be about humans working alongside increasingly capable intelligent systems.

The Next Great Explorers

Throughout history, exploration has expanded human understanding.

Explorers crossed oceans.

Scientists explored nature.

Astronauts explored space.

Future generations may explore frontiers that previous generations could barely imagine.

Some of these frontiers may involve AGI.

Others may involve biotechnology, quantum computing, robotics, sustainable energy, or interplanetary exploration.

Many of the students reading this book today may become the scientists, engineers, teachers, policymakers, entrepreneurs, and leaders who shape that future.

The decisions made by your generation may influence how AGI develops and how society benefits from it.

Your Role in the Story

One of the biggest misconceptions about technology is the belief that the future happens to people.

In reality, people create the future.

Every invention begins with a person asking a question.

Every discovery begins with curiosity.

Every breakthrough begins with someone willing to learn.

The future of AGI will not be determined solely by researchers working in laboratories.

It will be influenced by students, educators, families, communities, businesses, governments, and citizens around the world.

The future is not written yet.

The next chapter of history has not been completed.

The people reading this book today may help write it.

The Final Lesson

Throughout this book, you have explored some of the most important ideas surrounding Artificial General Intelligence.

You have learned how intelligent systems may:

- Set goals.
- Make decisions.

- Build plans.
- Learn from experience.
- Adapt to change.
- Reason through problems.
- Generate creative ideas.
- Build world models.
- Monitor their own performance.
- Explore new knowledge.

These capabilities may someday contribute to powerful forms of machine intelligence.

Yet the most important lesson is not about AGI.

The most important lesson is about humanity.

Technology reflects the choices of the people who build it.

The future of AGI will depend not only on intelligence, but also on wisdom.

Not only on capability, but also on responsibility.

Not only on innovation, but also on values.

The future will belong to those who continue learning, continue questioning, continue exploring, and continue striving to improve the world around them.

Because the ultimate purpose of intelligence—whether human or artificial—is not simply to know more.

It is to create a better future.

And that future begins with the choices we make today.

Learn AI. Understand AI. Shape the Future.

— Susie Hala, IntelliGloss Press

Chapter 16 Summary

The Human Future: Living Alongside AGI

This chapter served as the concluding chapter of the book and explored one of the most important questions surrounding Artificial General Intelligence (AGI): What does the future look like when humans and advanced intelligent systems live and work together?

Throughout history, transformative technologies such as the wheel, the printing press, electricity, and the internet changed how people lived, learned, worked, and communicated. AGI has the potential to become another transformational technology because it may contribute to problem-solving, scientific discovery, education, healthcare, transportation, environmental protection, and many other areas of society.

The chapter emphasized that while AGI may become increasingly capable, the future is ultimately about people rather than machines. Technology is a tool, and its impact depends on how humans choose to design, guide, and use it. The future of AGI will be shaped not only by technical innovation but also by human values, ethics, leadership, and responsibility.

Readers learned that intelligence and wisdom are not the same thing. Intelligence focuses on solving problems, processing information, and generating solutions. Wisdom involves judgment, ethics, responsibility, and understanding the broader consequences of decisions. As AGI becomes more powerful, wisdom may become increasingly important in guiding how intelligent systems are used.

The chapter introduced the concept of alignment, which refers to ensuring that AGI systems operate in ways that support human goals, values, and well-being. Alignment is considered one of the most important challenges in AGI development because powerful systems must be guided responsibly.

Another major theme was lifelong learning. The chapter explained that future generations will likely live in a world of continuous technological change. Success may depend on the ability to adapt, learn new skills, and remain curious throughout life. Just as AGI systems may learn continuously, humans must continue learning as well.

The chapter also highlighted the importance of human-AI collaboration. Rather than viewing AGI as a competitor, many experts believe that humans and intelligent systems may work together to solve problems and expand knowledge. Human strengths such as empathy, ethics, creativity, leadership, and wisdom can complement the analytical and computational strengths of AGI.

Finally, the chapter encouraged students to recognize their own role in shaping the future. The future of AGI is not predetermined. Students, educators, researchers, leaders, and citizens will all influence how intelligent technologies develop and how they are used to benefit society.

Key Concepts

- AGI
- Human-AI Collaboration
- Wisdom
- Intelligence
- Alignment
- Ethics
- Responsibility

- Lifelong Learning
- Adaptation
- Innovation
- Leadership
- Human Values
- Future Technologies
- Societal Impact

Chapter 16 Reflection

Shaping the Future Together

Throughout this book, you have explored many of the building blocks of Artificial General Intelligence. You have learned about autonomy, goals, planning, memory, learning, reasoning, creativity, world models, metacognition, curiosity, and discovery. Each of these capabilities contributes to our understanding of how advanced intelligence may develop in the future.

This final chapter shifts attention from machines to people. Technology does not determine the future on its own. Human decisions, values, and actions play a critical role in shaping how technologies are used and how society benefits from them.

As AGI continues to develop, future generations may face important questions about ethics, responsibility, leadership, and collaboration. The choices made by students today may influence the technologies, industries, and societies of tomorrow.

This chapter encourages readers to think about their own role in the future and how they can contribute to a world where technology supports human well-being and progress.

Reflection Questions

1. Why might AGI become one of the most transformative technologies in history?
2. What is the difference between intelligence and wisdom?
3. Why is alignment important in AGI development?
4. How can human values influence technology?
5. Why is lifelong learning important in a rapidly changing world?
6. How can humans and AGI work together effectively?
7. What strengths do humans possess that machines may not?
8. What responsibilities come with developing powerful technologies?
9. How might AGI affect future careers and industries?
10. What role do you hope to play in shaping the future?

Chapter 16 Worksheet

The Human Future: Living Alongside AGI

Part A: Vocabulary Matching

Match each term with its correct definition.

_____ 1. Alignment

_____ 2. Wisdom

_____ 3. Lifelong Learning

_____ 4. Collaboration

_____ 5. Responsibility

A. Working together toward shared goals

B. Continuous learning throughout life

C. Ensuring actions support human values and goals

D. The obligation to act carefully and ethically

E. Applying knowledge with sound judgment and ethics

Part B: True or False

Write TRUE or FALSE.

_____ 1. AGI may influence many areas of society.

_____ 2. Intelligence and wisdom mean exactly the same thing.

_____ 3. Alignment is an important topic in AGI development.

_____ 4. Lifelong learning may become increasingly important in the future.

_____ 5. Human-AI collaboration could create new opportunities.

Part C: Short Answer

1. What is alignment?

2. Why is wisdom important?

3. What is lifelong learning?

4. How can humans and AGI collaborate?

5. Why are human values important when developing AGI?

Part D: Scenario Analysis

Imagine you are a future leader helping your community adopt AGI technologies.

1. What benefits could AGI provide?

2. What risks should be considered?

3. How would you ensure AGI systems remain aligned with community values?

4. How could education help people prepare for the future?

Part E: My Future and AI

Imagine your life 20 years from now.

1. What career would you like to pursue?

2. How might AGI help in that career?

3. What human skills will remain important?

4. How will you continue learning throughout your life?

Chapter 16 Quiz

The Human Future: Living Alongside AGI

Multiple Choice

1. Why is AGI considered potentially transformative?

A. It only affects computers.

B. It may contribute to solving problems across many fields.

C. It replaces all human activity.

D. It eliminates learning.

2. What is wisdom?

A. Memorizing facts

B. Applying knowledge with judgment and ethical consideration

C. Storing information

D. Following instructions

3. What is alignment?

A. Improving internet speed

B. Ensuring AGI systems support human goals and values

C. Increasing memory storage

D. Reducing creativity

4. Why is lifelong learning important?

A. The world and technology continue to change.

B. Learning stops after graduation.

C. Technology never changes.

D. Knowledge never expands.

5. What is one benefit of human-AI collaboration?

A. Eliminating all challenges

B. Combining human strengths with machine capabilities

C. Replacing all workers

D. Preventing innovation

Short Answer

6. Explain the difference between intelligence and wisdom.
7. Why is alignment important for AGI?
8. What role do human values play in technology development?
9. Why may adaptability be important for future success?
10. How can students help shape the future of AGI?

Chapter 16 Answer Key

The Human Future: Living Alongside AGI

Multiple Choice

1. B — It may contribute to solving problems across many fields.
2. B — Applying knowledge with judgment and ethical consideration.
3. B — Ensuring AGI systems support human goals and values.
4. A — The world and technology continue to change.
5. B — Combining human strengths with machine capabilities.

Short Answer

6. Intelligence involves acquiring and applying knowledge, while wisdom involves making ethical, responsible, and thoughtful decisions using that knowledge.
7. Alignment helps ensure that AGI systems operate in ways that support human well-being, safety, and values.
8. Human values guide decisions about how technologies are designed, used, regulated, and applied within society.
9. Adaptability allows individuals to respond to changing technologies, careers, knowledge, and opportunities throughout life.
10. Students can shape the future by learning, asking questions, developing skills, participating in innovation, and making responsible decisions about technology.

Scoring Guide

9–10 Correct

Outstanding Understanding

7–8 Correct

Strong Understanding

5–6 Correct

Developing Understanding

Below 5 Correct

Review the chapter and retake the assessment.

Final Book Reflection

Looking Back, Looking Forward

Congratulations on completing this journey through **AUTONOMY: The Engine of Artificial General Intelligence**.

You explored how intelligent systems may:

- Set goals
- Make decisions
- Create plans
- Build memories
- Learn from experience
- Adapt to change
- Solve problems
- Generate creative ideas
- Construct world models
- Monitor their own thinking
- Explore new knowledge
- Collaborate with humans

Most importantly, you discovered that technology alone does not determine the future. Human choices, values, wisdom, and leadership will play a critical role in shaping how AGI develops and how society benefits from it.

The future of artificial intelligence is still being written.

The scientists, engineers, educators, leaders, entrepreneurs, and innovators who will shape that future may already be sitting in today's classrooms.

Perhaps one of them is you.

Final Reflection Questions

1. Which chapter impacted you the most and why?
2. What new ideas did you learn about AGI?
3. How has your understanding of intelligence changed?
4. What opportunities could AGI create for humanity?
5. What responsibilities come with creating powerful technologies?
6. How can ethics guide innovation?
7. What skills do you want to develop for the future?
8. How will you continue learning beyond this book?
9. What role would you like to play in an AI-powered world?
10. What does "Shape the Future" mean to you?

Learn AI. Understand AI. Shape the Future.

— Susie Hala, IntelliGloss Press

GLOSSARY

Letter A

1. Access Time

The amount of time it takes for an AI system or computer to locate and retrieve data from memory or storage. Access time affects how quickly megabytes of data can be used during AI processing.

2. Activation Data

Intermediate data generated inside an AI model while it is running. Activation data is stored temporarily in memory and often measured in megabytes during model execution.

3. Adaptive Storage

A storage approach that automatically adjusts how data is stored or moved based on usage patterns. In AI systems, adaptive storage helps manage large volumes of megabytes efficiently.

4. Algorithmic Data Size

The total amount of data an algorithm needs to operate effectively. In AI, this size is often measured in megabytes or larger units, depending on model complexity.

5. Allocation (Memory Allocation)

The process of assigning a specific number of megabytes in memory or storage for an AI task, model, or dataset.

6. Analytics Dataset

A structured collection of data used for analysis or AI training. The size of an analytics dataset is commonly measured in megabytes, gigabytes, or more.

7. Annotation Storage

The space required to store labels, tags, or explanations added to AI training data. These annotations contribute additional megabytes to total dataset size.

8. Artificial Neural Network (ANN) Size

The total memory footprint of a neural network, including weights, biases, and parameters. ANN size is often described in megabytes when discussing model efficiency.

9. Asset Compression

The process of reducing the number of megabytes required to store AI-related files such as models, images, or datasets without losing essential information.

10. Available Memory

The amount of free memory, measured in megabytes, that an AI system can still use to load data, run models, or perform computations.

ANI (Artificial Narrow Intelligence)

Artificial Narrow Intelligence refers to AI systems designed to perform **one specific task or a narrow set of tasks** rather than general intelligence. ANI systems rely on data stored and processed in memory and storage measured in **megabytes, gigabytes, or more**. Examples include image recognition, speech-to-text, recommendation systems, and chatbots. ANI does not understand beyond its training scope, but it can process large amounts of data efficiently within its defined function.

Letter B

1. Bandwidth

The amount of data that can be transferred between systems in a given time. In AI systems, bandwidth determines how quickly megabytes of data can move between storage, memory, and processors.

2. Batch Processing

A method where AI systems process large groups of data all at once instead of one item at a time. Batch processing often involves handling many megabytes of data in a single operation.

3. Binary Encoding

The process of representing information using binary values (0s and 1s). All megabytes of AI data are ultimately stored and transmitted using binary encoding.

4. Bit Depth

The number of bits used to represent a single piece of data, such as a pixel or audio sample. Higher bit depth increases data quality but also increases the number of megabytes required.

5. Bitmap Data

A type of image data where each pixel is stored as a set of bits. Bitmap images can quickly grow in size, consuming large numbers of megabytes in AI vision systems.

6. Buffer Memory

Temporary memory used to hold data while it is being transferred or processed. Buffers store data in chunks measured in megabytes to keep AI systems running smoothly.

7. Bulk Data Storage

Large-scale storage designed to hold massive datasets used for AI training or analysis. Bulk storage capacity is measured in megabytes, gigabytes, or larger units.

8. Byte Stream

A continuous flow of bytes transmitted or processed by a system. AI applications often analyze byte streams that accumulate into megabytes of data.

9. Bytecode

An intermediate form of program code that is easier for machines to execute than human-written code. Bytecode files occupy storage space measured in megabytes.

10. Byzantine Fault Tolerance (BFT)

A system property that allows AI or distributed systems to continue functioning even when some components fail or act unpredictably. Implementing BFT requires additional data handling and storage overhead measured in megabytes.

Letter C

1. Cache Memory

A small, high-speed memory area that stores frequently used data so the processor can access it faster. Cache helps reduce the time needed to move megabytes of data from main memory or storage.

2. Capacity Planning

The process of estimating how much memory and storage an AI system will need. Capacity planning ensures there are enough megabytes available to handle data, models, and future growth.

3. Checkpoint File

A saved snapshot of an AI model during training. Checkpoint files are stored in memory or storage and often consume many megabytes so training can resume without starting over.

4. Chunking

The practice of breaking large datasets into smaller pieces. Chunking helps AI systems process megabytes of data more efficiently by handling them in manageable parts.

5. Cloud Storage

A method of storing data on remote servers accessed through the internet. Cloud storage manages files measured in megabytes and allows AI systems to scale beyond local hardware limits.

6. Compression

The process of reducing the size of data so it uses fewer megabytes. Compression helps AI systems store, transfer, and process data more efficiently.

7. Compute Load

The amount of processing work required to run an AI task. Compute load often increases as the number of megabytes being processed grows.

8. Context Window

The amount of data an AI model can consider at one time. Context windows consume memory measured in megabytes, especially in language and vision models.

9. Corpus

A large collection of text or data used to train AI models. A corpus is usually measured in megabytes or larger units depending on its size.

10. CUDA Memory

Specialized memory used by GPUs to accelerate AI computations. CUDA memory holds model data and intermediate results measured in megabytes during processing.

Letter D

1. Data Allocation

The process of assigning a specific amount of memory or storage for data use. In AI systems, data allocation determines how many megabytes are reserved for datasets, models, or tasks.

2. Data Buffer

A temporary storage area that holds data while it is being transferred or processed. Data buffers manage megabytes of information to keep AI systems running smoothly.

3. Data Compression

A technique used to reduce the size of data so it consumes fewer megabytes. AI systems use data compression to save storage space and speed up data transfer.

4. Data Footprint

The total amount of data an AI system uses, including datasets, models, and temporary files. A data footprint is measured in megabytes, gigabytes, or more.

5. Data Loader

A software component that loads data into memory for AI training or inference. Data loaders handle batches of data measured in megabytes.

6. Data Migration

The process of moving data from one storage system to another. During AI system upgrades, data migration may involve transferring large numbers of megabytes.

7. Data Throughput

The rate at which data is processed or transferred by a system. Higher throughput allows AI systems to move more megabytes efficiently.

8. Dataset Size

The total amount of data in a dataset used for AI training or testing. Dataset size is commonly measured in megabytes or larger units.

9. Deep Learning Model Size

The amount of memory required to store a deep learning model, including its parameters and weights. Model size is often described in megabytes to assess efficiency.

10. Disk Storage

Long-term storage used to save files, datasets, and AI models. Disk storage capacity and usage are measured in megabytes, gigabytes, or terabytes.

Letter E

1. Edge Computing

A computing approach where data is processed closer to where it is generated rather than sent to a central server. Edge computing reduces how many megabytes must be transferred over networks.

2. Embedding Size

The amount of memory required to store vector representations used by AI models. Embedding size is often measured in megabytes and affects model performance and storage needs.

3. Encoded Data

Data that has been converted into a specific format for storage or transmission. Encoded data occupies megabytes depending on the encoding method used.

4. Encoding Scheme

A rule set that defines how data is represented digitally, such as text or images. Different encoding schemes can increase or reduce the number of megabytes required.

5. Encrypted Storage

Storage that protects data by converting it into a secure format. Encryption may slightly increase the number of megabytes used due to added security information.

6. End-to-End Data Pipeline

The full path data takes from collection to processing and storage. Each stage of the pipeline manages data volumes measured in megabytes.

7. Energy Efficiency (AI Systems)

A measure of how much energy an AI system uses to process data. Systems that move and store fewer megabytes are often more energy efficient.

8. Execution Memory

The memory required while a program or AI model is running. Execution memory usage is tracked in megabytes during runtime.

9. External Storage

Storage devices located outside a computer, such as USB drives or external hard drives. External storage capacity is measured in megabytes and larger units.

10. Extracted Features

Important data patterns identified by AI models during processing. Extracted features are stored temporarily or permanently in memory measured in megabytes.

Letter F

1. Feature Map

A structured output produced by AI models, especially in image and signal processing. Feature maps are stored in memory and can consume significant megabytes during computation.

2. Feature Scaling

The process of adjusting data values to a consistent range before training an AI model. Feature scaling affects how efficiently megabytes of data are processed and stored.

3. File Allocation Table (FAT)

A file system structure that tracks where files are stored on a disk. FAT helps manage how megabytes are organized and retrieved from storage.

4. File Compression Format

A standardized way to reduce file size so it uses fewer megabytes. Compression formats help AI systems store and transfer data efficiently.

5. File System Cache

A temporary memory area that stores frequently accessed files. File system caches reduce repeated access to storage and manage megabytes more efficiently.

6. Floating-Point Data

Numerical data that includes decimal values and is commonly used in AI calculations. Floating-point data requires more bits per value, increasing memory usage measured in megabytes.

7. Frame Buffer

A region of memory that stores image or video frames before they are displayed or processed. Frame buffers often consume large numbers of megabytes in AI vision systems.

8. Fragmentation

A condition where data is stored in scattered locations instead of one continuous block. Fragmentation can reduce storage efficiency even when megabytes appear available.

9. Free Memory

The amount of unused memory available for programs or AI tasks. Free memory is measured in megabytes and determines how much additional data can be loaded.

10. Full Dataset Load

The act of loading an entire dataset into memory at once. This approach can require large amounts of megabytes and is common in AI training scenarios.

Letter G

1. Garbage Collection

An automatic memory-management process that frees memory no longer in use. Garbage collection helps reclaim megabytes so AI programs can continue running efficiently.

2. Generalization Data

Data used to test how well an AI model performs on new, unseen inputs. Storing and evaluating generalization data requires additional megabytes beyond training data.

3. Gigabyte (GB)

A larger unit of data measurement equal to 1,024 megabytes (or commonly approximated as 1,000 MB). Gigabytes are used when datasets or models grow beyond megabyte scale.

4. Graph Data Structure

A way of organizing data using nodes and connections. Graph-based AI systems store graph data in memory and storage measured in megabytes.

5. GPU Memory

Specialized memory used by graphics processing units to accelerate AI workloads. GPU memory holds model parameters and data batches measured in megabytes.

6. Gradient Data

Numerical values calculated during AI training to update model parameters. Gradient data is stored temporarily in memory and contributes to overall megabyte usage.

7. Granularity

The level of detail at which data is stored or processed. Finer granularity often increases the number of megabytes required.

8. Greedy Algorithm

An algorithm that makes the best immediate choice at each step. Greedy algorithms may reduce memory usage by limiting how many megabytes of data must be stored at once.

9. Ground Truth Data

Correct, labeled data used to train or evaluate AI systems. Ground truth datasets are stored in files measured in megabytes or larger units.

10. Growth Rate (Data)

The speed at which data size increases over time. In AI systems, a high data growth rate means storage needs measured in megabytes can expand quickly.

Letter H

1. Hard Disk Capacity

The total amount of data a hard disk can store. Capacity is measured in megabytes and larger units.

2. Hardware Acceleration

The use of specialized hardware to speed up AI processing. Acceleration often reduces how long megabytes of data stay in memory.

3. Hash Table

A data structure that stores information for fast lookup. Hash tables occupy memory measured in megabytes in large AI systems.

4. Hierarchical Storage

A storage design that uses multiple layers such as RAM, disk, and cloud. Each layer manages data measured in megabytes.

5. High-Dimensional Data

Data with many features or variables. High-dimensional datasets often require large numbers of megabytes.

6. Host Memory

Main system memory used by the CPU. Host memory stores AI data and models measured in megabytes.

7. Hybrid Storage

A combination of different storage types working together. Hybrid storage systems manage megabytes across multiple devices.

8. Hyperparameter Storage

Memory used to store configuration values for AI models. These settings are saved in files measured in megabytes.

9. Hyperscale Data

Extremely large datasets used by major AI systems. Hyperscale data is tracked from megabytes up to much larger units.

10. Heuristic Data

Information used by AI systems to guide decision-making. Heuristic data contributes to the overall data size in megabytes.

Letter I

1. Image Dataset Size

The total amount of storage required for image data. Size is measured in megabytes or more.

2. Inference Memory

The memory used when an AI model is making predictions. Inference memory usage is tracked in megabytes.

3. Input Buffer

A temporary area where incoming data is stored. Input buffers hold megabytes before processing begins.

4. Intermediate Data

Data produced during processing steps. Intermediate data can significantly increase memory usage in megabytes.

5. Index File

A file that helps locate data quickly. Index files use additional megabytes to improve performance.

6. Information Density

The amount of useful data stored within a given size. Higher density means more information per megabyte.

7. Initialization Data

Data loaded when an AI system starts. Initialization data occupies memory measured in megabytes.

8. In-Memory Processing

Processing data directly in RAM instead of storage. This approach uses large amounts of memory measured in megabytes.

9. Input Feature Size

The amount of data required to represent input features. Feature size affects how many megabytes are needed.

10. Instruction Cache

A small memory area that stores frequently used instructions. Instruction caches manage small but critical megabytes.

Letter J

1. Job Queue

A list of tasks waiting to be processed. Job queues may store task data measured in megabytes.

2. Joint Dataset

A dataset created by combining multiple sources. Joint datasets often increase total size in megabytes.

3. JSON Data Size

The amount of storage required for data stored in JSON format. JSON files can grow quickly in megabytes.

4. Jitter Buffer

A temporary storage area that smooths data flow. Jitter buffers store megabytes during real-time processing.

5. Job Scheduler

A system that decides when tasks run. Schedulers manage memory and data measured in megabytes.

6. Just-in-Time Processing

Processing data only when needed. This approach can reduce how many megabytes are stored at once.

7. Joint Memory Allocation

Memory shared across multiple AI tasks. Joint allocation must carefully manage available megabytes.

8. Java Bytecode Size

The storage size of compiled Java programs. Bytecode files occupy megabytes on disk.

9. Job Metadata

Information describing AI tasks. Metadata adds additional megabytes to total system storage.

10. Junction Storage Point

A logical link between storage locations. Junctions help organize data measured in megabytes.

Letter K

1. Kernel Memory

Memory reserved for core system operations. Kernel memory usage is tracked in megabytes.

2. Key-Value Store

A data storage method that pairs keys with values. Large key-value stores consume many megabytes.

3. Knowledge Base Size

The total amount of stored knowledge in an AI system. Size is measured in megabytes or larger units.

4. K-Means Dataset Size

The amount of data used in clustering algorithms. Dataset size affects memory usage in megabytes.

5. Keras Model Size

The storage required for AI models built with Keras. Model size is measured in megabytes.

6. Keyframe Data

Important frames selected from video data. Keyframe storage contributes to total megabyte usage.

7. Kernel Cache

A cache used by the operating system kernel. Kernel caches store frequently used data in megabytes.

8. Knowledge Graph Storage

Memory used to store relationships between data points. Knowledge graphs require significant megabytes.

9. Kinetic Data Stream

Continuously changing data from sensors or systems. These streams generate growing megabytes over time.

10. K-Nearest Neighbor Memory Usage

The memory required by nearest-neighbor algorithms. Memory use increases as datasets grow in megabytes.

Letter L

1. **Latency**
   The delay between requesting data and receiving it. Latency affects how quickly megabytes move through AI systems.
2. **Layer Output Size**
   The amount of data produced by a neural network layer. Output size is measured in megabytes during processing.
3. **Load Balancing**
   Distributing work across systems so no single device is overloaded. Balancing helps manage megabytes efficiently.
4. **Local Storage**
   Data stored on a device rather than the cloud. Local storage capacity is measured in megabytes.
5. **Log File Size**
   The amount of storage used by system logs. Logs can accumulate many megabytes over time.
6. **Loss History Data**
   Stored values showing how model error changes during training. Loss history consumes megabytes.
7. **Low-Precision Data**
   Data stored using fewer bits per value. Low-precision formats reduce megabyte usage.
8. **Labeled Dataset**
   Data that includes tags or labels for AI training. Labels increase total dataset size in megabytes.
9. **Linear Model Size**
   The storage required for a linear AI model. Size is measured in megabytes.
10. **Load Time**
    The time required to bring data or models into memory. Load time depends on megabytes involved.

Letter M

1. **Memory Allocation**
   Assigning a specific amount of memory for tasks. Allocation is tracked in megabytes.
2. **Memory Footprint**
   The total memory an AI program uses. Footprint is measured in megabytes.
3. **Metadata Size**
   The storage used by descriptive information about data. Metadata adds extra megabytes.
4. **Mini-Batch Size**
   The amount of data processed at once during training. Batch size affects megabyte usage.
5. **Model Checkpoint Size**
   The storage required for saved training states. Checkpoints often consume many megabytes.
6. **Model Compression**
   Reducing model size while preserving performance. Compression lowers megabytes required.
7. **Model Parameters**
   Values learned by an AI model. Parameter storage contributes to total megabytes.
8. **Memory Bandwidth**
   The rate at which memory transfers data. Bandwidth affects how fast megabytes move.
9. **Multimodal Dataset**
   Data combining text, images, audio, or video. Multimodal data uses large megabytes.
10. **Mutable Data**
    Data that changes during processing. Mutable data can increase temporary megabyte usage.

Letter N

1. **Network Bandwidth**
   The capacity of a network connection. Bandwidth controls how many megabytes can be transferred.
2. **Neural Network Size**
   The total storage required for a neural network. Size is measured in megabytes.
3. **Node Memory**
   Memory available on a computing node. Node memory limits megabytes per task.
4. **Normalization Data**
   Values used to scale data consistently. Normalization adds to dataset megabytes.
5. **Non-Volatile Memory**
   Memory that retains data without power. Capacity is measured in megabytes.
6. **Numerical Precision**
   The detail level of stored numbers. Higher precision increases megabytes.
7. **Noise Data**
   Unwanted or random information in datasets. Noise increases data size in megabytes.
8. **Neural Activation Size**
   Memory used to store neuron outputs. Activation size is measured in megabytes.

9. **Network Transfer Size**
   The amount of data sent across a network. Transfer size is tracked in megabytes.
10. **Node Cache**
   Temporary storage on a node for faster access. Cache size uses megabytes.

Letter O

1. **Object Storage**
   A storage method that manages data as objects. Capacity is measured in megabytes.
2. **Offline Dataset**
   Data stored locally rather than streamed. Offline datasets occupy megabytes.
3. **On-Device Storage**
   Storage located on the AI device itself. On-device capacity is measured in megabytes.
4. **Operational Memory**
   Memory used during active AI operations. Usage is tracked in megabytes.
5. **Optimization Data**
   Information used to improve model performance. Optimization data uses megabytes.
6. **Output Buffer**
   Temporary storage for results before delivery. Buffers hold megabytes.
7. **Overhead Data**
   Extra data required for system operation. Overhead increases total megabytes.
8. **Object Detection Output Size**
   The amount of data produced by detection models. Output size is measured in megabytes.
9. **Online Storage**
   Storage accessible via the internet. Online storage limits are measured in megabytes.
10. **Open Dataset Size**
   The storage footprint of publicly available datasets. Size is measured in megabytes.

Letter P

1. **Parameter Count**
   The total number of model values. Count correlates with megabytes required.
2. **Persistent Storage**
   Long-term storage that retains data. Capacity is measured in megabytes.
3. **Pipeline Buffer**
   Temporary storage between processing stages. Buffers manage megabytes in motion.
4. **Preprocessing Data**
   Data created while preparing datasets. Preprocessing adds megabytes.
5. **Precision Reduction**
   Lowering numeric detail to save space. Reduction decreases megabyte usage.
6. **Prediction Output Size**
   The amount of data produced by model predictions. Size is measured in megabytes.

7. **Primary Memory**
   Main system memory used for processing. Capacity is measured in megabytes.
8. **Processing Overhead**
   Extra resources needed during computation. Overhead increases megabyte usage.
9. **Profiling Data**
   Information collected to analyze performance. Profiling data uses megabytes.
10. **Paged Memory**
    Memory divided into fixed-size blocks. Paging manages megabytes efficiently.

Letter Q

1. **Quantization**
   A technique that reduces numerical precision to lower memory usage. Quantization helps AI models use fewer megabytes.
2. **Query Cache**
   Stored results from previous searches or requests. Query caches save megabytes by avoiding repeated computation.
3. **Query Latency**
   The time it takes to retrieve data after a request. Latency depends on how many megabytes must be accessed.
4. **Queue Buffer**
   A temporary holding area for data waiting to be processed. Buffers store megabytes in order.
5. **Quick Access Memory**
   Memory designed for fast retrieval. It handles megabytes needed immediately by AI tasks.
6. **Quantitative Dataset**
   Data made up of numerical values. These datasets are stored and measured in megabytes.
7. **Query Result Size**
   The amount of data returned from a query. Result size is measured in megabytes.
8. **Quorum Storage**
   A distributed storage method requiring agreement across systems. Data is replicated in megabytes.
9. **Quality Metrics Data**
   Information used to measure model performance. Metrics consume storage in megabytes.
10. **Quantized Model Size**
    The reduced size of an AI model after quantization. Size is typically measured in megabytes.

Letter R

1. **RAM Usage**
   The amount of active memory in use. RAM usage is tracked in megabytes.
2. **Read Throughput**
   The speed at which data is read from storage. Throughput affects how fast megabytes are accessed.
3. **Real-Time Processing**
   Processing data immediately as it arrives. Real-time systems manage megabytes continuously.
4. **Recursive Memory Use**
   Memory consumption during repeated function calls. Usage accumulates in megabytes.
5. **Redundant Storage**
   Extra copies of data kept for reliability. Redundancy increases total megabytes stored.
6. **Resource Allocation**
   Assigning system resources like memory and storage. Allocation is measured in megabytes.
7. **Runtime Memory**
   Memory required while a program is running. Runtime memory usage is tracked in megabytes.
8. **Raw Dataset Size**
   The size of unprocessed data. Raw datasets often require many megabytes.
9. **Read-Only Memory Footprint**
   The storage space used by non-modifiable data. Footprint is measured in megabytes.
10. **Retrieval Speed**
    How quickly stored data can be accessed. Speed depends on the number of megabytes involved.

Letter S

1. **Sample Size**
   The number of data examples used in AI training. Larger samples increase megabytes.
2. **Scalable Storage**
   Storage that grows with demand. Scalability supports increasing megabytes.
3. **Serialized Data Size**
   The storage size of data converted into a transferable format. Size is measured in megabytes.
4. **Shared Memory**
   Memory accessible by multiple processes. Shared memory usage is tracked in megabytes.
5. **Snapshot Size**
   The storage required for saved system states. Snapshots consume megabytes.
6. **Sparse Data Representation**
   A storage method that saves space when data contains many empty values. Sparsity reduces megabytes.
7. **Storage Capacity**
   The total amount of data a system can store. Capacity is measured in megabytes or more.

8. **Streaming Data Buffer**
   Temporary storage for incoming data streams. Buffers handle megabytes in motion.
9. **System Cache**
   Memory that stores frequently used data. Caches manage megabytes for faster access.
10. **Synchronization Data**
    Information used to keep systems aligned. Sync data adds to total megabytes.

Letter T

1. **Temporary Storage**
   Short-term storage used during processing. Temporary storage holds megabytes briefly.
2. **Tensor Size**
   The memory required to store multidimensional data structures. Tensor size is measured in megabytes.
3. **Throughput Rate**
   The amount of data processed per unit time. Rate is often described in megabytes per second.
4. **Training Dataset Size**
   The total amount of data used to train AI models. Size is measured in megabytes.
5. **Transfer Buffer**
   Temporary memory used during data movement. Buffers hold megabytes during transfer.
6. **Transactional Storage**
   Storage that ensures data consistency. Transactions add overhead measured in megabytes.
7. **Thread Memory Usage**
   Memory consumed by execution threads. Usage is tracked in megabytes.
8. **Token Storage Size**
   The memory required to store processed tokens. Token data uses megabytes.
9. **Time-Series Data Size**
   The storage footprint of data collected over time. Size increases in megabytes.
10. **Training Checkpoint Size**
    The storage required for saved training states. Checkpoints are measured in megabytes.

Letter U

1. **Unified Memory**
   A memory system shared between CPU and GPU. Unified memory manages data in megabytes efficiently across processors.
2. **Upload Size**
   The amount of data sent to storage or the cloud. Upload size is measured in megabytes.
3. **User Data Storage**
   Storage allocated for user-generated files. Capacity is tracked in megabytes.

4. **Utilization Rate**
   The percentage of memory or storage currently in use. Utilization reflects how many megabytes are occupied.
5. **Uncompressed Data Size**
   The size of data before compression. Uncompressed data often uses more megabytes.
6. **Update Payload**
   Data sent during software or model updates. Payload size is measured in megabytes.
7. **Uptime Storage Logs**
   Logs recorded while systems run continuously. Logs accumulate megabytes over time.
8. **Unified Dataset**
   A dataset combined from multiple sources. Size is measured in megabytes.
9. **User Session Memory**
   Memory allocated for active users. Session memory uses megabytes dynamically.
10. **Usage Quota**
    A storage limit set for users or systems. Quotas are defined in megabytes or larger units.

Letter V

1. **Validation Dataset Size**
   The amount of data used to evaluate AI models. Size is measured in megabytes.
2. **Vector Embedding Size**
   The memory required to store numerical representations of data. Size is measured in megabytes.
3. **Virtual Memory**
   A system that extends RAM using disk storage. Virtual memory is managed in megabytes.
4. **Volatile Memory**
   Memory that loses data when power is off. Capacity is measured in megabytes.
5. **Video Dataset Size**
   The storage required for video data. Video datasets consume many megabytes.
6. **Versioned Storage**
   Storage that keeps multiple file versions. Versioning increases megabyte usage.
7. **Vision Model Size**
   The memory footprint of computer vision models. Size is measured in megabytes.
8. **Vector Database Storage**
   Storage used for similarity search data. Vector databases consume large megabytes.
9. **Virtualized Storage**
   Storage abstracted from physical hardware. Capacity is tracked in megabytes.
10. **Volume Capacity**
    The total size of a storage volume. Capacity is measured in megabytes or more.

Letter W

1. **Weight Parameters**
   Learned values in AI models. Weight storage contributes to megabytes used.
2. **Working Memory**
   Memory actively used during processing. Working memory usage is measured in megabytes.
3. **Write Throughput**
   The speed at which data is written to storage. Throughput affects megabytes per second.
4. **Warm Cache**
   Cached data that is already loaded. Warm caches reduce repeated megabyte transfers.
5. **Workflow Data Size**
   The total data used across an AI workflow. Size is measured in megabytes.
6. **Web Dataset Size**
   The storage required for web-based data. Size is tracked in megabytes.
7. **Weight Compression**
   Reducing model weight size to save memory. Compression lowers megabytes used.
8. **Window Size (AI Context)**
   The amount of data processed at once. Window size affects memory megabytes.
9. **Writable Storage**
   Storage that allows data modification. Capacity is measured in megabytes.
10. **Workload Memory Demand**
    The memory required for tasks. Demand is expressed in megabytes.

Letter X

1. **X-Axis Data Size**
   Data stored along one dimension of a dataset. Size contributes to megabytes used.
2. **XML Data Size**
   The storage footprint of XML-formatted data. XML files often use many megabytes.
3. **XOR Encoding**
   A binary operation used in data processing. Encoded data occupies megabytes.
4. **Execution Context Size**
   Memory required during task execution. Size is measured in megabytes.
5. **External Dataset Size**
   The size of data sourced externally. External datasets add megabytes.
6. **Expanded Memory Use**
   Memory growth during processing. Expansion increases megabytes consumed.
7. **Experimental Dataset**
   Data used for testing AI models. Size is measured in megabytes.
8. **Extraction Buffer**
   Temporary storage during data extraction. Buffers store megabytes briefly.
9. **Extended Storage Capacity**
   Additional storage added to a system. Capacity is measured in megabytes.
10. **Explainability Data Size**
    Data used to explain AI decisions. Explainability outputs consume megabytes.

Letter Y

1. **Yield Data Size**
   The amount of useful output data produced. Yield is measured in megabytes.
2. **Yearly Data Growth**
   Annual increase in stored data. Growth is tracked in megabytes.
3. **YAML File Size**
   The storage footprint of YAML configuration files. Size is measured in megabytes.
4. **Y-Axis Feature Size**
   Feature data along a dataset dimension. Size contributes to megabytes.
5. **Young Generation Memory**
   Memory area for newly created data. Usage is measured in megabytes.
6. **Yield Optimization Data**
   Data used to improve output efficiency. Stored in megabytes.
7. **YourAIStudyBuddy Dataset Size**
   The total data used by AI study tools. Size is measured in megabytes.
8. **Yottabyte Reference Scale**
   A conceptual upper scale of data measurement. Used for comparison beyond megabytes.
9. **Yield Metrics Storage**
   Storage used for performance metrics. Metrics consume megabytes.
10. **Yoked Memory Allocation**
    Linked memory regions used together. Allocation is measured in megabytes.

Letter Z

1. **Zero-Copy Memory**
   A method that avoids duplicating data. Zero-copy reduces megabytes in motion.
2. **Zipped Dataset Size**
   The storage size after compression. Zipped files use fewer megabytes.
3. **Zettabyte Scale (Reference)**
   A large-scale data concept. Used to compare growth beyond megabytes.
4. **Zone-Based Storage**
   Storage divided into regions. Zones manage megabytes efficiently.
5. **Z-Score Normalization Data**
   Statistical values used in preprocessing. Data adds megabytes.
6. **Zero Padding**
   Adding placeholder data to inputs. Padding increases memory megabytes.
7. **Zoomed Feature Maps**
   Scaled representations in vision models. Stored in megabytes.
8. **Zonal Cache**
   Cache divided by region. Cache size is measured in megabytes.

9. **Zero-Day Model Update Size**
   The storage required for emergency updates. Size is measured in megabytes.
10. **Zipped Model Archive**
   Compressed AI model files. Archives reduce megabytes required.

Teacher's Overview

AUTONOMY

The Engine of Artificial General Intelligence

By Susie Hala
IntelliGloss AI Education Series
Module 2: Artificial General Intelligence (AGI)

Overview

Artificial General Intelligence (AGI) represents the next major step in the evolution of artificial intelligence. While today's AI systems perform specific tasks extremely well, future AGI systems are expected to operate across many different areas of knowledge while learning, adapting, planning, and making decisions much like humans. One of the most important capabilities that will make this possible is **autonomy**.

Autonomy is the ability of an intelligent system to operate independently while pursuing goals, making decisions, learning from experience, adapting to change, and solving problems without requiring constant human instruction. Rather than simply following commands, autonomous systems evaluate situations, select appropriate actions, monitor results, and continuously improve their performance.

This book introduces students to one of the foundational building blocks of Artificial General Intelligence by explaining autonomy in simple, easy-to-understand language. Students will learn that autonomy is not a single technology but a collection of interconnected capabilities that allow intelligent systems to function independently in increasingly complex environments.

Throughout the sixteen chapters, students explore how autonomous systems set goals, make decisions, develop plans, remember past experiences, learn from feedback, adapt to changing situations, and improve over time. They also examine the relationship between autonomy, human values, ethics, safety, alignment, and the future development of AGI.

An important theme throughout this book is that autonomy does **not** mean replacing humans. Instead, it focuses on creating intelligent systems that can work alongside people to improve productivity, solve complex problems, and support human decision-making while remaining aligned with human goals and values.

This book also introduces students to one of the most exciting ideas in AGI research: that autonomy may eventually enable intelligent systems to improve themselves through continuous learning and recursive self-improvement. At the same time, students are encouraged to consider the ethical responsibilities that accompany increasingly capable intelligent machines.

Rather than presenting AGI as science fiction, this book explains emerging concepts using practical examples from everyday life, helping students connect advanced AI concepts to familiar experiences.

The ultimate goal is to help students understand not only **how autonomous intelligence works**, but **why responsible development, human oversight, and ethical decision-making will remain essential as AI continues to evolve.**

Learning Objectives

After completing this book, students should be able to:

- Define autonomy and explain its role in Artificial General Intelligence.
- Distinguish between traditional AI systems and autonomous intelligent systems.
- Explain why AGI requires independent decision-making capabilities.
- Describe the spectrum of autonomy from human-controlled systems to fully autonomous systems.
- Understand how goals, planning, and decision-making work together.
- Explain how memory, knowledge, and context support autonomous behavior.
- Describe how autonomous systems learn through experience and feedback.
- Explain the importance of adaptation in changing environments.
- Compare Agentic AI with Autonomous AI.
- Understand the importance of alignment, ethics, and human values.
- Explain recursive self-improvement and its possible role in future AGI.
- Discuss how autonomous intelligence may shape education, healthcare, science, transportation, and everyday life.

Who Should Read This Book?

This book is designed for:

- Middle school students
- High school students
- College readiness programs
- Career Technical Education (CTE)
- STEM classrooms
- Computer science courses
- Artificial Intelligence literacy programs
- Teachers introducing AGI concepts
- Parents learning alongside their children
- Anyone interested in understanding the future of intelligent systems

No programming experience is required.

The concepts are presented in plain English using relatable examples that make advanced AI topics accessible for all learners.

Teacher's Guide

Teaching Guide

Artificial intelligence is advancing rapidly, and autonomy represents one of the most significant developments in that evolution. As students begin hearing terms such as AGI, autonomous systems, intelligent agents, robotics, and self-improving AI in the news and popular media, they need accurate, balanced, and age-appropriate educational resources.

This book was written to support classroom discussions while encouraging curiosity, critical thinking, and responsible innovation.

Rather than memorizing technical definitions, students are encouraged to ask questions, compare ideas, analyze examples, and discuss the benefits and challenges associated with increasingly autonomous technologies.

Teachers do not need an advanced background in computer science to successfully teach this material. Each chapter introduces one major concept using familiar examples before gradually building toward more advanced AGI ideas.

Suggested Classroom Discussion Topics

Throughout this book, encourage students to discuss questions such as:

- What does it mean to act independently?
- Should every AI system be autonomous?
- What kinds of decisions should always require human oversight?
- How do humans learn from mistakes?
- How can machines learn from feedback?
- Why are ethics important when building intelligent systems?
- What responsibilities come with creating increasingly capable AI?
- How can autonomous systems improve society?
- Where should humans always remain in control?
- How can AI and humans collaborate successfully?

There are often no single correct answers. These discussions help students develop reasoning, communication, and ethical decision-making skills.

Cross-Curricular Connections

This book supports instruction across multiple subject areas, including:

Computer Science

- Artificial Intelligence
- Machine Learning
- Intelligent Agents
- Robotics

- Decision Systems

Science

- Observation
- Experimentation
- Systems Thinking
- Feedback Mechanisms

Mathematics

- Logic
- Algorithms
- Decision Trees
- Optimization

Engineering

- System Design
- Autonomous Robotics
- Safety Systems

Social Studies

- Technology and Society
- Public Policy
- Workforce Changes
- Economic Impact

Language Arts

- Informational Reading
- Critical Thinking
- Technical Vocabulary
- Analytical Writing

Classroom Activities

Teachers may extend learning through activities such as:

- Designing a simple autonomous robot on paper.
- Comparing human decision-making with AI decision-making.
- Debating the benefits and risks of autonomous technologies.
- Creating flowcharts that demonstrate autonomous decision processes.

- Researching real-world examples of autonomous systems used in healthcare, transportation, agriculture, manufacturing, and space exploration.
- Writing essays about how autonomy may change future careers.
- Discussing ethical scenarios involving autonomous AI.

Assessment Suggestions

Student understanding may be evaluated through:

- Chapter quizzes
- Reflection journals
- Classroom discussions
- Group presentations
- Vocabulary assessments
- Scenario-based problem solving
- Research projects
- Short essays
- Team debates
- Final presentations on future autonomous technologies

Assessment should emphasize understanding, communication, ethical reasoning, and problem-solving rather than memorization alone.

Preparing Students for the Future

Today's students will likely enter a world where autonomous intelligent systems assist people in education, healthcare, transportation, scientific research, manufacturing, environmental protection, finance, and countless other professions.

Understanding autonomy helps students prepare for careers that may not yet exist while developing skills that will remain valuable regardless of technological change. Curiosity, creativity, ethical judgment, communication, collaboration, adaptability, and lifelong learning will continue to distinguish human intelligence in an increasingly AI-assisted world.

The purpose of this book is not to predict the future with certainty, but to give students the knowledge and confidence to participate in shaping it responsibly.

As Artificial General Intelligence continues to evolve, one lesson remains clear:

Autonomy gives intelligent systems the ability to act independently. Human wisdom gives society the ability to decide how that independence should be used.

Together, they will help shape the future of intelligence.

Learn AI. Understand AI. Shape the Future.

— Susie Hala
IntelliGloss Press

www.ingramcontent.com/pod-product-compliance
Lightning Source LLC
Chambersburg PA
CBHW041752220926
51847CB00014B/176
9781972925263